Travels Through Time in Italy

Eight Cities Past and Present

David M. Addison

Other Books by
David M. Addison

A Meander in Menorca
Misadventures in Tuscany
Bananas About La Palma
An Innocent Abroad
Confessions of a Banffshire Loon
The Cuban Missus Crisis
Still Innocent Abroad
Exploring the NC500

TRAVELS THROUGH TIME IN ITALY

Eight Cities Past and Present

David M. Addison

EXTREMIS publishing

Travels Through Time in Italy: Eight Cities Past and Present by David M. Addison.

First edition published in Great Britain in 2017 by Extremis Publishing Ltd., Suite 218, Castle House, 1 Baker Street, Stirling, FK8 1AL, United Kingdom. *www.extremispublishing.com*

Extremis Publishing is a Private Limited Company registered in Scotland (SC509983) whose Registered Office is Suite 218, Castle House, 1 Baker Street, Stirling, FK8 1AL, United Kingdom.

A CIP catalogue record for this book is available from the British Library.

ISBN: 978-0-9934932-9-4

Typeset in Goudy Bookletter 1911, designed by The League of Moveable Type.
Printed and bound in Great Britain by IngramSpark, Chapter House, Pitfield, Kiln Farm, Milton Keynes, MK11 3LW, United Kingdom.

Front cover artwork is Copyright © JohnBello2015 & Momentmal at Pixabay.
Incidental stock images are Copyright © Pixabay.
Cover design and book design is Copyright © Thomas A. Christie.
Author images are Copyright © Fiona Addison.
Internal photographic illustrations are Copyright © David M. Addison and Fiona Addison, unless otherwise indicated.

Contents

Foreword
by Arup K. Chatterjee

He Made Me an Offer I Couldn't Refuse

I find myself often turning back to David Addison's monographs on Italy, as if editing them, publishing them, or sniggering in slow motion – respectively in that order – was not enough for me. I am tempted to say that his representation of Italy makes philistinism a work of art. But, frankly, what is more endearing, he makes the charge of philistinism – often leveled at the occasional tourist in Europe, especially more so in a polarized world today – a human creed.

What is it really that keeps me from feeling annoyed with yet another innocent abroad seeking "surprisingly sumptuous restaurants" in Florence? Surprisingly indeed, the Victorian architectural theorist, John Ruskin, comes to the rescue. According to him, the Italians were not embarrassed to embellish wall surfaces of their churches, as they dwelled in a juxtaposition of melancholia and philosophical elevation. To Ruskin, Venice was a golden city, writ on marble, paved with emerald, rippling with the thrill of silence. To Addison, Florence is misleadingly comprised of Tuscan marble, the pink too loud, like a child's inedible birthday cake, leaking with candle grease, and the air reeking of milling crowds and their competing cacophonies.

I do not recommend Ruskin to all due to what may be misconstrued as his archaisms. But I recommend Addison to all due to his refusal to be pretentiously modern. Ruskin found Venice, as Addison finds Florence. The former appeared to know more than anyone else about Italian architecture. The latter more than anyone else, is the best at his lack of comprehension, of the same:

> This is another Franciscan church but much more ornate than a Franciscan church ought to be. Far too fussy by half and the combination of pink and green marble does not appeal either... in the days of the rival city-states, you showed your wealth on the outside so travellers passing through would marvel and be impressed by how rich your city was. I suppose you could say this makes the church a weapon of mass deception.

In a world plagued by a race to secure borders or amass nuclear capital, architecture is the last thing we need. What we need is what Addison truly offers the reader. Ruskin made the Italian landscape more architectural than anyone. To that architecture, Addison serves irrepressible wit and laughter. I began rereading Ruskin as a guide to understanding Addison better. But I recommend Addison to all to enrich their Ruskin.

I would also recommend Addison as a contemporary guide to the humors of Oscar Wilde, Mark Twain or G.K. Chesterton. I have never quite understood, whether these authors were really born with some otherworldly finesse in wit, or unnatural grief, or just a childlike sense of wonder upon the world of masquerading adults. Consider Addison's necromanticism, and you will find he is not far from the mark. For like collectors of stamps specialize in species of the wild, Addison claims to specialize in species of tombstones of litterateurs.

Like some philatelists specialise in birds or bees, I specialise in literary graves and have collected amongst many others – Shakespeare, Wordsworth, and the spinster Jane Austen who, being interred in the floor of Winchester Cathedral, was treated to a view up my kilt when I was there for a wedding. I'm not so sure it was such a happy occasion for poor Jane, however. I have also been as close as I can to poor Charlotte and Emily in Haworth but Anne inconsiderately died and lies in Scarborough, so I have yet to do the full Brontë... [Now in Florence], four memorials further down, we come to Machiavelli. It seems curious to pay him the same honour as those other great men, but he was a writer and philosopher and he has certainly achieved immortality, though most would say, "immorality."

Listen to Addison, not if you think you are tired of trained eyes and lecturers who, however well-intentioned, exhaust the traveler's spirit in you. "I am afraid," he says, "I am not listening to Giulia anymore," who is his guide in Florence. He is more eager about his grave quest, and is on his way to Filippo Brunelleschi's tomb. He is now cowed down by the ancients he meets on the way, or hears of being name-dropped by fellow tourists and guides. It would have been rather easy to be overtly reverential or even detached. Addison is neither, but refreshingly unreal. The architectural realism of Italian buildings and frescoes is an underlying theme of Addison's travels in Italy. With so much erudition around him, the most real narrative possible would have been that which necessitates the reader sitting down with a dictionary meant for architectural historians. None of that will be needed here. I have not quite figured how Addison does it, and therefore I must turn back to his writings every once in a while.

It is not as if Addison does not follow the lessons on architecture at all. "The architecture is distinctly ancient Roman, reminiscent of a forum," he says, perhaps unable to resist the showing the fact that some of the discourses have rubbed on him too. But he follows it up by "I half expect to see someone in a toga emerging from behind a pillar, Cicero perhaps, pondering the imponderables, his philosophy becoming more concrete with each circuit. Perhaps that's why I like it so much – the feeling I have slipped through some portal into the past." Addison is here to meet the ancients, not necessarily scavenge on their legacies like a cultural aficionado. Although Giulia's voice keeps coming back to negotiate some artistic rationality back into Addison's journeys, the humorist compulsively pulls him back to his more loveable adventure, in Florence and elsewhere.

> The Crucifixion is indeed in a pretty bad state. Giulia says it is an important painting in the development of art because it shows the real suffering of Christ. He's suffering all right, and not just from the usual causes either but also, it seems, from some nasty disease which has left huge brown patches all over his body.

Perhaps Addison's publisher, or he himself, might like to believe that the author presents settings and landscapes of Italy as he sees them. Nothing could be farther from the truth. Many could have done much the same without capturing the dark comicality of Italian architecture. Worse still, many could have done much the same without even visiting Italy. What quintessentially defines Addison however – much in the same way as what defined Ruskin – is that he writes for his time, which is in need of education. Italy – its Florentine or Neapolitan cobbled streets feminized and cataracted by tourists – has become an opaque destination over the years, more so in the age of Mark Zuckerberg's global clientele. A seemingly benign photograph posted from Italy, or an account of its architecture, cuisine, or people, is not benign after all. It contains traces of the innate colonizer lurking within. But none could be charier of this worrisome spirit of capturing stock landscapes than Addison. He has successfully exorcised it, and has nearly no affectation of seeing the country from within. What he simply wants is to dwell with the ghosts of the men who crafted this land. It is a noble pursuit. And also a hilarious one. Beyond a point, I cannot take Wilde, Twain or Chesterton too seriously. The greats are never meant to be. I have just added Addison to that list. For instance, I can never ascribe sincerity or cunning to the following. No sooner do I interpret this as yet another case of the author's mischievous wit, I may be told, this was an exceptional statement of his honest wonder.

> Now we have reached the Piazza Plebiscito. Now this is what I call a piazza! It is vast! On our left is the Palazzo Reale, an austere edifice taking up one entire side, and on the right, the church of San Francesco di Paola. Now that is what I call a church!

Be that as it may, Addison's Italy is an offer you simply cannot refuse. I can assure you, having read it, both you and the ghosts of Cicero, Caesar or Michelangelo, would be rolling upon his book, with leisurely laughter. I certainly am.

Arup K. Chatterjee is Founding Editor-in-Chief at Coldnoon International Journal of Travel Writing and

Travelling Cultures (*coldnoon.com*), and Assistant Professor of English at O.P. Jindal Global University in Sonipat, India.

Map of Italy

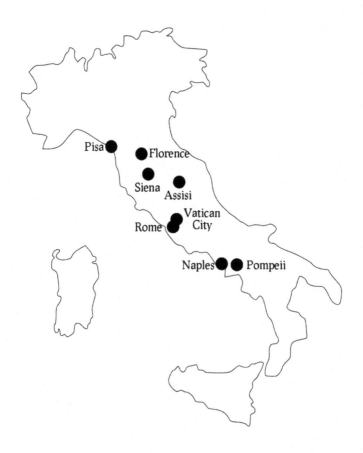

Pisa

Florence

Siena

Assisi

Vatican City

Rome

Naples

Pompeii

TRAVELS THROUGH TIME IN ITALY

Eight Cities Past and Present

David M. Addison

Prelude

L ONG before Thomas Cook made mass tourism to Italy possible in the 1860s there was the Grand Tour which, believe it or not, goes back a couple of centuries before that. Of course you had to be rich to do that and with plenty of time on your hands, so naturally it appealed to the young men of the aristocracy. Some young women also undertook the Tour, accompanied by a chaperone, naturally. Nice work if you can get it.

Arguably the most famous Grand Tourist of all was Goethe (1749-1842) who regaled his readers with his adventures in his *Italian Journey*. Seen as a sort of educational finishing school, the Tour took in the famous cities of Europe, particularly the Classical and Renaissance sights of Italy. They would visit Turin, Florence, Pisa, Padua, Bologna, Venice and Rome before finishing up in Naples and Pompeii.

I am neither young nor an aristocrat, just a wrinkly on a package tour, like hundreds of others – because they make it so easy for us nowadays.

Back then, the trip might last one or two years and was not without its dangers. My illustrious namesake, Joseph Addison, the founder of *The Spectator* is said to have made a spectacle of himself by falling into the harbour at Calais. History does not record if he was drunk or not. Well, that is not going to happen to me. I am not going to Calais.

We are going directly to Naples, my wife Iona, aka La Belle Dame Sans Merci, and me. Thus perversely and true to type, at least as far as I am concerned, on this modern-day Grand Tour of Italy, I set the tone right from the beginning, starting off where the real Grand Tourists finished.

Another major difference between our trip and those of yesteryear is that ours is only going to last two weeks rather than two years. How blessed is today's Grand Tourist who can be whisked off to Naples from Heathrow in three hours or less! In just one week, we shall be visiting Naples, Pompeii, Assisi, Florence, Pisa, Siena, and Rome. And then, after that, we shall be spending a second week in Sorrento, a stepping-stone to attractions such as Vesuvius, Herculaneum and the Amalfi coast. Thanks to the marvels of modern transport, we

Vesuvius and Harbour

can cram in much more in a fraction of the time it took to rat-
tle over those rough roads in carriages all those centuries ago.

But first we have to get from Edinburgh to Heathrow.
And that was where our troubles started. Troubles that the
original Grand Tourist never dreamed of – not even in his
worst nightmares...

Yes, they make it so easy for us nowadays.

Naples by Night

1
Neapolitan Street Party

I T would have been nice to have seen Naples for the first time from the sea, the way Nelson did in 1798 when he supported the King of Naples, sorted out the French and where an unintended consequence was meeting the love of his life, Emma Hamilton, which led to difficulties of another kind.

But now that we are in the old part, Naples is taking on its own individual character and unlike Goethe who was here in 1787 and who, in his *Italian Journey*, described it as "a paradise", my first impressions are not so favourable. The buildings may have had a certain glory once, but now they are dingy and dirty and many are crumbling. The whole place has an air of decadence, not helped by the fact that there does not appear to be any street lighting other than that coming from shop windows and car headlights. It gives the place a semi-deserted, half-shut sort of look, as if the inhabitants have had enough of all the squalor and are in the process of evacuation, turning off the lights one by one as they leave.

When I ask Angela, our guide, why there are no lights, she has a conversation with the driver and reports they are conserving electricity because of the drought. It has not rained since early May. We are more than half way through July.

From our position above and behind Enrico, the driver, even if the architecture is not very appealing, we have the compensation of a grandstand view of some fine examples of mad Italian driving.

It is not for the hesitant, driving in Naples. Those who are will never get anywhere, never mind lost. There appear to be no rules. Angela says the traffic lights are for decoration, pedestrian crossings are street paintings and nobody pays any attention to either. This also applies to Italy's attitude towards EU legislation.

"The Germans make the laws, the British obey them, the French ignore them and the Italians have never heard of them," Angela says, laughing. "They've just introduced a seatbelt law," she adds. (God knows how many years we've had that!) "They're also supposed to wear crash helmets on their scooters but no one bothers. You'll often see a man and his wife and his son, sometimes even a dog on a scooter and no one is wearing a crash helmet."

"Except for the dog," I remark to Angela, who is just across the passage.

It's not quite true though: there are one or two who are wearing crash helmets and here is a boy with bare feet standing on the platform behind the handlebars, holding on to them in a casual sort of way, as if he has been doing it for years – which he probably has ever since he was tall enough to reach them. Interestingly, the father *is* wearing a helmet. He has less faith in his driving than his son apparently or maybe he thinks there's no point in getting him one until he's fully grown – if he makes it that far.

The aim of driving in Naples seems to be to get as close as you can to the car in front without actually touching it, but this doesn't always work, judging by the number of vehicles with bashes in them. It's dodgems without the protective rubber bumpers. Amazingly, despite more close shaves than all the Wilkinson Swords in Italy, Enrico does not seem to mind all the cars and all the scooters in Naples cutting him up and having to brake sharply to avoid hitting them. Here size gives way to agility; might does not automatically secure the right of way. Enrico cannot bulldoze his way through the Neapolitan traffic willy-nilly. It's like Goliath taking on David and we all know who won that one.

Now Enrico wants to turn right up a narrow street but he can't because his bus is so long it will not allow him to make the manoeuvre without slicing the side off an abandoned car on the corner, like peeling back the lid of a sardine can.

A bar stands on the opposite corner. Seeing the problem, one of the customers comes over to give Enrico non-verbal directions by waving his arms about like those people with table tennis bats who semaphore to pilots where preciseley to park their planes. Enrico has opened the door and gives a full-throated response to what he thinks of that. It might be expletives for all I know. It certainly sounds like it. He might uncharitably be telling the would-be guide to mind his own business – or, and I am thinking this might just possibly be nearer the mark – if he'd kindly go and drag that moron of a motorist out of that bar, he'd happily disembowel him with his bare hands.

A crowd begins to gather as drinkers come to add their tuppenceworth. Suddenly the street has sprung to life with a multitude of voices.

Angela, over her microphone says, "Welcome to Neapolitan life! Now the whole street is going to become involved!"

She says it as if she relishes it and I have to admit, I do find it interesting. This is not the sort of scene which you would see in, say Glasgow, and certainly not in Aberdeen, the home of my *alma mater*, the granite city with the tough exterior where you would rather die than reveal your feelings. Besides, it's too bloody cold to hang about the streets there.

But these southern Europeans, hot-blooded with a superfluity of sun, cannot wait to get involved. The gentle Neapolitan air is filled with the sound of shouting. We haven't a clue what's being said and that is the romance of being in a foreign place. Are they cursing or giving helpful advice? There is a lot of gesticulating going on. Meanwhile Enrico carries on manoeuvring, moving forward until there seems to be a coat of paint only between the front of the bus and the car in front of him to the left, then the bus rocks on its brakes and Enrico switches his attention to his offside mirror and puts the bus into reverse. Iona is shutting her eyes and breathing in as if that would somehow make the bus narrower.

The Streets of Naples
(Image Credit: Pixabay)

"I don't like this seat," she says from between clenched teeth.

At the other side, where I can't see properly, there

seems to be a crowd gathered round the car on the right. The roof is rocking wildly. They seem to be bouncing it and lifting it to make a bit of extra room for the bus. It takes me back to years ago, when as a schoolboy, my colleagues bounced the French *assistant's* Citroen Deux Chevaux from the back of the school to the front. Any car that looks like an upturned pram is just asking to be rocked.

Here presumably, they can't find the owner, or maybe this is the more fun way of doing it and that's the owner over there who is shouting more vociferously than all the rest: *Hey, get your filthy hands off my car!* It looks as if a street fight could break out at any time but it's maybe just a Neapolitan street party. It's not every place you go where they throw an impromptu street party in your honour, but Angela has given us the feeling that this is the sort of thing you might expect to see here any day of the week.

At last Enrico manages to swing the bus past the offending car, and somewhat belatedly, the self-appointed director of traffic gestures to Enrico that he can get past. Enrico is saying something but it is impossible to judge by his tone what it might be or to whom it might be addressed but he doesn't give any sign of acknowledgement for the director's "help" so I assume Enrico has thought him a spare part all along.

We give Enrico a round of applause but his part is not over yet. A hundred yards or so up this street with cars to the left of us, and cars to the right of us like the cannons flanking the Six-Hundred in the Valley of Death and with us all holding in our breath as we pass up the middle, Enrico stops again. It is too narrow to pass. He gets out and folds back a wing mirror of a car on the left, then he inches forward, then shunts, comes forward, reverses again. By inches we are getting there. This time there is no audience to applaud the deed, and although Iona and I have ringside seats, she cannot bear to look. I notice that most of the cars, if they have wing mirrors at all, are folded in. The cars they belong to are bashed and covered in dust. Perhaps although it looks like a street, it's really a Neapolitan scrapyard.

But what, I wonder, happened as Enrico completed his manoeuvre and we left the onlookers behind in the street, still arguing? Did the party stop as suddenly as it had begun, or is there a different type of scrap going on at this very moment?

Neapolitan Evening Stroll

FROM the 7th floor towards heaven of our skyscraper hotel, but not visible from our room unfortunately, I am impressed by the sight of a very striking fort-like building. It turns out to be the Castel Nuovo which dates from 1279 and was much in the wars during the succeeding centuries, sometimes requiring extensive remodelling.

If there is one thing I can't resist it's a medieval castle, so despite the lateness of the hour and the weariness of the body after all the stresses of the day and which I won't bother you with except to say that our flight to Heathrow from Edinburgh was at first delayed and then cancelled due to industrial action by BA staff. We were very lucky to be able to get a couple of tickets from another carrier, albeit at enormous expense, because come hell and high water, we just had to get to Heathrow that evening in order to catch our connection to Naples the following day.

Yes, they make it so easy for the Grand Tourist nowadays.

We head out into the soft Neapolitan night. This is what I adore about the continent – to set out, to stroll in shirtsleeves

Castel Nuovo

and shorts into the velvet warmth of an evening that would be considered a blisteringly hot afternoon in Scotland.

We go through a park teeming with people; even little kids who should be in bed long ago, are still up. Now we need to cross the road but that is more easily said than done. Despite that zebra-striped piece of contemporary art which someone has gone to all the trouble of painting on the road, not a single driver slows down, let alone stops to acknowledge our presence, but thunders over it as if we (and it) weren't there. No, we are just not going to be able to cross here unless we want to end up being scraped off that black-and-white stripy thing like strawberry jam.

We retrace our steps and like the attackers of old, I imagine, come at the fort from a different angle – you can see the impact of where a cannonball has left a dent high up on one of the crenellated walls – and this time we are successful. Now we are as close as we can get due to the enormous moat which separates us. Apart from the soaring walls, what impresses me most is the way the immense round towers fan out at the bottom, like the pleats on a tennis skirt, something I have always found rather sexy.

Somewhere in the distance, down by the port, I hear the sound of music from an open-air concert. Some people would call it "music" I suppose, but I don't and I'm sure Rogers and Hammerstein wouldn't either – though I have to admit, it does add a certain ambience to the evening. To our left, a neon sign on a pharmacy broadcasts the time and the temperature for anyone who would care to look: *22:22 28°C.* Perfect. Just right for a little stroll.

But La Belle Dame Sans Merci puts her (weary) foot down – no way is she going to walk all the way round the Castel, as was my intention. And, I have to admit, now we

Castel Nuovo by night

have rounded one of the five massive crenellated towers and can see what lies ahead, it does look a bit of a trek. And being next to a busy street with the roar of traffic and the irritating buzz of Vespas for company, it doesn't seem the most appealing or romantic of walks either, so we turn around and in a short while come to a footbridge with an arch at the end of it. I just *have* to cross it to see where it leads but the tired and footsore lady is not going one step further than is necessary and that is flat! So leaving her alone and palely loitering, like the knight-at-arms in *La Belle Dame Sans Merci*, I set off to see what I shall see.

Once through the arch, I find myself standing at the front of the castle and facing three of the fat towers which make me think of upended giant cotton reels. Incongruously, linking the central two is a two-tiered marble arch. With its Corinthian pillars and elaborately-carved figures and not least, the contrasting whiteness against the austere brown of the plain, brick towers, it looks singularly out of place, like a brand-new tooth in a set of coffee-stained dentures.

It dates from 1443 when Alfonso V of Aragon became Alfonso I of Naples and Sicily. He seems to have collected places to rule over like other people collect postage stamps. Now be prepared to suspend your disbelief – he was also Alphonso III of Valencia; Alphonso II of Majorca, Sardinia and Corsica; Alphonso I of Sicily and finally, he was Count Alphonso V of Barcelona. But perhaps we shouldn't count that one.

It looks distinctly out of place, this fresh-faced triumphal arch squashed between the two fat, ancient, round, brown towers. Not a happy marriage this combination of styles and if I don't start heading back right away, it's not the only unhappy marriage there is going to be.

Soon we come across a couple of *scugnizzi*, small boys with two plastic washbasins full of empty beer bottles. Presumably they are collecting them to sell for a few cents somewhere. Unemployment in Naples is at a staggering 28% compared to 12% in the country generally and crime is rampant, so they say. As a matter of fact, I have noticed a number of cars displaying some very sturdy anti-theft devices. Yet I feel completely at ease and the warm air with its gentle breeze and the distant strains of the music from the concert create a very ambient atmosphere. The only crime I have seen so far is that crime against architecture, that incongruous and just too-too white triumphal arch, though I suppose what I really don't like about it is its location. As a piece of art per se, I'm sure it is very fine indeed.

At the top of the grassy Piazza Municipio which we had come through earlier, and occupying one whole side of it, is a very attractive pale-yellow building with olive-green windows. It is an elegant symphony to symmetry. Some flags are lazily stirring over the entrance and a brass plaque in Italian, but which I can work out thanks to the little Latin remaining to me, tells me it's the Town Hall (1819-25).

Our hotel, on the other hand, has nothing to recommend it architecturally, being no more than a rectangular cornflake box with perforations for windows, but it does have the advantage of height and its flat roof does make an excellent vantage point, so just before we turn in, I suggest we go up (it's only two flights up the staircase from our floor) to soak in a little more of the atmosphere.

The floodlit Castel Nuovo dominates. Despite its glaringly-white triumphal arch, I think it is one of the most splendid buildings of its type I have ever seen. Away down in the park where the lighting is soft and yellow in contrast to the stark-white illumination of the Castel, the sound of the laughter of the ant-like children comes filtering through the trees. Further away, down by the port, obscured by darkness, the sound of the concert is wafted up on the breeze which even the thrumming of the nearby myriad of invisible cicadas fails to drown out. Some twelve hours ago I doubted if I would ever see the sights and sounds of Naples this day but here I am, breathing in the warm wisteria-scented air. It feels good to be alive.

Virgil it was who first remarked: "Videre Neapolim et Mori", and not a lot of people realise that the phrase adopted by Goethe in his *Italian Journey*, "See Naples and die", is actually a pun revolving around the Italian *mori* meaning "die" and Mori, a small village outside Neapolis (literally "new city") in Virgil's day.

So said those two great poets. My poet, Keats, after whose famous character I named my trouble and strife, said unequivocally:

Now more than ever seems it rich to die,
To cease upon the midnight with no pain...

I wouldn't go quite so far as that but my feet are killing me and we're not far off the bewitching hour. Time for bed.

We have a long way to go tomorrow. Back to 79 AD in fact, and Pompeii.

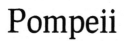

Pompeii

3

The Human Standard Lamp

UNLIKE Jane Eyre, there is every possibility of *us* taking a walk today. The alarm bell, really our telephone, began our day by ringing at 7:30. We are being picked up at 8:30 for our half-day trip to Pompeii and in the afternoon we have a walking tour of Naples, so we shall be doing plenty of walking, both in the past and the present.

When we get to Pompeii, we have a problem. Angela is on her mobile because our guide has not turned up. She tells us he is on his way, that there has been a misunderstanding.

Meanwhile we evacuate the bus and loiter at the street corner. Most people are in the shade, but I hang about at the edge of the group, in the sun. There are a few stalls selling books and souvenirs and, across the road, a stall selling water. Whilst Iona looks at the books, I go across to get some more water. Judging by the heat already, it looks like we will need it.

"Una grande acqua freddo, per favore." I have no idea how correct that is but I do know that confusingly, in Italian, *caldo,* which you would expect to mean "cold", actually means "hot". I also think I might be confusing my little Spanish with my little Italian. But it seems to be good enough because the vendor rattles off the price in Italian so fast I haven't a clue how much it is. So much for trying to embrace the language.

I can only look back at him like an idiot. "Eh?" I am conscious of sounding and feeling like Manuel in *Fawlty Towers*.

He repeats it just as rapidly as before. I nod sagely, as if I had understood and rake about in my pouch for some coins. I can't get at them for some notes, so I take them out and put them down on a wooden table nearby. I hand over some coins and he gives some of them back to me. This could be the dearest water in Italy – I haven't had time to get used to the euro and haven't a clue what I gave him or what I got back. I slip the change into my pouch, zip it up and turn to go. I've only gone a couple of steps when I suddenly remember the notes. Phew! That *really* would have been the dearest water in Italy.

Meanwhile, Iona has bought a book which shows Pompeii then and now. It's a great idea. There is a colour photo of a ruin as it is now and on the facing page, a colour transparency which you slip over the scene and, hey presto! an artist's impression of what it looked like before the eruption. Brilliant! She shows it to some of our fellow tourists who like it so much they buy one for themselves. (Pity she wasn't on commission.)

We hang about in the broiling heat waiting for our guide. At last he arrives. His name is Marco and he expresses his apologies in a lilting sort of voice, placing the stress at the end of each sentence. I suppose that's the Italian way. It seems the site employees have been staging half-day strikes and he had been told one was scheduled for this morning rather than this afternoon. He is carrying a hat rolled up like a scroll and when he uncurls it and plonks it on his head, I can't help thinking it looks like a pleated lampshade.

We set off towards the *Scavi* but before we get there, he stops and gives us a talk about the eruption and how Pompeii's fate differed from that of Herculaneum. Whilst Pompeii was buried under a ceaseless downpour of ash and cinders, Herculaneum was engulfed by a pyroclastic surge, a mixture of mud and gases as hot as 500° C. It boiled the victims' blood and split their skulls wide open when their brains expanded. No doubt about it, had I been given the choice in 79 AD, I'd rather have been a resident of Pompeii. On that fateful day, 24th August, restoration was still not complete from an earthquake in 62 AD. That's what it's like living in the shadow of an active volcano though they didn't know they were until then.

Standing under the shade of some pines, if we look to our right along the grove of oleander, we can it see sleeping peacefully now. It has been having a nap since 1944 but one of these days it is going to rouse itself again. What no-one knows is when that day will come, but come it will. Probably the first sign will be an earthquake.

I hope it will not be when we are here. At a conservative estimate, 2,000 people died that day in Pompeii alone, including some gladiators who were chained up and unable to flee. Can you imagine the panic there would be today, if alerted by the early warning system, the 3 million and more residents of the metropolitan area of Naples tried to put as much distance as they could between them and the volcano – the roads choked with traffic, the harbour clogged with ships. As hopeless a flight for their lives as that fight for their lives those poor gladiators never got the chance to make.

Before we get to the ticket booths, Marco picks up a book just like the one Iona had bought but does not pay for it and tells us this is the last chance to buy water. There are only 18 of us. It's a good number because we can all gather around Marco without him having to project his voice as if he were addressing a public meeting, as Queen Victoria complained about Gladstone.

It is a bit disappointing to enter the city along a wooden ramp instead of treading where Roman sandals trod nearly two millennia ago but I needn't have worried. Once through an arch, actually the Porta Marina, we are on the actual cobblestones, though to call them "cobblestones" calls to mind our puny little ones and which doesn't do these monsters justice. I'd like to see rioters digging these up and throwing them at the police! They are enormous and irregular with gaps between them which must have made riding in a wagon or cart such a bone-shaking experience that it's a wonder that everyone didn't get out and walk.

Marco enters a side street and ushers his flock into the shade, though I am able to find a spot in the sun within hearing range. He points out some ruts where the carts have worn grooves in the stone. Further along the street are massive blocks of stone which would seem to obstruct vehicular passage but actually are stepping stones so that people carrying heavy loads, suspended from poles over their shoulders, didn't have to step off the high pavements and climb up again and break their necks in the process. And here's the cunning part; the height of the stones is sufficiently low to allow clearance for the axles of the carts to pass through. And the reason that the pavements are so high is because the streets doubled as a drainage and sewage system. Yes, well, maybe that's not such a nice idea.

It is easy to project oneself back two thousand years and imagine ordinary life, the hustle and the bustle there must have been on this street for it is bustling now and still sandal-trod. But what would the citizens make of those, like some in our group, who are wearing shorts with sandals *and* socks? Some strange new cult? And what would the punishment be for such sartorial impropriety? Exile or death? Anyway, shockingly socked-and-sandaled or not, as the case may be, we set off to follow in the footsteps of the last inhabitants of Pompeii and explore their town.

The first stop is the Basilica. This, of course, was long before Christianity became the major world religion it is now, so it has nothing do with churches, though the architects pinched the idea for the great cathedrals. This is a secular building, a meeting place, but principally, the law courts. An immense structure, intimidating in itself, but with the podium where the magistrates sat so high up it must have made any defendant standing beneath it feel like an insignificant little worm upon whom the full weight of the law was just about to descend: *You are charged with wearing socks and sandals and making yourself look a right pleb. Sentenced to 200 hours community service for offending public decency. Take him down!*

The place is pretty-much ruined now, one of the places they didn't quite get round to restoring completely after the earthquake of 62 BC, never mind the catastrophic events seventeen years later, so Iona's book with the transparency comes in pretty useful as I can see just how awe-inspiring it was in its heyday.

But apart from the huge scale of the building, the thing that captures my interest particularly is because of its ruinous state, you can see the construction of a Roman pillar. Made of

The Basilica

cheap brick, the whole thing is then covered in plaster and then given a coating of marble dust and – transformation! You have what looks like a column of marble! Put a lot of these together and you create a place of elegance and apparent affluence, perhaps even opulence.

Now imagine all those northern industrial streets with the back-to-back red brick houses being given a veneer of powdered marble! Now that really would be something, wouldn't it?

Street in Pompeii showing cobbles, cart tracks, high pavements and stepping stones

4

Pompeii:
Baths, Bodies and Bread

WE'RE off to see the Forum along the Via dell'Abbondanza, that great artery than runs through the city from east to west. Then, as now, the Forum is a large open rectangular area – the heart of the city, a market place and also where religious and civic functions took place. At the northern end once stood the Temple of Jupiter and behind the ruins, looking surprisingly near, shouldering into the cloudless azure sky, is the hulking presence of Vesuvius.

Three massive blocks of stone, not stepping stones these, ensure the Forum is a pedestrian precinct: this far can the vehicular traffic come and no further. Turning must have been a nightmare as there is no turning circle. And if another cart was beside you, and another twenty behind, what did you do? Traffic jams: yet another idea we got from the Romans. I can imagine them all, shouting and gesticulating, telling the cart driver how to manoeuvre, like Enrico with his bus. It makes me wonder if they had rules of the road then, or did they just do what they pleased, like the Italian drivers of today? Perhaps we should understand that that was how it was then and that is why it is as it is today. *Plus ça change* and all that.

In one of the market places off to the right of the Forum are some faded frescoes but more interesting and grim, enshrined in two glass cases, two victims of the eruption have been put on display. The first of these, we are told, is a boy of about 15. The expression on his face is one of agony as he gasped his last breath. In his contorted posture, it is a reminder of how awful it must have been that day, how great the panic, how desperate the struggle to flee, to take to the ships, to escape what must have seemed to them, the wrath of the gods. From his extended hand, I can see the bones of his fingers emerging from the grey plaster: for this is how he has

The Forum and Vesuvius

been resurrected. He lay covered in ash for eighteen-hundred years until the first archaeologists poured plaster into the cavity created by the decomposed flesh and thus preserved him forever for us to gawk at.

It reminds me of a similar idea I saw a number of years ago in the Dordogne. A dead pig had been immersed in running water and slowly the corpse was being calcified due to the heavy concentration of limestone in the water. I thought then and still think now, what a wonderful way to dispose of a corpse! I'd like that: I could be put out in the garden as an ornament – think of the variety of artistic poses I could be twisted into once rigor mortis had worn off. Or instead of an artistic use, I could be something practical, like a hat or an umbrella stand. Or think of the fun the grandchildren could have playing hoopla with Grumpa!

Next stop are the baths or *thermae*. We are going to the Stabian baths, the oldest in Pompeii, dating from the 4th or 5th century BC. I am already familiar with the principle behind Roman baths, having been to Bath and many other Roman baths besides, though as expected, these are in a much better state of preservation.

First there is the *apodyterium* or dressing room, but it should really be the undressing room. Here you can see the holes in the walls where once were the shelves where the patrons placed their clothes and belongings. Next is the *tepidarium* (work it out for yourself) then the *calidarium* (hot room, remember) containing the *alveus* or hot tub and the *laconicum* or steam bath, what we call a sauna. The whole system is operated by a hypocaust, an ingenious underfloor heating system (another idea we nicked from the Romans).

There are men's and women's sections: none of your mixed bathing here, and no funny business either. It is a common misconception that Roman baths were scenes of debauchery and depravity. That only happened in the latter days of the Empire and Pompeii never survived to see that.

The baths are swarming with people, and bizarrely, two hot dogs, their sides heaving rhythmically in deep slumber with their tongues lolling out, their method of sweating. It beats me why they should choose this location for a nap amongst the constant tramp of feet just centimetres from their ears, not to mention the Babel's Tower of guides' voices. If anything, it shows just how dog-tired they must be. A bit like me actually. Like the hitchhiker said in *The Grapes of Wrath,* "My dogs are pooped out." Like him, I'm footsore already and if I were a dog, my tongue would be hanging out too as it's as hot as Hades in here.

It is quite hard to hear Marco amongst all this mêlée, so it's as well that this is the area of Roman architecture I need to learn least about. However, the one thing I do learn, which intrigues me, is that the roof in the *calidarium* is grooved, like a Nissen hut in the Second World War which allows the condensation to run down the channels instead of dripping onto the patrons below. These Romans seem to have thought of everything.

The Stabian baths are near the brothels (so you are nice and clean – apparently already aware of sexually transmitted diseases) and that's where we are off to next, via the House of the Vettii.

We can't get in there today as it is under restoration, but Marco takes us up a side street so we can peer through an iron-grilled window at a famous pornographic fresco. It looks like a grocer weighing a leek and a couple of onions but in fact, it is Priapus casually weighing his phallus, as you do. It is poking out obscenely from beneath his tunic and reaches his knees. He's not looking too happy so I presume it's lost a bit of weight.

Actually, I think he should be more cheerful. I don't know what effect his weapon of mass reproduction had on the horses, unless it was to make them jealous, but I bet it frightened the ladies to death. A ding-a-ling like that don't mean a thing even if it could swing like a scythe at a sickle party. The more I think about it, the more I am convinced that the reason for his glum expression is that he has realised, through experience, that like Enrico's bus, size isn't everything – a curse even.

Marco wants to know what Iona thinks of it. She gives it a brief glance and him short shrift.

"Disgusting!"

Marco seems disappointed and says that it is only recently that women have been allowed to see this fresco and others of an erotic content, implying Iona is very lucky indeed. If he had hoped she would find it arousing, he's sadly mistaken.

Modest, Priapus is not, but next stop for us is Modestum's bakery. You can see the holes where the shafts of wood were threaded through the grindstones to be turned by the slaves, poor devils. The oven is still here too. In fact, the whole place must have been like an oven when you take into account the baking temperature outside.

Amazingly, archaeologists found 81 carbonised loaves here. Marco shows us a picture of one in the book which Iona has bought. It is divided into segments like a sponge cake and I must admit that although it looks a trifle well-fired, I like the look of it a whole lot better than the loaves Iona bakes in her bread machine. We are on our third one now and I think currently, a loaf is working out at something like £27.10.

Modestum's Bakery

Anyway, man cannot live by bread alone, and we're on our way to the *lupanar* or brothel – at long last. My tongue has been practically hanging out to go there.

5

Pompeii:
House of Ill-Repute and
Other Houses

I T'S like the lunchtime queue outside the baker's at home,
only worse. But we are not outside Modestum's bakery
now: we are outside the brothel. Was it like this then, I
wonder? It's at a three-way intersection and they are queuing
up from each direction. Did the punters, as Milton didn't
quite write centuries later, stand and wait to be served in a
queue as long as this? Most of the streets in Pompeii are built
in a grid design (another thing we got from the Romans) but
this brothel is on one of the few twisty streets in Pompeii.
Marco says it's so people couldn't see where you were making
for. As if they wouldn't have guessed if they saw you on that
street!

Never mind the goings-on inside; the building itself is very
interesting. Forming two arms of a Y, it's a two-storey affair

The Lupanar

and shaped like the prow of a ship, the upper storey hanging over the ground floor and extending so far as to over-shadow the narrow pavement. I bet this place was high on the list for restoration after the earthquake of 62 and by the looks of it, appears to have been given a lot of attention since the disaster of 79. It looks the newest building in Pompeii, as if the restorers knew this is what would draw the crowds. There must be something about brothels which intrigue us; even the baths were not as busy as this, and everyone has been to the baths.

When we eventually get inside, our time is regrettably all too short as we are processed along a conveyer belt of humanity along the ground floor only. There isn't time to stop and look properly into a room unless you want to be trampled underfoot by the perpetual motion of the stream pushing to get in from behind, so to speak.

Above each door is an erotic fresco. Here is one of a woman with very small breasts sitting astride her client. Unfortunately, or fortunately as far as Iona is concerned, the fresco is badly damaged in the vital area. He has his right hand raised as if in a cheery greeting to someone who has just come into the room, but more likely he is saying *Hold! Enough!* – only in Latin, of course. Or else he is waving cheerily at someone who has just come into the room: *Hello, dear, it's not what you think. I'm just doing a bit of research for my novel.*

It's a windowless and cramped cell and although that unappealing hard stone bed (like something out of *The Flintstones*) would have had a palliasse on it, it looks far from inviting. Had these walls ears, what sounds would they have heard? Had they eyes, what sights would they have witnessed? It couldn't have been very erotic, I reflect, especially with other patrons passing by within feet of you, although there presumably was at least a curtain, so they didn't get a free show.

In and out, done and dusted and before we know it, we are back out into the baking sun and off for a more cultured place of entertainment. We are off to the theatres. Yes, theatres. Pompeii had two, side by side and a porticoed quadrangle behind them (later turned into a gladiators' barracks) where patrons could take a stroll during intermissions. The big theatre, seating about 5,000, staged dramas, whilst the smaller Odeon, seating about 1,200, was used for musical concerts and poetry readings. How cultured were the ancient Romans! And how barbaric too! The Ying and the Yang.

And how modern! They had fast-food shops, so close to the road that you could purchase a snack without getting out of your cart if you didn't feel like it. And to think I was misguided enough to once believe that it was the Americans who had dreamed up the notion of drive-in takeaways! You can see the marble counters in which are set the *amphorae* which once held the hot food but which now contain the killer ash. Marco says they did that as tourists were using the *amphorae* as rubbish bins. I take out a lump and put it in my pocket to take home as a souvenir. It's not as if it's rubbish. Besides, there's plenty more where that came from.

Marco the Guide with his lamp-shade hat at a fast-food place

And if the Romans were advanced in the matter of take-aways, when it comes to the matter of housing, those of the rich make my modest dwelling look like a slum. But then I am by no means a man of means.

The basic structure consists of an entrance hallway which they called the *vestibulum*, which leads to the *atrium*, a porti-coed area open to the elements with its *impluvium* to catch the rainwater. Then there is the *peristilium* which would have been my favourite part of the house. This is an open courtyard area, a sort of inner garden off which the other rooms opened. What a grand design to have a garden inside your house and how cool in both the literal and modern par-lance of the word which signifies excellence, to have a water feature too! Totally impractical in Scotland, of course.

As we pass "The House of The Tragic Poet", so called be-cause of a mosaic in the *tablinum,* or main room, used for receiving guests, I notice a black-and-white mosaic behind another of those grilles like at the House of The Vettii. It depicts a fierce dog with teeth bared, straining against his chain. At the bottom is written: *Cave Canem*. I know it well from my Latin textbook and it sends a tingle down my spine to see it for real.

Next we visit "The House of The Faun" so called because there is a diminutive bronze statue of a naked bearded bloke prancing about in the middle of the *impluvium*. Bizarrely, he has a ponytail sprouting from the middle of his back. Fortunately there is a transparency in the book and I can see just how sumptuous the house is. What's special about it is that it contains not one, but two *peristyles* and an *exedra,* a recess with seats, where lofty conversation could take place in the peace and tranquillity of pleasant surroundings.

It must have seemed a million miles from the Via Della Fortuna which is the main thoroughfare on which it stands. I adore its open spaciousness, how you can look from the atrium to see the peristyles beyond and when you think of all the mosaics and frescoes which would have surrounded you,

The Faun

it must have seemed like paradise. These Romans knew how to live, I think. Wonderful houses, public baths and theatres, and plumbing better than in French campsites today. But of course you would have to have been rich, and I would have been one of those poor slaves pushing the grindstone at the bakery or a porter tripping over the stepping stones with a heavy load and not enough money to go to the bordello at the end of the week, so there's no point in feeling jealous – especially if you happened to be there in 79AD.

On the way to our exit through the badly damaged Temple of Venus, Marco points out a public drinking fountain (another idea we adopted but, no doubt due to the advent of the canned drink, is an endangered species these days) and embedded in the pavement, a sign. It is a phallus with its blunt tip pointing to the left to indicate to visitors that the way to the brothel is the first street on the left. How thoughtful! Avoids the embarrassment of strangers tramping around aimlessly looking for it and eventually, in desperation, having to ask directions from someone whom you think is not going to be morally outraged. Or if you are a resident, what a great thing to be able to keep your head down (just in case you bump into someone who might recognise you) and at the same time make sure you are heading in the right direction. These Romans think of everything!

Marco hands his book with the transparencies back to the vendor from whom he borrowed it. Ah, so this is how it works! The vendor tells us that we can buy this book for less than the marked price. Damn! Why didn't we wait? But it's all right. It's the same price as we paid. They mark it up then reduce the price and everyone's happy: the tourists think they've got a bargain, the vendors get a sale and they all agree on the same price, so it doesn't matter where you buy it.

It's time to say *ciao* to Marco – our trip to Pompeii is over. But we haven't seen half of it! It should have been a whole-day excursion. Only we couldn't anyway because of the strike. Having said that, my feet are *loupin'* as we say in Scotland. We must have walked for miles and on unforgiving hard surfaces too, but more tiring still was when we were standing listening to Marco, not because what he said was boring, far from it, but because I was more conscious of the weight on my legs.

I watch as his slim, lanky frame with the lampshade hat on the top disappears down the street, for all the world like a walking standard lamp. There he goes, as Burns said of Holy Willie, "a burning and a shining light", having illuminated for me some of the fascinating history of Pompeii.

Naples by Day

6

Traffic Police and Pizzas

THERE are still hours to go before our afternoon walk. Our feet are recovered from the pavements of Pompeii, so we decide to pound those of Napoli instead. The objective is to go to the National Archaelogical Museum to see the artefacts which were removed from Pompeii. I think it is a pity they haven't built a museum in the vicinity of the *Scavi*, it would have been fitting to have spent the afternoon there, having visited the places where they actually came from.

The trouble is, I can't find any information about buses and I'm too poor to afford a taxi after having to stump up £320 for the emergency flight to Heathrow. Actually, to tell the truth, I'd rather not have the hassle of negotiating a price with a taxi driver because I think I may as well have *I'm a tourist, rip me off* written across my T-shirt.

According to a digital display on the Via Monteoliveto, it is 34°C. It's as if we are not together, Iona and I. We are the *chiaroscuro* pair: I walk on the sunny side of the street whilst she walks in the shade. Apart from this arrangement matching my, oh, so sunny disposition, I like to feel the warmth of the sun on my back. Of course it makes conversation a bit difficult but there is nothing to say, unless it is to comment on the tattiness of the buildings or, as we pass the side streets, the yards of washing hanging like bunting from the tenement flats.

At the junction with the Via Toledo, police are lying in wait for unsuspecting motorists. Now they have actually heard of it, it seems the Italians really are taking this seat belt legislation seriously and with the zeal of the newly-converted. Here's one poor devil being flagged down by a cop holding what looks like a table-tennis bat. He's directed round the corner where another policeman, armed with a clipboard, confronts the hapless victim. This could be interesting so I loiter about to see what happens. It doesn't look like it's just a warning as pages of paperwork are being completed, which, to my disappointment, the transgressor takes with Anglo-Saxon sang-froid, not southern Italian hot-headedness.

Leaving him to his fate, we arrive at the Piazza Dante. This would be a very attractive square but for two things. Firstly there is an extremely ugly Metro station, all Perspex and tubular grey steel and secondly, there is some exhibition or other going on, so, like the Louvre with its pesky pyramid, it's impossible to get an uninterrupted view of the very fine curved façade of the Convitto Nazionale Vittorio Emanuele with its massive pillars and triumphal arch. The roof has a balustrade dotted with statues, said to be allegories of the virtues of Charles VII of Naples, all 26 of them. They may have considered him a good king but can anyone really be as good as that? It's just as well they thought so, as he was also Charles III of Spain and Charles V of Sicily. Isn't that being a bit greedy? And isn't greed a vice, if gluttony is a sin?

The exhibition will go, but the Metro is there to stay. Dante, on his pedestal, has his back to the exhibition but is looking down on the Metro in both senses of the expression. He has a very sour expression on his face while his left arm is raised in a gesture of resignation as if to say: *Would you just look at that monstrosity? But what can you do?*

The Museo Archeologico Nazionale is a grand, pink building. A big banner strung across the front proclaims a special Pompeii exhibition. Great! We didn't know it was on, but it's exactly what we want. It's €10 for the museum and €6 for the special exhibition. There's a ticket kiosk and a separate one which has tickets for the Secret Cabinet which is where they have put all the erotic art from Pompeii and Herculaneum so as not to offend the sensibilities of the ladies.

I show the cashier a leaflet Iona had picked up. I point to where it says €6. "*Due, per favore.*"

The LED on his till says €32.

"No! No! This one. €6."

He shakes his head and points to the screen. It must mean that the special exhibition is six in admission to the admission fee. We've only got an hour before we are due back for our guided walk. It doesn't seem very long to go the main museum, never mind all three exhibitions, even if La Belle Dame Sans Merci says there is absolutely no need to visit the last.

I don't know what he's going to do with the sale he's rung up and I don't want him to tell me, so I smile apologetically, shake my head and beat a shameful retreat. My back prickles as I feel the daggers he is throwing at my back.

So we have come all this way for nothing. But never mind, we can always come back next week when we are staying across the bay in Sorrento. As we are leaving, someone thrusts a leaflet into Iona's hand. It is a flyer for a restaurant

offering a pizza with beer for €5 and as an additional entice-
ment, it declares that it is in "pleasant gardens, surrounded by
greens". We had decided that since Naples is the home of the
pizza, that's what we were going to have tonight anyway and
who could resist sitting in a garden surrounded by cabbage,
broccoli and Brussels sprouts – especially at that price?

We retrace our steps down the Via Santa Maria de Con-
stantinopoli which has a pavement wide enough for Iona to
walk in the shade and for me to walk out of it. Down a side
street to our right, we can see some greenery which should be
the pizza place, so we decide to check it out. It looks as if it
would be pleasant enough, sitting outside, even although the
promised greens are only leylandii and oleander. But in the
meantime, my eye is attracted by a huge arcade at the top of
some steps off to the right. Leaving Iona sitting at the botton
of them to study the map, I set off to see what it can be.

It's like entering a cathedral. Built in the shape of a cross,
it's a cathedral to shopping and a hymn to architecture. It is
eerily quiet. Apart from the litter strewn across the inlaid
marble floor, I have the place all to myself. It's a Sunday and
all the shops are shut. Each arm of the cross has a richly-
decorated triumphal arch but it's the ceiling that is the most
breathtaking – a delicate dome of iron and glass which is echoed in the curved roof of each of the radiating arms.

Iona is still sitting where I left her, which is strange really
as there is a big comfy armchair on the pavement at the bottom of the steps. There really is! I'd dearly love to sit in it and
have Iona push me back to the hotel but it doesn't have a seat
belt and we'd probably get pulled up by the cops when we hit
the Via Toledo. And, in their newfound zeal, they'd probably
throw the book at me for not wearing a crash helmet whilst

being a passenger in a moving armchair, so I don't bother to suggest it.

In fact they *are* still pulling people over for not wearing seat belts as we carry on down the Via Toledo and when we come to the painted cannon balls and the rusty windmill, we know that is the top of our street. We only have a few minutes to take the weight off our feet before our guide comes to take us on the walking tour.

Oh my poor feet, or as the Neapolitan song has it: *O sole mio.*

Neopolitan Residences (Image Credit: Pixabay)

7

A Walk in the Centre of Naples

W E are in the Galleria Umberto I, which was completed in 1891. From the roof of our hotel, I had assumed it must be the Botanical Gardens because of the glass roof. It's like the galleria near the Museo Archaeologico although it differs in some important respects. Built in the same cross-shape, here the arms of the cross are of equal lengths. It is altogether much bigger and the marble floor is much more ornate with geometric patterns and designs and although the façades of the shops (three tiers here instead of two), are much less decorated, they are all the better for that.

Also it is far from empty. Street traders are trying to tempt passers-by with leather goods and handbags as well as jewellery and trinkets which are displayed on a blanket in front of them. According to Sophia, our guide, if a policeman came along they'd sweep the whole lot into the blanket, sling it over their shoulder and leg it, like a burglar making off with the swag. Well maybe, but it seems to me they could easily be

The Galleria Umberto I

arrested if the cops really put their minds to it and I suspect it's just another law that the Italians choose to ignore. Probably they'll get fed up of catching motorists not wearing seatbelts soon too and life can get back to normal.

We came in by the entrance facing the Teatro di San Carlo, the oldest opera house still operating in the world, if you pardon the pun. It's attached to the Royal Palace and the Charles after whom it was named was the Bourbon Charles III of Spain, or Charles VII of Naples, or Charles V of Sicily. Take your pick, but since we are in Naples, I'm going to go for the middle one and although he was three times a king, I can't quite see somehow how that elevates him to the sainthood. Anyway, the theatre was completed in 1737 which makes it some 40 years older than La Scala in Milan. So put that in your pipe and smoke it, Milano – not that I'm suggesting that city wars are still alive and well in Italy, of course.

When we leave the Galleria we find ourselves once more on the Via Toledo, this time near where it ends at a roundabout on the Piazza Trieste e Trento. Sophia tells us that Rossini lived on this street and had to be locked in his room by the theatre manager because the maestro was more interested in sampling the delights of Naples rather than getting on with his composing. I presume that means he was addicted to pizza and ice cream with three flavours, though not necessarily at the same time.

At the other side of the piazza is the aforementioned Teatro di San Carlo. It's just as well that's not on our itinerary as the piazza is immense and crossing a street, never mind an entire piazza, is a death-defying experience in Naples at the best of times. But just in case we should wish to attempt it, a car has been parked on the pedestrian crossing just to make it a bit more challenging.

We pass the Caffè Gambrinus where waiters with long aprons are flitting amongst the patrons sitting at the pavement tables. It dates from 1860. I mention it, because as well as being the present-day haunt of artists, musicians and writers, it was frequented by two of my literary heroes, Guy de Maupassant and Oscar Wilde.

Now we have reached the Piazza Plebiscito. Now this is what I call a piazza! It is vast! On our left is the Palazzo Reale, an austere edifice taking up one entire side, and on the right, the church of San Francesco di Paola. Now that is what I call a church!

The problem is there has been a concert here last night. (What! Here – and the one down by the port as well?) It's hard to hear Sophia over the intrusive sound of cascading scaffolding. But why, oh why, is it you can only see the best buildings Naples has to offer except through a screen of 21st

century clutter and scaffolding? And what was the concert performed here last night? Verdi? Puccini? Mozart? Or was it some rock concert whose amplified bass notes made the very foundations of this magnificent building tremble to their core, never mind recoiling in horror at the "music" it was forced to endure?

Despite being seen through this spider's web of steel, the San Francesco di Paola is the best building I have seen in Naples so far and I have seen some pretty good ones it has to be said. Perhaps it has something to do with scale; in fact, I am sure it does. It is so huge it's staggering, but it also has a lot to do with contrast. The Palazzo Reale is so austere, so plain, that it is hopelessly upstaged by the classical lines of the church.

It is modelled after the Pantheon in Rome and there is something immensely pleasing about the combination of the magnificent portico with its columns and the graceful curves of the cupola rising behind the pediment like a moon – but for me it is the great sweep of the colonnades on each side, embracing the piazza like welcoming arms that gives the building its awesome elegance and appeal. We are told it was conceived by Murat, Napoleon's brother-in-law, but unfortunately for him he never saw it, the French being booted out of Naples in 1815. His loss is our gain. *Merci, M. Murat, merci mille fois!*

The Palazzo Reale was begun in 1600 and not completed until 1843. Not so surprising when you look at its vast scale. It's difficult to hear Sophia as yet another piece of scaffolding strikes its fellows down below with a clang like a giant glockenspiel and continues to resonate long after the blow was struck – but to be honest, I am not that interested anyway. I am still in awe of the San Francesco di Paola. The façade of the palace is so plain the beauty must all be on the inside. What is of some interest though are the statues of the kings of Naples in niches all along the bottom of the building and even if the names mean nothing, it's a parade, in stone, of fashion through the ages, particularly the headgear. Which is fine if you are a follower of fashion, but if you are like the "baby" in Nina Simone's song who didn't "care for clothes", you won't even find that interesting. It begins with the unlikey-named Roger of Sicily (1031-1101) and finishes with Vittorio Emanule II who was actually King of Italy, which title he assumed in 1861. Incredibly, he was the first king of the unified country since the 6th century.

Sophia tells us if we want a pleasant walk in the evening, we should walk this way, past the Palazzo and follow the bay round to the Castel dell'Ovo or Egg Castle, so-called because of a magic egg supposedly supporting its foundations of all places. Some chicken, some egg, as Winston Churchill didn't quite remark in a put-down to Marshal Pétain's prediction that the Nazis would invade Britain and pretty damn soon too.

According to legend, this egg had a spell cast on it by Virgil, and it was believed that as long as the egg remained intact, the castle, and Naples, would be protected from disaster. The oldest part of the castle dates from the 9th century whilst Virgil's dates are 70BC-19BC. That's a long time to keep an egg and where it had been all that time I cannot tell you. Anyway it worked very well until, in 1503, the castle was practically razed to the ground by Ferdinand II of Spain.

Perhaps some careless person had scrambled eggs for breakfast. They were under siege from Ferdinand after all.

8

The Spaccanapoli and the Saint

WE are trailing up the Via Toledo again, this time making for the Spaccanapoli, a narrow street that cleaves its way through Naples, straight as a die, like the slash from a sword. The Romans called it the *decumanus*, the east-west road in any city. Now it is famous for its churches, but we are only going to be visiting two.

The first is the 16th Century Gesù Nuovo. I wouldn't call the façade beautiful, but with its top-to-toe diamond-point rustication it definitely makes a point – about 2,000 of them, I would guess. It certainly pokes you in the eye.

A service is in process, and as quiet as nuns, we follow Sophia as she skirts the nave and leads us to a chapel beyond where we find a man on his knees. He is praying to Naples' very own saint, a very recent one, Guiseppe Moscati, who died in 1927 and was canonized in 1987. We can see his study and bedroom preserved here behind glass, including the arm-

The Spaccanapoli (Image Credit: Pixabay)

chair in which he died. (What! He didn't *really* work and sleep here, did he?)

He was enormously pious and had a reputation as something of a miracle worker, bringing about impossible cures, as commemorated above. His sainthood was assured when the mother of a young man who was dying of leukaemia dreamed of a man in a white coat visiting her son. Shortly after his visit, he went into full remission. When shown a photograph of the man in white, she identified Dr Moscati.

The ceiling is covered from floor to ceiling with ornaments – except they aren't exactly ornaments. They are replica body parts that have been placed here in thanks for a cure: legs, arms, breasts like poached eggs, even guts and brains – any part you care to mention (yes, even *them*) – all are here, so many that the walls glow with a silvery luminescence. What's more, they have run out of space because bundles of them are hanging on hooks, like on a chatelaine's keyring. I take a closer look at one. It's paper-thin and made of aluminium, if I'm not much mistaken.

If there is anything else of interest in the church, we are not going to be shown it, maybe because of the service still in progress or maybe because Sophia's time is almost up. I suspect this may be the case, as when we cross the street to the exceedingly plain Santa Chiara, which, in contrast to its pointy neighbour, seems to make a point of being deliberately self-effacing. It dates from the 14th century, so Sophia tells us, and doesn't bother to take us in but leaves us to our own devices instead. I don't mind in the slightest because my feet are dropping off and if I don't get my weight off them soon I'm going to end up having to buy a pair of metal replicas.

Having come this far, we may as well go in. Its Franciscan simplicity is very pleasing, better by far than the Baroque Gesù Nuovo. In the middle of the back wall is the tomb of Robert of Anjou (1277-1343). I suppose, as one of the kings of Naples, he was a famous person in his day, but I've never heard of him before so I don't count him as a worthy addition to my collection. You should know I'm no ordinary tourist, but a bit of a thanatourist besides – my special interest being the graves of men and women of letters, like some philatelists specialise in birds for example.

In a chapel off to the right is another tomb, that of Philip of Bourbon. Pity I wasn't collecting obscure royalty – they would have been a couple of good ones. He was the "idiot" son of Charles III, so the guidebook says. That's a bit harsh and a fine way to be remembered I must say! He had learning difficulties and suffered from epilepsy, poor sod.

Leaving the church (and the rest of the group behind), we walk a little way down the Spaccanapoli, past the little church of Santa Marta and the altogether much grander San Domenico Maggiore. We are heading for the restaurant with the bargain beer and pizza for €5 which is near here somewhere.

Wouldn't you know it! It's not open yet but a café further up is. With relief, I take a seat and order a *birra grande* and a glass of white wine for Iona whilst we study the menu. We should have a Margherita I suppose. It was for the queen of Umberto I that this pizza was invented. Up until this time, the pizza was the food of the poor with a topping of tomatoes only, but for the Queen, mozzarella and basil were added to mimic the national colours. Food fit for a queen it may be and it may look pretty enough to eat but it sounds a bit boring to me, so in the end I opt for a *calzone* which I've never tried before. When in Naples...

It takes an age to come, so I order another beer, this time a *media* because by now I have seen the price and a *grande* costs as much as our whole meal would have at the other place. The *calzone* itself costs €7.50 (much dearer than a Margheri-ta, ironically the cheapest on the menu) and when it comes, I see why it has been so long – they have been lovingly burning it to a crisp. I cut off the worst bits and open it up to remove all the nasty mushrooms.

I would have been better off having a Margarita and a *grande*.

* * *

Now we are rested, night has fallen and I want to go out again, to take Sophia's advice, to walk down to the Castel dell'Ovo and drop in to the Gambrinus on the way back. La Belle Dame Sans Merci reluctantly comes along to keep an eye on me.

The Piazza Plebiscito is mobbed. It looks as if all Naples and his wife and children are here, most heading the same way we are, towards the bay and the castle. But then I have heard that Italian television is the worst in Europe, where even game shows with housewives taking their clothes off fail to attract viewers. But you can see why: this is where the real action is. Everywhere you look (though I try very hard not to) lovers are eating each other's faces off.

Presently we turn onto the Via Partenope. There are some very swanky hotels here and in their reflected light, a flotilla of boats and yachts are bobbing gently while Vesuvius looms darkly in the distance. And up there, floodlit, is the bulk of the Castel dell'Ovo sitting on its own little promontory like a galleon turned to stone by the Gorgon as it was heading out to sea. It's impressive, like the Palazzo Reale, but it is too square to be really interesting, architecturally speaking, and the buildings on the top look decidedly modern. A bit of a disappointment, but I've still got the Caffè Gambrinus to look forward to.

There is a door at the side off the Piazza Plebiscito. Inside, it is all marble and mirrors and gilt chandeliers – and not a single soul about. What's a tramp like me doing in a posh place like this? Before someone comes along wanting to know what I'm doing here and throws me out on a torrent of irate Italian, I swiftly rejoin Iona who was too cowardly but wise enough not to follow me in. The entire clientèle, apparently, is here on the pavement. I just can't imagine Oscar and Guy sitting here somehow, lapping up their lattes. There's no sense of their presence; their ghosts have gone.

I have made the fatal mistake of looking forward to this expedition far too much but before I turn in, I go up to the roof for one last look at Naples by night. A myriad lights are twinkling all round the bay as far as Sorrento and in the dark distance I can just make out the brooding hulk of Vesuvius.

This, at least, does not disappoint. It's the image I take with me to bed. I hope I will not die in the night but if I do, this image of Naples will be the one they find imprinted on my retina.

The Spaccanapoli from above (Image Credit: Pixabay)

Assisi

9

Santa Chiara and Poor Clare

A T last we leave the A1 at Orto and head north on the E45 *superstrade*. There is nothing super about it except the bumps and potholes. The Appian Way could scarcely have been less bumpy. The pneumatic seat of our new driver, Giancarlo, is bobbing rhythmically like a cork on water.

Assisi is visible for miles, tumbling down from its elevated position on a ridge high to our left on the vast Umbrian plain. If Pompeii was my most anticipated highlight of the trip, Assisi was my least. Churches are not one of my favourite things, nor religious art for that matter, unless it is by Hieronymus Bosch. That said, I am looking forward to seeing Giotto's famous frescoes, though they would have to be quite outstanding to rival Pinturicchio's which we had seen in the Piccolomini Library in the Duomo of Siena last Easter. Painted in the early 16th century, the colours look as fresh as if he had just laid down his brush yesterday. But who has heard of Pinturicchio? (Well I hadn't before, anyway.) And who hasn't, of Giotto?

We pass the Basilica degli Angeli, according to Angela, the seventh largest church in the world. From the distance, we had seen the gold statue of Mary over the entrance, flashing in the strong sunlight, like the beam from a lighthouse. (Come to me! Come to me!) But it's not its size that interests me so much (I've seen bigger in Malta and who says size matters anyway?) – it's the place where St. Francis died. Incorporated within it like a matryoshka doll, is the *Porziuncola*, the humble little church where St. Francis founded the Franciscan order and where he died in 1226. The massive basilica which swallowed it up took a whole century to build and was completed in 1679. We are not going there, but I don't mind that as long as we visit the tomb, for I am a grave man (though I would prefer to be called a thanatourist or a taphophile).

Our guide, Paolo, is waiting for us. The good thing about

Assisi

this visit is that we are going to start at the top and work our way down. Just as well: the temperature today is 36°C, so he informs us. The bus has taken us quite high, but in response to requests from American visitors there is an escalator to take us further up. (Actually I just made that up about the Americans, but it could be true for all that.) I can't remember being on an escalator in the open air before, though this is more like being levitated through a tunnel of leafy vegetation. No matter who was responsible for it, I am very grateful, as it's a pretty steep climb, heat or no heat.

We enter Assisi through the Porta Nuova and make our way down the Via Borgo Aretino. It's an attractive street with window-boxes of geraniums a splash of red against the warm brown stonework. At the end of the street two spindly cranes rear into the cloudless blue sky. Apparently reconstruction after the earthquakes of 1997 is still progressing.

In the shade of the enormous flying buttresses of Santa Chiara, Paolo points out where the damage had been repaired and explains that they gave the church a facelift while they were at it. It's a bit difficult to hear him as there is some sort of commotion, chanting and cheering coming from the piazza just round the corner. As we move round I can see what it is. Some American students are trying to build a human pyramid on the central fountain and making more noise than a combined choir from Bedlam as one of them tries to take their photograph if only they would stand still long enough. I can imagine it in the album later: *Here we are really getting up the noses of all the tourists in Assisi by acting like assholes.* Thankfully they finally get their photograph and boisterously go off to annoy some other tourists somewhere else, and the piazza returns to relative peace and quiet.

Turning my attention to the church, what draws the eye most is a beautiful rose window, like a lace doily, set high up on the plain façade which is composed of alternate layers of pink and white stone. The entrance is through a simple Romanesque doorway. The flying buttresses on the left are equalised by the convent on the right, fortunately, or it would have looked distinctly unbalanced. As it is, it still does not look quite right – the buttresses too thick and solid for the delicate façade, whilst their curves are not echoed in the squat, square shape of the convent.

Having said that, I find its simplicity enormously appealing. I get the feeling that I am seeing it as the builders saw it after its completion in 1265 but I have to imagine it without the buttresses as they were only added in 1351. I like the buttresses. I am sorry they had the bother of them, but I think they are very impressive: I'm not sure if I don't almost prefer them to the church itself. I am sorry about the earthquake too, but I am glad that I can see the church in its newly-restored freshness. Just like the poor people of Pompeii, their disaster is our good fortune.

It's dedicated to St Clare, the founder of the Poor Clares, the distaff side of the Franciscans. We are going in to see a cross which supposedly spoke to St Francis. What it said, three times, just to make sure there could be no mistake – that he wasn't hallucinating after an excess of *Lachrimae Christi* the night before – was to repair the church which had fallen into disrepair. Francis took this to mean his local church, not the much grander plan that the cross might have had in mind – the church with a capital "C" which was, in fact, what the cross actually meant. (Some people are a bit slow on the uptake.) And let me be not misunderstood either – my comment on the wine was not facetious. Before he got religion, Francis

68

lived a life of privilege (his father was a rich cloth merchant) and he was a bit of a tearaway, drinking and partying until the wee small hours, long after curfew.

There are frescoes of Biblical scenes and scenes from the life of St Clare on each side of the nave, but we walk straight past them as if they weren't there. Imagine that! Some poor devil has put his heart and soul into painting these scenes and quickly too, before the plaster dried, and we hardly spare them a glance, let alone stop and look at a single one! But time is limited and Paulo probably doesn't want to give us fresco fatigue before we get to Giotto's.

We make straight for the cross, known as the San Dami-ano Cross. The artist is unknown but it is reckoned to date from the early 12th century and is painted in the Byzantine tradition, featuring a lot of other figures associated with the grisly scene – on the left, Mary and St John the Evangelist, on the right, Mary Mag-dalene, Mary the mother of James, and the Roman centurion who asked Jesus to heal his servant. We know who they are

The San Damiano Cross
(Image Credit: Pixabay)

because their names are written below their figues. I have to say I am somewhat surprised to see the centurion given such a prominent position.

On the bottom left is a the tiny figure of Loginus holding his spear after having done the deed, for the blood is sprouting out of, and flowing down, Christ's side. It's also running down His right arm from the wound in His palm and dripping off His elbow. He may not have blood on his hands but any moment now, Longinus is going to have it on his head. Serve him right, though we are told the cruel act was done out of kindness. According to one version of the story (which are as many as you can shake a spear at), as a punishment, Longinus was banished to a cave where he was mauled daily by a lion, his wounds miraculously healing so the process could begin all over again the next day, forever.

In another version, he was blind, and when the sacred blood fell on his eyes, his blindness was cured, the scales fell from his eyes so to speak, and he was instantly converted to Christianity. In due course, he became a saint and his body parts were scattered to the four corners of the empire.

On the right is Stephaton, the soldier who offered Jesus the sponge soaked in vinegar, another kindly act, but Jesus turned his head away in order not to prolong the agony. Speaking of which, the crosses also used to have a ledge on the upright, a sort of seat where the victims could take the excruciating weight off their arms. Not an act of kindness; quite the reverse. It was designed to prolong the agony.

At the top is the noticeboard they mockingly put on Christ's cross which bore the inscription, in Latin: *Jesus of Nazareth, King of the Jews.* That's what the Romans did – put a board at the top of the crosses so citizens knew who had done what (if they could read). This notice gave the T-shape on which the victim was crucified the appearance of the four-armed cross with which we are so familiar today.

In the painting, above the notice, the artist has shown us Jesus bearing his instrument of torture, now turned into a staff and symbol of the new religion and at His feet, another symbol, which, says Paolo, is a bird. It's not very clear what sort of species exactly: some say it's a cockerel, reminding us of the story of how Peter denied Jesus three times, while others say it's meant to be a peacock which, in early Christian art, stood for eternity. Whilst both would be appropriate, it seems to me the peacock would be the more fitting of the two – Christ on His way to everlasting life in heaven. He is waving cheerily, supposedly at a host of heavenly angels (well, ten of them), some of whom have hands outstretched in welcome, but actually He is facing the spectator. Is it another example of the artist's lack of skill, or is it perhaps another deliberate ambiguity on the artist's behalf – Christ waving goodbye to us rather than in greeting to the heavenly host?

For what it's worth, and this may give you an idea of the quality of the artist's skill – I think the fowl aforesaid is actually a lamb! That would be appropriate too.

At the very top, the Hand of God is giving His blessing with two fingers directing our gaze to the grisly scene below. It was all in His divine plan, all that indescribable suffering inflicted upon His Son because He so loved the world.

There is no mistaking the awe of reverence which permeates this chapel. It seems as if the very air is imbued with it. Whether the cross actually "talked" to St Francis or not, he certainly *thought* it did. What is certain is he saw it and prayed before it. It's about the only thing left in Assisi that he *would* recognise. It's extremely unlikely he would approve of the enormous basilica built in his honour and much else besides if he were to see it now – which he may or may not be able to do.

I bet St Clare can. Since 1958, she's the patron saint of television. She has this dubious honour – especially in the case of Italian TV – because it is said she foretold the time and circumstances of her death, describing it in glorious Technicolor as if watching it on a screen.

Poor Clare indeed.

Santa Chiara

The Flying Buttresses of Santa Chiara

10

Sound and Silence in the Pursuit of St Francis

WE make our way through the throng up the gentle slope of the Corso Mazzini until we emerge in the Piazza del Comune. Forget the Basilica of St Francis: this place immediately takes your breath away. I love the rustic warm brown stone and the style and character of the buildings. It's a charming place, worth coming to Assisi for its own sake. Pity about the people. You wouldn't mind them so much if they only did it quietly.

To tell the truth, I'm starting to form a bit of a grudge against St Francis. For one thing, I'm beginning to develop a nappy rash. I am wearing long trousers in this stifling heat lest bare knees were considered disrespectful and I was banned from the basilica. I also hold him responsible for bringing all these people here, including me of course, but I don't count: it's the other tourists that are the problem.

Long before you enter the piazza, you see the early 14th century Torre del Popolo appear, bit by bit. With its crenellations and two tiers of windows looking like keyholes, it is very pleasing indeed. And so is the Town Hall to which it is attached. If only ours had been built in the 13th century instead of the 20th it might have had a chance of looking as attractive as this instead of looking like a packet of abandoned condoms with holes in them.

Once in the square, your attention is drawn from the Torre to the adjacent building. It looks like a Roman temple with its six massive Corinthian pillars and pediment. In fact it *was* a Roman temple, the Temple of Minerva, and predates the birth of Christ by a century. It's a church now: the Christian religion was grafted on, in many cases, to the existing pagan beliefs. Never mind St Francis' reactions to how Assisi has changed; what would the Romans make of their temple now?

Maybe not that much actually, given the way in which the Christian religion became implanted, in a manner of speaking, within the pagan system of worship. Minerva was the goddess of industry, commerce and the arts. Now it's the Virgin Mary who's in charge, but whether they changed the job description when they rededicated the church to her I do not know.

**The Torre del Popolo
and the Templo di Minerva**

76

The Templo di Minerva

Embedded on the wall of the Torre are encapsulated medieval weights and measures, written in stone so to speak. Paolo
says the long iron rod is a cubit, but there is so much noise
from passing vehicles and chattering tourists I can't quite
make out what else he's saying. It's annoying, as it might have
given me an idea of how big Noah's ark was, if he had reminded me how many cubits it was in the first place. And
maybe that's what he was saying, only I couldn't hear.

We take the Via Portica out of the square. The houses, of
weathered brown stone look warm and inviting in the sunshine, the side where I am walking. Everyone else is walking
on the shady side of the street. There are boxes of geraniums
everywhere and terracotta pots over-spilling with them to add
to the general ambience. It's so easy to like Assisi.

Before very long it turns into the Via San Francesco and
here there is an ancient fountain, a trough with a badly-

weathered coat of arms out of which the pipes emerge. We arrive at the same time as a party of backpackers, recently released from the hush of the basilica, now shouting at each other, and adolescent girls screaming in that ear-splitting way that only they and stuck pigs can. I'd cheerfully like to hold the heads of each and every noisy brat under the water. One thing about Assisi, it's certainly not quiet and I think even the Saint himself might approve of my giving this lot a ducking, if it restored the peace and tranquillity he was reputedly to have held so dear. Are you turning in your grave, Francesco?

We pass the Oratorio dei Pellegrini, or Pilgrims' Hostel with its overhanging roof of ancient beams and a faded fresco over the entrance. There are frescoes inside too, but we're not going to bother with them either. Just then, a backpacking Franciscan friar strides past, unconscious of any incongruity between his ancient habit and the 21st century rucksack on his back. So that's what the well-dressed pilgrim is wearing nowadays. I notice he is wearing sandals *without* socks. And quite right too.

Presently we come to a very interesting little house. It may be medieval but it looks good to me. I wouldn't mind living there despite the sanitary arrangements. It has diamond-shaped, lead-paned windows with the ubiquitous geraniums suspended between them. I can imagine how the estate agents would present it: *Bijou residence, own toilet, ceramic, portable, with handy carrying handle and in case of noisy tourists – empty over their heads.* Much more efficacious than a ducking I would have thought. It's the Casa dei Maestri Comacini. Their coat of arms is visible beneath the floor of the projecting upper storey.

From here we can see the *campanile* of the basilica peeping over the rooftops and now Paolo gathers us around him and issues us with gadgets like hearing aids. It's called "Talking in Whispers" and the idea is that when we enter the basilica, he is able to talk to us in a low voice and we can all hear him. It's to create an atmosphere of awe and reverence, to preserve a sense of the numinous and quiet in this hallowed place.

From the vast piazza in front of the church you can peer down over the colonnades of the even more vast Piazza Inferiore to where the lower church is – for the basilica is built on two levels, three if you count the crypt – you can see the vast Umbrian plain stretching out towards the hazy blue hills in the far distance to the Santa Maria degli Angeli with the gold statue on the top, looking like a pimple ready to burst.

It's here, in the Piazza Superiore, I should see the beggars. I am half-expecting them because of Norman McCaig's poem *Assisi* which, as every school pupil in Scotland knows, satirises the attitude of the Catholic church to the poor.

As soon as we enter the basilica we hear a sibilant SSSH! which would have stunned us into silence, had we been saying anything. I can't see who said it but it's so loud it must have been through speakers and so fierce everyone instantly falls silent – even the guides who are "Talking in Whispers". It's probably some fierce nun who took lessons in crowd control from the Captain Bligh school of discipline. Or is it like the *Wizard of Oz* and in reality it's just a tiny wee wifie whom if you met face to face, wouldn't say boo to a goose?

Now what's going on? Someone has just come up to Paolo and whispered something in his ear and into my shell-like a moment later comes: *Take your hat off!* I hadn't realised I was still wearing it but the whole group of course gets the broadcast and La Belle Dame Sans Merci gives me one of her Viagra looks. I am happy to take my hat off but I do object to all those men allowed to wear shorts when I am not.

On either side of the nave, there are 28 frescoes on the life of St Francis, attributed to Giotto (1266-1337), but now some scholars think are from the school of Pietro Cavallini in Rome. One thing is beyond dispute – the whole church is frescoed like Ray Bradbury's *Illustrated Man* was tattooed, leaving no part uncovered. It's not so much a church as an art gallery, and we are invited to sit in the pews whilst Paolo gives us an art lesson pointing out the details with the help of a laser pen. Confucius would say *Man who have sweaty botty should sit in own pew* but we are a group and we must crowd together as closely as we can so Paolo can whisper. Fortunately, I find myself next to the Guttings who are in the clothes they came with as their luggage has gone missing and therefore we cancel each other out.

SSSHHH! An anonymous and sibilant whisper booms out.

The frescoes have been restored and the colours are quite vivid, more vivid than I had been expecting. Paolo tells us Giotto was the first to depict life-like human figures with a real sense of movement and perspective. From this distance, it's hard to see if Paulo is right, but I'll take his word for it.

(SSSSHHHH!) Is it just my imagination or is that scary nun getting more irritated?

Paolo picks out some of the frescoes for our attention. If we discussed them all, we'd be here all day, but here's the one with the Talking Cross, the actual one we saw just a few minutes ago. Right enough, the figures on that didn't look too realistic, especially the one of the bird – if that's what it was.

And so we go round both sides of the church and that's the story of the life of Saint Francis, told in pictures so the illiterate could understand. Reader, I will not trouble you with the details, apart from his dates. He was born in 1181 or 1182 and died in 1226 aged 44 or 45, depending.

Happily, apart from some frescoes in the vault which were destroyed, the others were largely unaffected by the quakes. Above the entrance there is a big crack which is in the process of being restored. Truth to tell, the frescoes there are so high up, if that's what it took for the others to be refreshed and Santa Chiara given a facelift into the bargain, well, maybe that was the shock that was needed to restore their unique heritage.

It means I am probably seeing the frescoes as the Grand Tourists saw them 200 years ago, maybe even better, apart from Goethe, who perversely avoided the place. Well actually, I can see where he was coming from. Did I not express the same sentiments myself about visiting churches?

But surely, out of curiosity alone, you must come to see the cradle of modern art, mustn't you?

View of the Upper Church from the Via San Francesco

11

Seeking the Bones of St Francis

WE'RE in the lower church now and, like the upper, it is full of frescoes but a gloomy building compared to the bright and airy one above. Taken together, these two churches have such an array of frescoes by such a variety of artists, you can trace the development of Italian art through the centuries. Paolo shows us some Byzantine frescoes, pointing out how stiff and formal the figures are. He was right earlier – Giotto's *are* far more natural.

He stops before a fresco by Cimabue and tells us this is a true likeness of Francis himself, not an idealised portrait. I can believe that. You'd make him a lot more handsome than this poor fellow if that were the case. Of course, the tonsure doesn't help. It's not the sort of hairstyle that flatters any man (nor does the more radical version with the fringe shaved off). Perhaps it was a style deliberately adopted by him after he'd reformed, to keep the birds away, unless of course we are talking about the feathered variety. He has a massive pair of ears

– the left, in particular, would not look out of place on a milk jug.

There are some frescoes of St Clare too. She has a face as long as a wet Sunday afternoon in Scotland, but probably that is exaggerated and she might actually have been quite comely. One thing though: both of them look pretty miserable. A saint's life is not a barrel of laughs evidently. I've never sat for a portrait, funnily enough, but equally strangely, I think I may possibly be designed for sainthood myself because in every photograph ever taken of me, I look as miserable as an alligator with the toothache. And recently, I have been suffering from a very itchy back in the region of my shoulder blades and once there was a feather in my bed although the bedding is synthetic. If I am a saint in waiting I need to perform some miracles to give others a sign. The Miracle of Leaping out of Bed first thing in the morning would be a good start, but the Miracle of the Giving up of the Chilean Cabernet Sauvignon or the Miracle of the Abstaining from Malt Whisky would truly be miraclous.

I have to confess I'm frescoed out and I'm not really listening to Paolo any more, although I can hear him clearly through my earpiece. I do perk up, however, at the famous fresco of Francis preaching to the birds. It's by an unknown artist, so they call him the "Maestro di San Francesco". The fact is I have seen a sign pointing to the saint's tomb. Surely we are going to pay it a visit? After all, he's the very reason why we are here, why practically everybody in Assisi is.

But, incredibly, it looks as if we are not. Paolo is already leading us towards the exit. I hurry after him.

"Are we not going to the tomb?"

That stops Paolo in his tracks. He blinks at me, startled ino speechlessness.

"Is it OK if I go?" I ask in as casual a tone as I can muster.

Paolo glances at his watch. "Yes, but you don't have long."

He clearly does not want me to go, but I'm off already, obeying the laws of Italian logic by going down the exit stairs as they are nearest. Just before I make my descent I hear him say: *Give me back your earpieces* then I lose radio contact with him.

I was confident I would recognise the tomb when I saw it. But I don't. Perplexed, I rush around the crypt in increasing panic as I fail to find anything that looks remotely like it. I start again at the entrance, the way I should have come in – without success. Where *could* the blighter be hiding? He's *got* to be down here somewhere! I had thought I would only be a matter of minutes and I simply daren't spend any more time keeping the others waiting. I feel the sweat break out on my brow at the very thought. Deeply disappointed, feeling frustrated and internalising involuntary curses, a terrible thing to do in this art gallery of a church, I make my way with the traffic this time out of the church.

When I plunge from that cool dimness into the searing heat of the sunshine, there is not the slightest trace of my fellow travellers to be seen! Where could they have gone? Surely they couldn't possibly have made their way down the entire Piazza Inferiore in such a short period of time? And why didn't they wait for me? And something else. Earlier, the piazzas were as crowded with people as a Lowry cityscape but now the entire place is eerily empty and silent. I get the uneasy feeling that somehow I'm the only living person in Assisi...

I'm in too much of a panic to admire the emptiness of the scene, the magnificent colonnades running down both sides of the piazza and looking over my shoulder, the bulk of the basil-

The Piazza Inferiore

ica with its *campanile* blocking off one end and at the other, the arch which must lead down to the town. I set off towards it at a gallop. If I were in a cartoon, it would show my little trotters revolving in a blur.

I reckon I must have gone halfway down the piazza before I hear a familiar voice calling my name. I hear, but I cannot see her. Perhaps I have actually died, been struck down for cursing in the church, albeit to myself, and have gone to hell and it's Iona calling me from the other side. Then I see her emerging from the shadowy depths of the colonnades to the left, waving at me furiously, in both senses of the word. It seems that's where the toilets are and that's where they all are too.

"You didn't hand your earpiece in," Iona accuses. "Paolo has been looking for you." It sounds ominous, like something out of a Mafia film. But it's better by far than the apocalyptic sci-fi movie I thought I was in a moment ago.

But Paolo isn't here. He's gone ahead to hand them in which means I'm not going to be very popular when he comes back. Angela is not in the best of moods either. We have only fifty minutes' parking time and the toilet stop is taking an age. At least it means that she wasn't kept waiting for me, I think selfishly. I'm in enough trouble already.

When Paolo returns I offer humble and abject apologies. I wouldn't blame him for wanting to strangle me and when he says it doesn't matter, it does sound a trifle strangulated. I can tell he's struggling not to express his opinion on some stupid buffoon who wanted to go and see where some dead saint is buried. Without saying anything futher, he takes the earpiece and strides back towards the town again. I call after him that I hope he doesn't have to go too far but with each step, he's probably thinking of all the ways he'd like to kill me before he buries *me* in a concealed grave somewhere. As for me, I'm cursing this waste of time, time in which, surely by now, I would have managed to winkle out the shy saint from his hidey-hole.

When Paolo comes back, the toilet stop is *still* in progress and Angela is becoming increasingly agitated – wetting her knickers, as I might improperly put it. We have been encouraged to drink lots of water and it seems there's only one toilet for all the ladies, according not only to the laws of Italian logic, but everywhere in the world of men.

At long last we set off at a cracking pace, but it doesn't matter how fast Angela marches us, the group begins to stretch out and soon some stragglers are trailing far behind. For one thing, the heat is not conducive to such a blistering pace and, for another, there are too many photo opportunities.

It's just too good to rush. There is one splendid view in particular, looking back up at the churches from below with oleander bushes in the foreground. It's too tempting not to stop and stare.

We are one of the first to be where the bus is already waiting for us and climb aboard. Angela is looking at her watch and walking up the aisle counting heads. Suddenly, there is a commotion.

"You can't eat that in here!"

I turn my head to the back of the bus and see that other chiaroscuro pair, the dark-skinned man and the blonde woman, walking sheepishly down the aisle holding ice creams. Clearly the strain has been getting to Angela. Who would be a travel rep with hooligans like that to deal with and people who are late and with deadlines to meet, and nutters who want to meet dead people? It's still not as bad as being in charge of a school trip though, as I know from personal experience.

At last we are all together. We hurriedly say goodbye to Paolo and in a scatter of dust and a residue of diesel fumes, we leave him and Assisi behind.

But he has left a legacy. Whilst I had been in search of St Francis, Iona had taken the opportunity to do some unsupervised shopping and had bought a book recommended by Paolo. As I flick through it, I make the happy discovery that I have visited the tomb after all. I recognise the picture with the caption: *The tomb of St Francis.* His bones lie in a sarcophagus at the top of a pillar. I hadn't thought, in my haste and mounting panic, to look *up*. We scarcely ever do, in our daily lives, especially when we are feeling depressed.

According to the book, his body was hidden beneath the floor of the church in 1230 to prevent it from being hacked to pieces and bits being sold all over the place as miracle cures – a practice to which medieval Catholics were rather prone. Then in 1818, Pius VII permitted a crypt to be hewn out of the solid rock. It was opened to the public two years later, leaving Francis stranded high and dry on his pillar of stone.

If that is good news, there is some bad news too, at least for me. I may have bagged the bones of St Francis, but I have missed those of St Clare. She's in the crypt of Santa Chiara along with her sister, St Agnes.

Just two more reasons why I'm going to have to come back to Assisi.

Florence

12

Dining Alfresco in Florence

W E are in Florence, or maybe it's a field in Flanders.
We're outside our hotel but there are earthworks
and ditches with purple and yellow plastic entrails
being disgorged from them. We are in a three-star hotel here,
one star less in the firmament in which we normally revolve,
at least as far as this tour is concerned. Angela warns us it is
not up to the standard of the Golfo di Napoli, but it is clean.
It sounds more like an apology than a recommendation.

I am surprised to hear how compact Florence is. Somehow,
I had imagined it to be vast and sprawling but Angela says it's
only 10 or 15 minutes' walk to the city centre where there is a
variety of eating-places. We decide we'll keep the delights of
the city until the following day. In any case, the restaurants in
the town centre sound flashy and expensive whereas if we
stay in this locality, we should get just as good a meal for a
fraction of the price, in the sort of place that is patronised by
locals, not tourists. Angela says if we turn right out of the
hotel and then right again we should come to a *trattoria*.

At the top of the street stands an enormous structure
which looks as if it had, in a former life, been one of the city

gates. Now its attendant walls have gone and it has a distinctly stranded appearance in a new role as a roundabout. We can see the *trattoria* down the street a little way. We pause outside to examine the menu. I am not much enlightened. For one thing it's entirely in Italian, and secondly it is handwritten which taken together make it a dangerous place to eat. What if I got tripe or liver or kidneys or something else awful?

We decide to walk on and try somewhere else, but it soon becomes apparent there *is* nowhere else. The street is long and straight and there are no neon signs proclaiming another restaurant, or any other signs of one for that matter. When we come to the first intersection and see nothing up that street either, we decide to head back. It's not all bad though because we can dine alfresco as I prefer to do when on the continent. The tables are set out on a makeshift dais made of pallets.

There is one diner, a solitary local crouching over his half bottle of wine and his meal, looking as if it would choke him. I recall an Italian proverb which I had picked up in Sicily last October: *He who eats alone strangles himself.* How true! I'd rather eat alone in my lonely garret than put myself under public gaze like that, letting the whole world see you haven't any friends.

The menu arrives. Iona, whose language skills are more honed than mine, can work out some things but most of it is incomprehensible even to her. And the bits that I can understand, like *Salad Toscana*, I don't know what it actually *is*. I order it anyway (when in Tuscany...) and since I am not a pasta fan, the *gnocchi* in a tomato sauce as Iona says it is made from potatoes.

The main event, as far as I am concerned, is the wine. I order *Vernaccia di San Gimignano*, not so much because it's the cheapest (€12), but because from my previous trip to Tuscany, I know it's not only one of the best wine-producing areas of Italy, but one of the most enchanting places I have ever been to in my life, with more towers left standing from medieval times than phallic factory chimneys in a Lowry painting.

When the salad comes, I look at in dismay. It is a cold-meat platter consisting of something that looks suspiciously like liver sausage that has been run over by a road-roller. It has great chunks of white fat in it. In fact, there is so much fat, it should be called "fat sausage" so as not to contravene the Trades Description Act. But of course the Italians have never heard of such a thing.

Whilst I am surgically removing the white stuff, Tom, Dick and Harriet come past, and seeing us there – and before I can say "fat sausage" – take this as a recommendation and ensconce themselves forthwith, but not at an adjacent table. A few minutes later, Gordon and Blondie come along, and seeing us and Tom, Dick and Harriet, decide to walk on. Quite right too. A bit like Groucho Marx who wouldn't want

Florence (Image Credit: Pixabay)

to be a member of a club that would accept him, I wouldn't want to be seen in a restaurant where the only clientele are people like me. However, in a few minutes, back they come, as I knew they would.

Now we are seven, as A.A. Milne nearly wrote. If we keep this quiet from the rest of the group, we could be the Secret Seven and perhaps we could have a jolly exciting adventure together. But there is no chance of that, for along with the *gnocchi* come the Yorkshire couple. His face has a lived-in look, like W.H. Auden's, only his seems to have been inexpertly ironed. Some creases have been erased while others are as deeply etched as striations on a block of sandstone.

He says something to me. He has a bit of a cast in one eye so I'm not quite sure if it is me he is addressing or someone over my shoulder, but since there is no-one behind me, I nod and say it's all right and there's nowhere else anyway. I assume he has been asking me what this place is like. His accent, which is very thick, has now got another level of obfuscation as it appears to be delivered through a mouthful of cotton wool. I have a suspicion he may be inebriated. Amazing! All those hundreds of people I saw on the *passeggiata* in Naples and not a single one drunk or even slightly the worse for wear! Yes, it takes an Englishman in Florence to show these wimpy Italians how to drink.

They sit down at an empty table on the other side of the lonely Italian.

"Whadyizbindoinzisevn?" He is determined to be friendly. Not waiting for a reply, he volunteers the information that they've been in their room "Havnfewwhishkies". I thought as much. My national drink has made him loquacious and friendly, as it can do sometimes. At other times, it makes some people want to fight the entire world. Tonight he is in mellow mood. Fortunately, the waiter interrupts us before this distant and difficult conversation can really get into its stride.

The *gnocchi* in tomato sauce is edible, but there is rather a lot of it and I'm struggling a bit. Meanwhile, the waiter is bringing something that looks very tasty and interesting to Tom, Dick and Harriet. I wish I'd ordered that, but then I always like the look of what other people choose better.

Now new arrivals are choosing a table to our right. When her food comes, she gets the sort of thing I would have dreaded – a mound of steaming dark green vegetation, the sort of thing that looks as if it had been freshly deposited by a not-very-well cow. I don't know what it is called in Italian, but it looks like cooked spinach. Imagine eating it at all, never mind a whole plate of it by itself!

My food may not be all that special, but the wine is. I give up on the *gnocchi* although it is against my twin principles of waste and getting value for money, refill my glass and savour what Keats called:

a beaker full of the warm South,
Full of the true, the blushful Hippocrene

before turning to a study of my fellow diners.

Ironic really. Now that the lone Italian has gone, all the customers, apart from the new arrivals, are Brits. And I had thought I was going to avoid the tourists by coming here! The Yorkies are attacking their *coperto*, Gordon and Blondie are sitting next to Tom, Dick and Harriet and seem to be getting on very well together. It's a little corner of England in this little corner of Florence.

When the wine is finished, the bill and tip paid, the latter out of habit rather than for services rendered, we have to make our way past our travelling companions. I can see Harriet is eating some sort of meat dish smothered in gravy.

"That looks good," I remark. "How did you know what to ask for?"

She flashes me a surprised look, as if to say, "What sort of stupid question is that!" What she actually said was, "I just asked the waiter what the menu said in English."

You can carry this "when in Florence, Tuscany, Italy" thing a bit too far sometimes, I reflect, as we make our way back to the hotel.

There is too much light pollution to see the stars, but by some optical illusion, there appear to be two moons – the old and the new. The lines from that great Scots ballad, Sir Patrick Spens, come floating into my mind:

I saw the new moon late yestreen
Wi' the auld moon in her airm
And if we gang to sea, maister,
I fear we'll come to hairm.

What does it mean? I have a horrible feeling that disaster may be lurking around the corner – not that I am superstitious of course, but it is our 31st wedding anniversary tomorrow and 31 is only 13 turned.

I have a sudden feeling of foreboding...

13

Meeting the Dead
in Santa Croce

O UR first stop is going to be the church of Santa Croce, but first we have to negotiate the Florentine traffic which means we have to walk a hundred yards in
the opposite direction so we can cross the broad boulevard of
the Viale della Giovine Italia in relative safety. Giulia, our
guide, says we have exactly thirty seconds to cross before the
torrent of traffic pours down again upon the hapless pedestrians. I wonder what the elderly and infirm do. There are only
eighteen of us, so Giulia has hopes of getting all of us across at
one sprinting. She must be assuming we are all reasonably
sprightly and doesn't ask if any of us are suffering from a heart
condition.

When the red light comes, frustrated by having been held
up by this valuable half-a-minute, I notice the motorists' fingers drumming impatiently on their steering wheels and hear
the revving of their engines, like the start of a Grand Prix. No
quarter is going to be given here. It's a case of *de'il tak' the*

hindmost as we are out of the starting blocks and a moment later, all of us are safely gathered to the other side. Had we been twenty, we might have been down to eighteen. The racing track is off again, roaring in our ears.

We make our way down the leafy shade of the boulevard and presently come to the Piazza Piave. Giulia tells us the structure ahead of us is where, in medieval times, people were publicly executed. It's a bit like the gate we had seen on the way to our *trattoria* last night, a city gate in need of a wall, and indeed that is what it is. The road which we are following is called the Via dei Malcontenti because this is the way that those poor unfortunates, about to meet their Maker, made their last walk and, unsurprisingly enough, were less than happy about the prospect.

Suddenly we emerge on the Piazza di Santa Croce. The church is on our left and we had not seen it coming, so we are denied a view of its façade from the distance. A statue of Dante stands to the left of the entrance at the top of some steps. It once occupied a position of prominence in the centre of the square but was later moved to its present position after the flood of 1996.

This is another Franciscan church, but much more ornate than a Franciscan church ought to be. Far too fussy by half and the combination of pink and green marble does not appeal either. Giulia explains that in the days of the rival city-states, you showed your wealth on the outside so travellers passing through would marvel and be impressed by how rich your city was. I suppose you could say this makes the church a weapon of mass deception. In Scotland we have the expression *fur coat and nae knickers* to describe a lady who is full of outward show but of little substance. I couldn't possibly comment.

The inside of the church is much better and plainer. Both sides of the nave have massive pillars on which the tidemarks of the flood are clearly visible – twelve feet high at least. Incredible to think of the whole piazza and much else besides, under water. This year there is a drought.

As far as I am concerned, the best thing about Santa Croce is it is home to lots of famous dead people so for a thanatourust like me it is a very good place indeed to augment my collection. I hadn't done this part of the homework before we left, so it is a very pleasant surprise that the first thing I see when I enter the church, over to my left, is a monument to that arch-heretic, Galileo, who in 1737, a century after his death, was given a Christian burial here. The memorial is intricately carved with a bust of the great man with jutting, bearded jaw above a marble sarcophagus. There is a Latin inscription below: *Galilaeivs Galileivs.* So good they named him twice. Giulia explains he is not really there at all, but down below in the crypt. That doesn't matter to me – it still counts as a grave visit.

Galileo's Memorial

The bust shows him looking heavenward, appropriately enough. The even more elaborate memorial directly opposite him is that of Michelangelo – *Michaeli Angelo Buonarroti* according to the inscription. That's some name too – the sort of name that would surely get you into heaven. The tomb was designed by Vasari who was a great artist in his own right and who wrote *Lives of the Great Artists*. At the bottom of the faux sarcophagus are the figures of Painting, Architecture and Sculpture, just three of the things in which the multi-talented Michelangelo dabbled.

Next but one down, we have Dante. This is exciting because he's a really good one for my collection. Like some philatelists specialise in birds or bees, I specialise in literary graves and have collected – amongst many others – Shakespeare, Wordsworth, and the spinster Jane Austen who, being interred in the floor of Winchester Cathedral, was treated to a view up my kilt when I was there for a wedding. I'm not so sure it was such a happy occasion for poor Jane, however. I have also been as close as I can to poor Charlotte and Emily in Haworth, but Anne inconsiderately died and lies in Scarborough, so I have yet to do the full Brontë.

But wait a moment; Giulia is explaining that Dante was exiled and died in Ravenna in 1321, where he is buried. In more recent times, letters from the mayor of Florence to the mayor of Ravenna asking for their boy back fell, as you might expect, on deaf ears. It brings a new meaning to the expression *habeus corpus*. City wars are alive and well in Italy. They had to be content with erecting a monument to him, which they did five hundred years later. Even Galileo didn't have to wait that long.

The thing about Dante is, apart from being arguably Italy's greatest poet, he was also the one who unified the language, so that the Italian of today and thus perhaps indirectly, the unification of the country, is thanks to him. But now some in Italy would like to see the rich north secede from the poor south and who's to say that given the length of time it takes the Florentines to erect a memorial to one of their most prestigious geniuses, that it couldn't happen, European Union or no European Union? If it happens anywhere, Italy could be the place.

Four memorials further down, we come to Machiavelli. It seems curious to pay him the same honour as those other great men, but he was a writer and philosopher and he has certainly achieved immortality, though most would say, "immorality" would be more *le mot juste*, his name being synonymous with duplicity and cunning.

Now we are standing in front of the memorial to Gioachino Rossini, who had to be locked in his room in Naples to make him get down to some composing instead of partying. Now he lies decomposing in the crypt of Santa Croce in Florence. I wonder if he's happy about his proximity to Machiavelli? Maybe he's not rubbing shoulders with him down there though. Rossini might have made it to heaven, his peccadilloes notwithstanding, but it's hard to imagine old Niccolò up there looking up the angels' skirts. Much more likely, he's warming his behind at Auld Nick's fire which is *bleezin' finely.*

Rossini was the last to be buried here and that wasn't yesterday – 1868 in fact, and only at the insistence of his loving widow. It's thanks to her then, he's got this grand memorial in Santa Croce. It prompts me to wonder what memorial, on what windy hillside, Mrs Addison will provide for me. It would be small of course, but big enough to have my name and dates (though I never had many of them), with a suitable epitaph. In hope and expectation, and to save her the trouble,

I have already composed a verse in the style of that of Lester Moore and others whose poor bones lie under the poor dusty soil of Boot Hill Cemetery, Tombstone, Arizona:

My name was Dave
I was a sexual slave.
I am lying below
And I am lying above.

14

Cloisters, Cimabue's Crucifixion, and a Corridor

ARGUABLY the most famous treasure in Santa Croce is Cimabue's *Crucifixion*, which was the most famous victim of the 1996 floods. Actually it doesn't look in the least damaged and is suspended from the ceiling, very high up, well above the watermark. So how come? Unfortunately what we're looking at is a copy. By bad luck, just two months before the flood, they had finally got around to beginning the restoration and had laid it flat in the refectory. Ironically, two-thirds of it is damaged now.

Behind it, at the back of the church, are two chapels which contain frescoes by Giotto that Giulia wants us to see. They do not have the strong, bright colours of those in Assisi however, looking more like a Victorian sepia photograph. I don't know if Giulia knows we've just been there, but she invites us to observe the realism of the faces, the lines and wrinkles, and points out what we already know – that it was a great leap forward from the Byzantine, and without Giotto the rest of

Italian art would not have been possible. They do indeed look like real people with individually recognisable faces, though having said that, they look decidedly fresher-faced than their grey hair and corpulent figures would suggest. In those days, if I'd wanted a flattering portrait of myself, I'd have chosen Giotto to do it. Actually, put me in a brown dressing gown and I could have been mistaken for one of these acolytes of St Francis. I've got their hairstyle for a start. Not by choice, I may add.

We're on our way out now, and it is a very pleasing prospect looking down the entire length of the nave. Wide and spacious, with a relatively plain wooden ceiling echoing the serried ranks of pews on the floor, it is a complete contrast to the exterior. That was due to some vandal in the nineteenth century under the misguided impression that the fussier the detail, the greater glory to God. I wonder what it was like before these "improvements". I bet St. Francis was having a fit in heaven whilst it was going on. Had his teaching all been in vain? Had they learned nothing at all?

Coming out of the church, we descend some steps and enter the cloisters. With two tiers of slim elegant pictures, they are breathtakingly beautiful. I'd rather be out here than in the church, but I daren't admit it to anyone, especially Giulia. The architecture is distinctly ancient Roman, reminiscent of a forum. I half expect to see someone in a toga emerging from behind a pillar, Cicero perhaps, pondering the imponderables, his philosophy becoming more concrete with each circuit. Perhaps that's why I like it so much – the feeling I have slipped through some portal into the past.

Shade is provided (for those who want it) by tall cypresses, their dark greenness picked up by two inviting carpets of lighter-green grass bisected by a path. This cool green oasis in

The Cloisters of Santa Croce

the heart of the city is given further emphasis by the twitter-
ing of invisible birds. Not a single sound from a Vespa is allowed in here to disturb the peace.

Alas, we're not allowed to loiter in this tranquil place.
Surprising as it may seem, this is not the object of our visit.
We are entering the Cappella dei Pazzi, designed by Brunelleschi, who even I know, also designed the famous dome of
the Duomo. According to Giulia, this is a perfect example of
early Renaissance art. It's based on geometrical multiples of
seven. Perhaps just a shade too mathematically precise and,
with its grey paint, perhaps a bit too cold and formal for my
taste. But for all that, I like the domed ceiling, the arches and
Corinthian pillars, and anticipating Wedgwood, the blue-and-
white roundels of the saints below the metopes which form a
frieze around the walls.

The de' Pazzi family were rivals of the famous and powerful de' Medici family. In the Pazzi conspiracy of 1478, the family attempted to assassinate Lorenzo de' Medici, the so-called "Magnificent". They only wounded him but succeeded in killing his brother, Giuliano. Naturally the Medicis did not take too kindly to this and somewhat disproportionately, wreaked their revenge. They banished the Pazzi from Florence, executed eighty or more conspirators and obliterated the Pazzi name and coat of arms wherever it occurred in the city. This prompted that war-like Pope, Sixtus IV, with the help of the King of Naples, to declare war on the de' Medicis and on Florence for good measure. Thus the Pazzi plan to eliminate Lorenzo had unintended and far-reaching consequences. In retrospect it turned out to be a pretty stupid thing to do, giving rise to the present-day word *pazzo* which means "insane" or "crazy".

Looking back at the Cappella from the cypress trees, I can see the façade which we had not seen before, having approached it from the side, as we did the Santa Croce. Much, much better. The dome rises, moonlike, over a loggia with a balcony and a tiled roof like a fringe on the top. It must be great to look down on the cloisters from there, or even better, to look back at the Capella from the length of the cloisters. For architectural ambience and harmony there is nothing to beat it.

Whilst I have been admiring this, the group has moved on to see the damaged *Crucifixion*. This place must have been a refectory once – there is a fresco of *The Last Supper* at the far end – probably where the *Crucifixion* was damaged. Perhaps Giulia has told my fellow travellers about it, but I don't think so – she wouldn't have had time. Just another case of some poor sod painting away for all he's worth before the plaster dries and, when he's finished, no-one spares it more than a glance. Like a writer bashing out his immortal prose which no-one bothers to read. Not that I would know anything about that, of course.

The *Crucifixion* is indeed in a pretty bad state. Giulia says it is an important painting in the development of art because it shows the real suffering of Christ. He's suffering all right, and not just from the usual causes either but also, it seems, from some nasty disease which has left huge brown patches all over his body.

As we make our way out of the cloisters, two classical statues stand on either side of the gate, identical apart from their size. The larger one is of Florence Nightingale, whose father was an ambassador here and was inspired to name his daughter after the city of her birth, apparently. The smaller figure is Elizabeth Barrett Browning who died here. Maybe she's smaller because the Florentines deem it a greater honour to be born in Florence than to die there. Quite rightly. Any-one can choose to die in Florence but to be born there is some-thing over which you have absolutely no control.

Just time for one last, lingering look back at the cloisters – at the elegantly thin pillars, the carpet of grass, the solitary statues and the cluster of cypresses with the Cappella de' Pazzi at the end. Quite heavenly!

It's back down to earth in the Piazza Santa Croce where the noise assaults the ears like a pneumatic drill. An accelerat-ing Vespa roars past like an angry wasp. This is the real Flor-ence of clamour, crowds and commotion. Before we set off to wherever we are going next, I wander down the piazza a little to study the façade of the Santa Croce, full frontal. No, I real-ly don't like it at all. With its variegated marble, it is too sug-ary by half, a confectioner's concoction that might have made

Hansel and Gretel's mouth water, but as far as I'm concerned, it's the height of bad taste.

We wander along the Via della Ninna towards the Uffizi and the Palazzo Vecchio. The Uffizi is not on our tour, or at least the interior isn't. If we want to see it, we will have to go on our own. It's another of Vasari's efforts. In 1560, Duke Cosimo I commissioned him to design a block of government offices and of course, now I come to think of it, "Uffizi" means "offices". It's quite obvious once you know. After Vasari died, succeeding Medici generations turned it into the art gallery we know today.

Giulia points out an arch, very white and new-looking high above our head with windows so huge, it's more windows than arch. She says this is the Corridoio Vasariano, more than a mile long and which runs from the Palazzo Vecchio behind us, right through the Uffizi, across the Ponte Vecchio, before it ends up in the Palazzo Pitti on the other side of the Arno. All this just so the Medicis, so high and mighty, did not have to mix with the riff-raff in the streets. Probably a good idea if there were *pazzo* Pazzis around every corner, trying to do you in.

I would do it too if it got me out of range of what were the equivalent of those infernal Vespas in those days. Horse poo, I imagine. The nose, not noise, was what you had to worry about most then.

15

Statues and Squares

WE are walking down the Piazzale degli Uffizi towards the river. In niches, on either side of us, are statues of the famous: Giotto, hooded and looking like something out of *The Canterbury Tales*; Donatello, with a hat like a pudding basin, as if he's about to have the escaping curls chopped off; Leonardo da Vinci, looking very hairy, with the best hat so far, like something Jean Shrimpton wore in the Sixties; Michelangelo Buonarroti, short-haired and hat-less and looking pensive, with his back slightly towards his rival, Leonardo. Dante Alighieri looking furious at having the worst headgear of all – a cloth cap like the leather helmets WWII pilots used to wear with padded ears, and then the crowning glory – a wreath of laurel leaves, Roman style, balanced on top. No wonder he's mad. Giovanni Boccaccio in drag, holding up his skirts and also sporting laurel leaves, but this time on top of a hooded cape and strangely enough, not looking if he minds too much being caught cross-dressing. Good old Niccolò Machiavelli is there too, hair cut down to the wood, looking like he's devising another scheme, or wondering where he's put his hat. There are many, many more. It's like being in a petrified open-air Madame Tussaud's.

Turning to look back at the way I have just come, it's a surprise, though it shouldn't be, to see, at the top of the street, behind a building completely shrouded in a white sheet and scaffolding, two segments of the famous Brunelleschi dome – my first ever sighting of it in real life. It's not seen to its best advantage from this vantage point and I can scarcely contain my impatience to get there. Patience is not really one of my attributes and I would certainly need more of it than the little I've got if I were one of those in the queue for the Uffizi. Giulia says the space between each column of the building represents a twenty-minute wait. The queue extends in an untidy snake from the entrance, down one side, round the corner, crosses a short stretch of the Corridoio Vasariano (which links the two arms of the Uffizi), runs parallel with the Arno for a good ten yards or more before it finally tails to an end. Not only that, but this multi-lingual human snake bulges hugely in places, like a boa constrictor that has just swallowed something very fat.

Because of these bulges and lack of columns to measure it by, it's impossible to estimate just how long it would take to get into the Uffizi, except a very long time indeed. Much as I would like to visit it, this is my first visit to Florence and I can think of better things to do than stand for three hours in a queue in the shade, not to mention another two or three inside trying to peer at paintings over the heads of other punters. Either that or being processed along a human conveyor belt as in the brothel at Pompeii.

We carry on and in a few moments come to the Arno, where up to the right, it's a thrill to see the famous medieval Ponte Vecchio. It makes a perfect photograph – the Corridoio

Vasariano on the top, the three broad arches on the bottom and the raggle-taggle of shops in the middle providing a splash of green, yellow ochre and terracotta which are reflected in the languid, lazy waters of the Arno. And while it's doing that, the bridge can also reflect on its lucky escape. It was the only one not blown up by the Nazis as they retreated in August 1944, thanks to a brave decision by the German commander in charge, Gerhard Wolf.

That was just a glimpse. We are on our way to the Piazza della Signoria.

Thank God for the Uffizi, for the hundreds in the queue and the hundreds inside because it means they can't be here. The piazza is heaving with humanity and so noisy it's almost impossible to hear Giulia over the competing babble of other guides and tourists shouting to each other in what amounts to a multilingual cacophony. It must be hell to be a Florentine, your beloved city invaded by tourists so thick on the ground you can hardly make your way across the piazza.

I don't need Giulia to tell me – I instantly recognise Michelangelo's *David*, standing totally naked and unashamed in front of the Palazzo Vecchio whose façade, unfortunately, is masked by a skeleton of scaffolding. *David* himself is caged in a wooden frame and not looking too happy, perhaps at the prospect of a good scrubbing. He looks as if he could do with it. His smooth marble skin is streaked and grimy and it doesn't look as if you could blame it entirely on the pigeons either. But not to worry, this is just a copy. The real one is in the Galleria dell' Academia.

From what we can see of the palazzo, it looks like a very fine building indeed with its arched windows and crenellated battlements from which rises the offset tower of the *campanile*, which I also find very appealing – plain at the bottom then

David, packed and ready to go

halfway up, thickening out in a similar style to the battlements. Here the great bell told the people to foregather for public announcements, such as: *Hide the kids! Here come the Neapolitans again selling their bloody ice creams.*

David is sightlessly gazing across the square at another fine building – the Loggia dei Lanzi which contains a number of other interesting stat-ues. In fact, the whole piazza is another free open-air sculpture gallery. Nearest *David* is Cellini's bronze statue of *Perseus* standing on the body of Medusa and triumphantly holding her severed head aloft. The message, meant to shock the ene-my, is: *See what'll happen to you if you meddle with us!* Nowadays, the enemy of the statues and indeed outdoor stat-ues the world over, are the pigeons, but *Perseus* has a shock for *them.* Apparently he has a copper wire somewhere and when the pigeons land, they get a shock. It's carefully cali-brated to frighten them but not so much that they lose control of their bowels. It seems to work as *Perseus* is pigeon-dropping free.

We are not going to have a closer look at the statues, we can do that on our own later, but the one that captures my attention is fortunately at the front – *The Rape of the Sabine Women.* This was Giambologna's last work, carved out of a single piece of marble. Maybe after creating a masterpiece like this, he thought he may as well lay down his chisel – he could never equal it, never mind surpass it. The figures are a writhing entwined knot, spiralling upwards to the fingertips on the outstretched protesting arm of the violated woman who is being lifted aloft by her nude attacker whilst her husband cowers horror-stricken between the rude attacker's legs. No wonder! Looking up at his dangles from that angle, not a pretty sight. Giulia tells us this is typical of the Mannerist school which likes spiralling forms. I more than like it. I think it is the most amazing, wonderful statue I have ever seen.

On our way out of the piazza we pass another Mannerist sculpture, though I would never have recognised it as such. It is Ammannati's nude statue of *Neptune* surrounded by water nymphs. He bears a rather offended expression. My guess is he has heard someone mocking his dangly bits. Even for a mere man they are on the miniscule side; for a god they are embarrassingly ridiculous. I quite like the statue but the Florentines didn't, notably Michelangelo who taunted Ammannati with having destroyed a fine block of marble. Just his luck to be a contemporary of arguably the greatest artist the world has ever seen. Unless of

Neptune, Piazza della Signoria

Palazzo Vecchio

course, you count Leonardo.

At some distance away is another piece of work by Giambologna – an equestrian statue of Cosimo I, but we are too far away to see it in detail. A pity, as he is said to have been the model for *Neptune.* I presume they are referring to the head only. In 1537 Cosimo de' Medici became the 2nd Duke of Florence and the head of a dynasty which was to last for two centuries. In 1569 he was elevated to the first Duke of Tuscany by Pope Pius V. This irresistible rise of the Medicis must have been utterly maddening for the Pazzis.

We exit the piazza by the Via Calimaruzza and presently come to the Mercato Nuovo. Believe it or not, it's more crowded than the Piazza della Signoria and the Uffizi queue put together. As well as being a busy market, the attraction here is a big bronze boar with scores of people milling around it, but it's just possible to see its nose is a bright, shiny gold colour unlike the rest, which is a dark brown. Giulia explains that if you rub the nose, your wish will be granted. I have a wish. I wish all these tourists would disappear so I could get close enough to give that nose a stroke as I have a wish, another wish, which I am not going to tell you what it is as it wouldn't work if I did.

But there's no chance – we're off again, this time down the Via Calimala. I'll try and get back to the boar this afternoon, not that I'm superstitious of course, but if there's any chance of my wish being granted, I may as well give it a try as nothing else seems to have worked so far.

Ponte Vecchio

Ponte Vecchio from a distance

16

On Being Perverse

WE are walking down the Via Calimala. About twelve feet beneath our feet lies the old Roman road. Presently it takes us into the Piazza della Repubblica which used to be the site of the old Roman forum. Now it is a pleasant-enough square, bounded on three sides by rather ordinary buildings, but on the other side dominated by a massive three-tiered triumphal arch of golden-brown stone towering over the others. On the topmost tier is a slab of white marble where is inscribed the legend:

> *L'ANTICO CENTRO DELLA CITTA*
> *DA SECOLARE SQUALLORE*
> *A VITA NUOVA RESTITUITO*

I don't need Giulia's help with this one. It seems the square was built upon the squalid remains of the old town by which they mean the much more recent past rather than the Roman era which I'm sure would have looked utterly splendid. I think it's meant to be a pedestrian precinct except this being Italy, a white car is crossing it now, cutting a swathe

Triumphal Arch in the Piazza della Repubblica

through the strollers and scattering them in all directions, like chickens chased by a fox. According to Giulia, through the arch is where all the expensive shops are – Gucci, Armani and all that sort of rubbish. Whatever else we do in Florence, we won't be going there. I may not know much, but I do know that for certain. I have made up my mind.

As we turn into the Piazza di San Giovanni, I give an involuntary gasp at the sight before me. I had expected to see the Duomo but instead, obscuring it, I see something which is so hideous it takes my breath away. I suppose another way to put it is I don't care for it very much. Octagonal and fussily decorated with green and white marble stripes and arches, it is none other than the Baptistery, famous for its golden doors. It's not its fault that it obscures the Duomo, however, as it was here first, as early as the 5th century, though what we see now dates from the 11th century.

We are not going into this either – it looks closed anyway, but the inside can scarcely be worse than the outside, so perhaps it is a pity we are not going inside as it might serve as a bit of an antidote, like the interior of the Santa Croce is much superior to the exterior. The beauty might lie within, if it lies anywhere. The reason for the Baptistery, Giulia says, is the church which once stood on the site of where the cathedral now stands, was considered too holy for the unbaptised to enter.

As everywhere else in Florence, crowds are milling around, especially in front of the golden doors. These were executed by Lorenzo Ghiberti who defeated Brunelleschi in a competition to design them. What we see, not surprisingly, are copies, the originals being in the Museo dell'Opera. Over the heads and the voices of the three-deep crowd in front of us, Giulia tries to tell us about the scenes from the Old Tes-

Panel from Ghiberti's Door to the Baptistery

tament which are depicted on the panels, but it's a bit of an exercise in futility as we are too far away to see the detail and it's difficult to filter out what she is saying from the competing cacophony. What we are meant to be noticing is the naturalism of the figures and the use of perspective which make these panels prime examples of early Renaissance art.

And so to the Duomo. I have to admit, I am bitterly disappointed – no, horrified would be a better word for it. If the façade of Santa Croce was bad, this is a thousand times worse. Also like it, it is constructed of white, green and pink Tuscan marble but it is the pink that draws the eye most. It looks like some kid's fantasy birthday cake, smothered in icing which has run like candle grease down a bottle. The overall effect is so sweet and sickly-looking that if it were a cake it would be stomach-churningly inedible to all but the sweetest of palates. As a piece of architecture, it is merely appallingly over-the-top, with its adjacent matching bell tower (designed by Giotto, no less) the proverbial cherry on the top.

I keep my sacrilegious thoughts to myself. I can't decide which is the worst – the Baptistery (golden doors excepted), the façade of the Duomo, or the *Campanile*. Am I the only one who thinks like this? Do the tens of thousands of tourists who come here gaze in awe and wonder and are struck dumb in breathless admiration, or am I merely being perverse? It's well worth coming to see, undoubtedly, but it leaves me feeling profoundly shocked like those who watch a horror film hope they will be. At least they know what to expect whereas I came totally unprepared for these three triple X-rated architectural abominations.

I wonder if Messrs Brunelleschi and Giotto would agree with me, for like the Santa Croce, the exterior of the Duomo is a nineteenth century "improvement". I might be mistaken, but I can see them *birling* in their graves at 1,000 revs a minute. In all the photographs, in all the postcards I'd seen of it, nothing had prepared me for this. That's because they all seem to have been taken from a distance where the iconic dome was the most prominent feature and I had not noticed all the fussiness below. It's a great disappointment. Once again it vindicates my philosophy of life: *Never look forward to anything too much, for you will be disappointed. Always look on the worst side of life, for it will never turn out as bad as you fear.*

There is a queue to get inside, a queue which extends almost as far as the Loggia del Bigallo on the other side of the piazza. Now that's a much better building by far, at least what I can see of it from where I am standing. I like the overhanging roof supported by timbers, the arches, the plain white façade relieved by a dark brown strip two-thirds of the way up and the three pairs of shuttered windows above that. It was here, in the 15th century, that abandoned babies were displayed for three days. At the end of that time, if they were still unclaimed, they were fostered out. It's good to know the Florentines had a thriving child-care policy all those centuries ago.

Although the queue is long, it is moving relatively quickly, for the Duomo is apparently the fourth largest cathedral in the world and soaks up people like blotting paper.

Talk about the beautiful inner self! If the outside of the Duomo was meant to impress (and it didn't me), then I must agree with Iona and admit I am perverse, for it is a relief to step inside and see just how plain the interior is. If plain can be beautiful, this is it. The side chapels are unadorned, illuminated by pointed windows imitating the shape of the arches beneath them. Very nice.

The Duomo showing Dome, Façade, Campanile and part of the
Baptistery

Turning round to face the entrance, the first thing Giulia
points out to us is a clock, decorated by Paolo Uccello in the
15th century. It is unusual on two accounts – firstly it has only
one hand, though I have seen that sort of thing before, but
what makes it really unusual, aberrant even, is it goes *anti-
clockwise*! Just imagine all the wheels and cogs whirring away
unseen making this thing tick backwards! It only serves to
reaffirm my impression of Italian logic, although it also appeals
to my love of the eccentric. Also, how perverse of Giulia to
tell us who decorated the clock but not who made it, which,
to my mind, is a far greater achievement. Perhaps it's that
typical Florentine thing again: outward show triumphing over
inner beauty.

If there are points of artistic interest here, then we are not
going to be told about them – we are making straight for the

cupola. When we get there, after several minutes' march, what can I say? Nothing! I am struck totally dumb by the wonder of it, just as I was only a few moments ago by the horror of the Baptistery. It is octagonal, light beaming in from a window at its zenith like a searchlight and around which swirls, in a myriad of colours, a multitude of figures. It's the handiwork of that man Vasari again. It might just be my ignorance, but it seems to me a pity he is not better known, famous as being the geezer who painted the frescoes on the cupola of Florence Cathedral, in the same way Michelangelo is as the bloke who painted the ceiling of the Sistine Chapel.

I suppose the difference might be the roof of the Sistine Chapel is not anything to write home about whereas the roof of the Duomo most certainly is. It's that Florentine thing again.

17

To the Top of the Dome

I am afraid I am not listening to Giulia any more. I have the binoculars out and am focusing on Vasari's frescoes, particularly on the bottom level to my right where horned devils are pitch-forking poor souls into the eternal flames – their reward for enjoying themselves when they were alive. I get the message. I will try to mend my ways – but not yet. I'll try to postpone my reformation until nearer the time.

Here's a curious thing. Three angels are sitting on a cloud, the middle one garbed in golden raiment and beneath him, at the bottom of the cloud, are a couple of cherubs on either side of what looks like an automatic washing machine! No wonder those angels have such blindingly white clothes! I wonder if it's a special one, being celestial, that does feathers. Maybe that's what it is: a tumble dryer for their wings – assuming they are detachable. I am reminded of a plane I once saw painted on the frieze of a temple in Egypt. At least it *looked* like a plane, but of course *had* to be something else. Likewise, this is actually an open book with a big round hole that had supported Vasari's scaffolding.

Looking further up, my attention is drawn to the very top tier beneath the octagonal window. Figures are sitting in alcoves looking down on the scene below as if in private boxes at the theatre. Only these are the most relaxed spectators ever and who have dressed down, rather than up, for the occasion. Some are wearing nothing but a strategically-placed piece of chiffon and are sitting astride the balcony as if at any moment they might hurl themselves into the abyss. Through the binoculars, it's a 3D effect and it's all I can do to stop my self from crying out: *Don't do it!* Incredible to think that it's all painted on a curved surface.

Beneath the frescoes the area is illuminated by eight portholes beneath which are the mammoth pillars and arches which support the enormous weight of the dome – except not exactly, for the dome, and this is Brunelleschi's crowning achievement, is built with an inner and outer layer. The thicker, inner layer supports the thinner, outer layer, the bricks of which are laid in a herringbone pattern so they are self supporting. No doubt about it, the man was a genius and, what's more, he got the ambitious Florentines out of a hole too, for in what seemed a bit of reckless one-upmanship over the Pisans and Sienese, they started building a *duomo* bigger and therefore better than theirs and left the problem of how they would crown the 40 metre hole in the roof till later. Fortunately Brunelleschi happened to be born at the right time and solved the problem.

Giulia says if we want to climb to the top of the dome, it will require an hour – twenty minutes to the top via a spiral staircase, twenty to come back down and twenty to admire the view. I'm sure I could trim some time off two of those at least. There are 463 steps. She says they are not very high but the passage is narrow and warns us that once embarked on the mission, there is no return as it is a one-way system.

That's our guided tour of Florence finished. Giulia ushers us outside, says goodbye and is soon lost in the throng. Iona and I sit down on the steps of the Duomo in the brilliant sunshine and as we do so, the bells begin pealing with an intensity that seems to

Brunelleschi's Dome

shake the ground and which lasts a long time. It's a wonderfully atmospheric sound that must have echoed down the centuries to reach all strata of society: poor men, beggar men and thieves as well as the good and the great. And it's great to be here, hearing the same sound clamouring into the air.

But before I make the ascent, I must go down, down to the crypt because I saw a sign that said *TOMBA di PHILLIPO BRUNELLESCHI*. As far as I know, he's the only one of note down there as the Florentines are pretty picky about whom they bury in that place. I am glad to see they recognise their debt to the maestro.

The grave is barred by a gate, but through the bars I can see a slab on the floor with a frame, like a blank painting, and behind it a rectangular slab with a marble plaque, which in

Latin says something about poor Bruneschelli's bones. In addition to that there are a couple of wreaths, a big bronze cross and a couple of candles. And that's it. Not for him the pretentious monuments in the Santa Croce. This is nice and modest. I like it.

I don't mind the long wait in the queue for the top of the dome so much as the fact that for most of it I am in the shade. It seems a waste of sunshine but it does give me time to study this side of the cathedral. It's not to be recommended. They haven't got round to restoring it yet and the green marble is black with dirt and encrusted with inches of pigeon guano. Some scaffolding has been erected though, so it's only a matter of time.

After some time, we come to a place which widens out and where there are some statues of what look like cardinals but could be popes, as well as some bits of masonry behind grilles. Can they really imagine anyone is going to nick one of these, carry it to the top of the dome and down again? It's good to pretend to be interested in them, to study the carving minutely until the heaving in the chest dies down, the pain leaves the thighs and it's possible to speak again. Here also is an ominous sign in four languages. There is an arrow and beneath, in English: *TO THE SUMMIT*. It makes it sound like a mountain expedition.

I don't know how many more steps we climb before we emerge onto a gallery from where there is a bird's eye view of the floor. Beneath the cupola it is possible to see how the octagonal shape has been echoed in the floor with dark and light strips of marble radiating out towards the chapels. It makes me giddy to look down on the nave and see the people moving about below. From here they don't really look like people at all, just black specks.

Vasari's frescoes, however, are much, much closer. Jesus is radiating a golden light with a prayerful Mary at his knee and a heavenly choir of angels gathered around them. Every square inch of plaster has been covered and so much is going on it's impossible to take it all in, or indeed to know where to begin looking. We are also very close to a beautiful stained glass window of red, green, purple and blue, but what still intrigues me most is the topmost gallery with one figure who had better be very careful indeed or else, like the *careless fella* in Harry Graham's witty ditty, might overbalance and *land upon my nut.*

We are achieving our goal now: we have reached the part where we are between the two domes. I can see the curve of the inner dome sweeping up and away in a graceful arc. Brunelleschi's patent. Apparently, before he died, he burnt all his papers so no-one would copy his ideas. In fact, he was so terrified he would die before the dome was finished, the workers were paid extra to stay up in the dome and their wine watered down in case they fell and plunged to a premature death. He need not have worried. The dome was completed in 1436 but he did not hand in his dinner pail until 1455.

To step out into the bright Florentine sunlight with the orange roofs of the city laid out below us is an awesome sight. More than half-a-millennium later, this is still the highest point in the city. The functional, yet attractive ribs of the dome, steeply curving to the ground seem inviting. I have an insane desire to sit on one, like a boy sliding down banisters but I manage to resist the temptation. Some poor unsuspecting soul would get more than a headache if he broke my fall.

From here, the *campanile* puncturing the sky actually looks quite elegant and even the Santa Croce looks good, now that distance means the fussy details are indistinguishable. I recognise the Piazza del Repubblica and in the distance, the pencil-like tower on the Palazzo Vecchio. The Ponte Vecchio looks like an insect-infested gap between buildings but curiously, the river isn't visible at all. On the other side, squat and brown, like a toad, sits the Pitti Palace and the Boboli Gardens.

On the way down, we come to another gallery, higher than the one on our way up, and which brings us in even closer proximity to the frescoes of the devils shovelling the souls into the everlasting bonfire. We are so close to them, in fact, it's difficult to see the big picture and they appear more as swirling patches of colour. There is one fellow whom I had noticed particularly from below, and now I am within feet of him. He has a double-yolked head with Mr Spock ears and a fine pair of antelope horns and an incongruously bushy ginger moustache. Apart from those ears and the growths on his head, he could be somebody's uncle.

We continue our descent. The whole of Florence awaits. So much to see and so little time. The afternoon lies ahead of us. Where shall we head for next?

18

Funny Things on the Way to the Boboli Gardens

BILL and Pat have gone to spend the rest of the day in the queue at the Uffizi. We have decided not to bother. I would like to go and stroke that boar's nose but can't admit it, so instead I tell them I want to find Dante's house. If I can't visit his grave at least I can see where he lived. The Casa di Dante is located – strangely enough, considering the Italians' disregard for logic as far as I have found it – on the Via Dante Alighieri.

It's a bit of a disappointment. There is a coat of arms on the wall with his name on it and that's all to show he lived there. It's a tower house with great barred windows making it look like a prison. It's well and truly shut up and like a lot of buildings in Florence, most of the surface is obscured by scaffolding.

Across the road we spot Tom, Dick and Harriet lapping up *gelati*. They too are on their way to the Pitti Palace and complaining about the heat. Iona agrees; she doesn't cope well in hot climates. We buy a couple of *gelati* too and try to eat them before they run down our arms as we make our way towards the Piazza della Signoria to have a closer look at *David* and the other statues. For my money (and that is the good thing about this place, you don't need any), *The Rape of the Sabine Women* beats *David* hands down. It has so much going on: so

The Casa di Dante

much interest, so much movement, so much drama. *David* merely looks forlorn, about to do battle with Goliath and doesn't reckon his chances too much.

When I tear my eyes away from Giambologna's masterpiece, I can see no sign of Iona. As before, the piazza is swarming with people. I scan the crowds with a mounting sense of panic as I fail to spot her. How will I ever find her again in this throng? How will she find me? Maybe she doesn't want to. Perhaps she's done a runner.

It would make a good thriller – how I went about trying to find her in a strange city with no map and no money. I would go back to the hotel room and find all our stuff gone and everyone else on the tour gone too. And the friendly, pretty receptionist says she's never seen me before in her life. And what's more, I gave her my passport and all I have are the clothes I stand up in – my shirt and swimming trunks.

What would I do next? All this I think as I stand alone and palely loiter like the knight-at-arms in the poem waiting for my Belle Dame Sans Merci in the hope she will turn up again. And she does – eventually.

United once more, we stroll down the Piazzale degli Uffizi. I am curious to find out how much progress Bill and Pat have made. We find them in the U that joins the two arms of the Uffizi. They haven't even made it as far as the columns where they can begin to estimate how many hours it will take them to get to the entrance. They don't seem despondent however.

We turn right and walk along the side of the river towards the Ponte Vecchio. Not as easy as it sounds, as most of the pavement has been commandeered by people selling handbags and other leather items. It would be much easier to walk along the Corridoio Vasariano like a Medici. A man is sticking wire into a crack in the parapet and bending it into the shape of a motorbike. Quite clever really. He has a few parked along the top of the wall, but like the leather sellers, no-one is buying.

It's difficult to get a view from the bridge as the handbag sellers are out in strength here too, their wares strewn all over the pavement. I can imagine the same hustle and bustle in medieval times, though thank God, it doesn't smell like it must have done then. In those days, the shops were butchers and tanners, but now nearly all are goldsmiths. The jewellery is not to my taste – big, heavy and chunky, the rings more like knuckledusters than pieces of adornment. You could give someone a nasty smack on the mouth wearing one of those.

It's not far from here to the Palazzo Pitti. Iona hugs the shade as much as she can but in the vast piazza in which the palazzo stands, there is no hiding place – the sun bakes it with a blistering intensity, far greater heat than any we have experienced so far on this trip and we've had some pretty hot days. If you can trust it, a green light on a pharmacy flashes 39°C. I believe it.

Massive and muddy brown, severe and stolid, the palazzo looks more barracks than palace. Windows and doors stand in regular, serried rows like soldiers on parade. It is impressive, but only by its size and its dominating position in the piazza, a giant dwarfing the pigmy buildings facing it. According to our guide – a book which Iona carries in a backpack along with sundry other items now we don't have Giulia – the façade was designed by no less a person than Brunelleschi.

How could someone who built the dome on the Duomo, design something like this! To be fair to him, it was later extended to three times its original length and wings added later still in the 19th century. Perhaps in the beginning, Brunelleschi's building may have looked more appealing, but I don't think so somehow – it's only a matter of scale.

It was the former home of the Pitti family, bitter rivals of the Medici, who tried to keep up with them by building this pile and who bankrupted themselves in the process. To add insult to injury, the Medici bought it from them, no doubt at a knockdown price, extended it and in due course it became *their* main residence. Pity those who tried to take on the Medicis.

The entrance is in the middle of the building but in another instance of impeccable Italian logic, we have to leave that queue, cross the piazza and join another queue to purchase our tickets before we can begin queuing all over again.

A menu of attractions is on offer. We can have an all-inclusive ticket which admits us to everything: The Galleria d'Arte Moderna, the Galleria del Costume, the Museo degli Argenti, the Museo delle Porcellane, the Galleria Palantina and the Boboli Gardens, a name which conjures up images of trees and hedges being trimmed by topiarists into fluffy balls like the heads of dandelions.

Although we have only come for the gardens, we have to buy a ticket for the Porcelain Museum as well. It is closed however, so we are just going to the gardens anyway. It's no less than I expect from Italian logic.

In the entrance queue we encounter Tom, Dick and Harriet and direct them to the ticket office. They show no signs of even mild outrage at having wasted time standing in the broiling heat and eventually we reach the entry kiosk, flash our tickets and pass through to a colonnaded courtyard. So where are the gardens? Strangely, there is no sign of them and no signs to them.

At the end of the courtyard, bounded by a high wall, we climb a curving ramp and find ourselves in the garden at last. Or is it? Where have all the other people gone? Facing us is a huge amphitheatre with tiers of seats, Roman style, with hedges and trees behind them. It was from here the stone was quarried to build the palazzo. The curious thing however, is that here, in this open setting, the stone has a honeyed appearance and a warmness and attractiveness which is entirely lacking in the palace.

The gardens are shaped like an isosceles triangle. If we turn to our right and follow the yellow sign that says *To the gardens*, we should come to what's called L'Isolotto or small island at the point and from where we can make our way back up the other arm. We begin walking across a gravelled rectangle towards a huge stage with battens of lights and speakers as tall (or short) as me. Obviously a concert of some description is held here in the evenings, though I have not seen any advertisements to indicate what it might be. Something incredibly noisy, if the speakers are anything to go by.

In the distance, to our right, a woman is gesturing furiously at us, indicating that we should go back the way we have come. Iona looks at the windmilling arms in disbelief and dismay. The thought of retracing her steps over that baking griddle makes her feel weak at the knees.

Should we not be here? Certainly no-one else is in sight. The garden seems to have swallowed up all the other visitors without trace. How bizarre!

We keep calm and continue on regardless, crossing the area in the front of the stage, at which point the woman becomes more animated, signalling frantically as if we were unwary travellers heading towards quicksands. I can see no reason why we *should* go back. I wave back as if I had misconstrued all this as a friendly greeting. She stops waving, her fists now belligerently resting on her ample hips. Then she turns on her heel and stomps back into the building from which she has emerged.

Perhaps she has gone to call security.

19

Hot Stuff in the Boboli Gardens

IN a couple of moments after leaving the gravel path and entering a wooded area, we come to another path with a mighty big gate barring the way. Was that what the woman's signalling was all about? It's not much of a problem as we can make our way up a shady incline to our left and Iona is glad to be out of the blistering sun.

It's very pleasant, surrounded by all this greenery, the sound of birdsong, the hum of insects and no danger of the ears being assaulted by a Vespa, let alone being run down by one. These gardens are the lungs of the city, a very far cry indeed from the crowded piazzas. We could be the only two people in Florence. It seems incredible – unless the reason is we are not meant to be here after all.

At last the trees thin out and we join a path which brings us eventually to an avenue of cypresses. We know where we are now. This is the Viottolone, planted in 1637 and which forms the spine of the triangle, pointing like a dagger at the

In the Gardens

heart of L'Isolotto. At regular intervals, classical statues have
been set into alcoves in the hedge bordering the avenue.
Apart from that, it lacks interest since it is so long and
straight. It's only partially shady since the sun is still high in
the sky and so, at one of the intersections, we take the greater
shade it may offer. Suddenly we are no longer alone. There,
on benches in the shade, we discover pairs of lovers. Unwit-
tingly we seem to have turned into Lovers' Lane.

We hurry past, eyes down, though our presence does not
seem to alter their behaviour in any way. Perhaps it's true
that love is blind. As it happens, today is our wedding anniversary but you'll never catch us indulging in any of that nonsense. We are Scots with cold blood in our veins, not hot-
blooded Latin lovers like these appear to be.

When we get to L'Isolotto it is to emerge from the relatively cool of our shady walk into the full glare of the sun

again. The lake is oval and we can walk round it, but, unfortunately, not across the path which bisects it to the island in the middle as the way is blocked by ornate gates at each end. This is annoying, as according to our guidebook, on that island is the *Oceanus Fountain* by my new-found hero, Giambologna. It's a copy, which doesn't bother me, but what does is the fact I can't get close enough to see it at closer range.

Having said that, it is only a minor disappointment as this is a lovely place, providing the only splash of colour we've seen so far. It's as if the designer of the gardens had told the Pittis, in the style of Henry Ford: *You can have any colour you like as long as it's green.* Except, of course, in Henry's case the preferred colour was black.

There is a splash of pink on the island but the main colour is provided by terracotta pots on the paths to it on which geraniums, strumpet-like, are spilling their scarlet petals over the rims and which are reflected in the still, emerald-green waters of the moat. Also reflected are the arches of the path to form

The Pitti Palace from the Steps

a perfect oval. Out of the green, a horse is rearing with a bare-backed rider holding an arm aloft in a victory salute. A photo in our guidebook shows the same statue, but there, the water is just clearing the horse's front hooves and lapping at the feet of the rider. Now, the whole belly of the horse is exposed and more, as I can tell it's a stallion – sure evidence of the drought that has been going on for months.

It's a perfectly idyllic scene. We sit on a bench in the shade to drink it in.

A couple of blonde women approach. Scandinavian, if I'm not much mistaken. Iona, pink and perspiring, is slugging some water and fanning herself with the very efficient fan she bought in China. We watch them stroll past, golden-limbed, sylphlike, lithe and laughing, not a bead of sweat to be seen, as if this baking heat doesn't trouble them at all, as if they were used to hot, sunny days in their northern climes every day of their lives.

"It's just not fair!" Iona protests after their retreating (shapely) figures. "They've not got the right to look so cool when they are so fair-skinned. I can understand how the Latin types stay cool, but the Scandinavians have no right to be. Just look at me – I'm a pink blob."

I chuckle until I turn to look at her and see she is weeping behind her sunglasses.

As we leave the lake behind, we take a path to the right, a beautifully green, shady path that looks as if it should be full of sylvan coolness. Shady it may be, but cool it certainly is not. It is uphill and interesting because it is meandering. But soon we sacrifice the meander: Iona because she wants to get to the top of the hill with as little walking as possible and me, be-cause I want to get out into the sun again. So a few minutes later, I am plodding up the steep and sunny incline of the

Viottolone whilst Iona struggles up the shady path to my right.

"David!"

"What?"

"I've got to stop. I don't feel right. I think I'm going to faint."

It's like being on the other side of a dual carriageway. I can't get across to help her. I can't even see her.

"Can you make it up to the next intersection?" I call through the screen of trees.

There is no answer, but I can hear her footsteps resuming so I assume she is conserving her energy. A few minutes later we come to another intersection with a bench in the shade. Fortunately we don't have to turf out any lovers to make room for the invalid. She collapses upon it and hangs her head down. She's pinker than ever. I hand her some water.

"It's so hot. I feel dizzy. I've had nothing to eat."

True, we've had nothing since breakfast apart from the *gelati* and she hadn't taken the precaution of filling up on the breakfast which was also my lunch. It might not have mattered had it not been for this extraordinary heat. And God knows how far we've walked, not to mention the hundreds of steps to the top of the Duomo (and down).

After a time she recovers and at long last, we reach the top of the Viottolone. A path to the right leads to the Porcelain Museum and the Forte di Belvedere, the one I want to take. It's either that or the one to the left, back down towards the exit, the stage and the scary woman. The question is which woman am I scared of most?

The dilemma is resolved when Iona feels fit enough to continue now the terrain is flatter and so we direct our steps towards the Porcelain Museum. No point in going there, so we sweep round to the right and come, in a short time, to a splendid vista. From the top of the steps we can look down the entire length of the gardens to the palazzo. In the immediate foreground, a pond as green as the water in L'Isolotto, and in the middle, according to our guidebook, *The Neptune Fountain*, by Lorenzi. It looks just like a rock to me. Neptune has gone fishin' evidently. Or gone to cool down.

Below the pond are some formal gardens, then the amphitheatre, ending finally with the palazzo. However, instead of making our way in that direction, we turn to the left and head towards the fort. The walls rise sheer above us and we can't see any way in, which is a pity as I'm sure there would have been a good view of Florence from there. The very place, I suspect, where all the postcards you've ever seen of the Duomo are taken.

As we make our way downhill through trees, we come across what's known as the *Kaffeehaus* which our guidebook tells us was built in 1776. It also says it is open during the summer. To me it looks as if it has been closed for two centuries. Another pity, as we might have got a cup of coffee and something sugary to sustain Iona.

There is, however, a good view across the city to Brunelleschi's dome which rises so hugely out of the tangle of roofs it seems you could almost reach out and touch it. Over to the left, I can see a mini Brunelleschi dome except the ribs are not picked out in white. It's the church of San Lorenzo where the Medicis worshipped and are buried. Their tombs were designed by Michelangelo and the dome by Buontalenti. It sounds more like an advertising slogan than a name but the dome is very much a copy of the master's despite Brunelleschi's best efforts for his not to be imitated. I don't think he would be flattered.

To save a long trail round by the path, we make our way down a steep embankment, me going first to make sure Iona has a soft landing on top of me should she slip, and on some steps at the back of the palace, we sit and get our breath back and take in some water. Now we are faced with the long trek back to the hotel. We could get a taxi but that would leave us open to the possibility of being ripped off by an unscrupulous driver who could take us all round Florence first whilst the meter ate up our money. Besides, by a direct route, it doesn't look so terribly far and a terrible waste of sunshine, only for us to skulk for ages in our room with nothing else to do.

The decision is made. Footsore and weary, hot and sweating, we hobble out of the Boboli Gardens.

The Duomo from the Gardens

20

Strange Goings On

W E have not gone far past the non-diminishing queues at the Uffizi before Iona says she can't take the heat. She wants to walk through the town so she can get some shade from the buildings, whilst I, on the other hand, want to walk along the banks of the Arno, where the sun can beat down on my back and the backs of my legs. We agree to meet at the end of the street which we came down this morning. She shows me it is the third street on the left, takes the map and a slug of water because the bottle is too heavy for her to carry and disappears into the maze of streets on our left while I set off along the riverbank.

It's a bit annoying that the parapet is just a little bit too high or I'm too short to see the river easily but the sun is very warm and it's quite pleasant and uncrowded here, which is just as well, as the pavement is very narrow. A group is coming towards me and seeing the pavement is not going to take us all, I make room for the advancing party. However, just as we draw abreast, one of them, who is carrying a map, addresses me.

"You speak Italian?"

The Uffizi (Image Credit: Pixabay)

Stout and perspiring profusely, he must be in his thirties. He looks as if he has caught a bit of sunburn. Shocks of straw-coloured hair are escaping from a bashed and disreputable hat. Obviously a tourist. No-one else would wear such headgear where there was the slightest chance anyone might recognise him.

I say no and am about to pass on when he says, "Do you speak English?" That's what we've been speaking up to now and it's a pretty safe bet that someone wearing a Panama hat and dressed in swimming trunks that look like shorts and a shirt of Lincoln green probably speaks English like Robin Hood. "Can you tell me the way to the railway station?" he continues without missing a beat.

"I'm afraid not. I'm a stranger here myself."

"Well, in that case, can you tell me where we are now?"

That's something I *can* do. "Oh, that's easy! That's the Ponte Vecchio over there." I turn to point it out to him.

He seems to be straining to see it although he is taller than me. "Can you show me on the map?" he asks.

"Certainly."

"Let's cross over the street," he says.

I suppose it is a bit narrow here and the other side may be fractionally wider, but he doesn't know I'll be able to tell him where we are very quickly and it's not worth crossing over, but he's already moving off so I follow him. He opens the map out.

"Right, let me see... There's the river so the Ponte Vecchio must be there... there it is, so we must be here." Simple really. If we hadn't crossed the street, he would have been able to see the bridge for himself.

"Show me your papers. Police."

What? The speaker is a swarthy young man in a baseball cap with two days' growth of stubble. He's dressed in black trousers and a navy polo shirt. He's with a companion who looks older and stouter, wearing lighter clothes and a straw hat, like a tourist, but that's all I see of him before he disappears behind me.

Since my passport is in the hotel, I have visions of being hauled down to the police station and it taking hours to get sorted out whilst Iona loiters increasingly pinkly at the rendezvous wondering where I have been all this time. She should never have let me out of her sight. I always seem to get into trouble when she is not with me. I remember the double moon of last night. It *was* an omen after all.

To my astonishment, the man with the map has produced his passport out of nowhere like a conjuror. I only had a glimpse of it as he handed it over, but it seemed to me the writing on it was in the Cyrillic alphabet. Wordlessly, the young cop takes it and flicks through it.

"Your papers," he repeats.

I shake my head. "I don't have them with me. At the hotel." My mouth has suddenly gone dry though strangely, I suddenly feel sweatier than ever.

He looks me up and down with a stern expression. "I have the right. I'm an undercover cop. Your papers!" he says again, this time with a hardened edge to his voice.

Until a moment ago I was considering myself very lucky indeed that the cops should happen to have swooped at that moment, it coming to me in a blinding flash that all that rigmarole about asking the way to the railway station had just been a ruse to preoccupy me whilst I was pick-pocketed. But no sooner had I thought this than another, more worrying thought sprang to mind. What if they are crooks too and they are all in it together? I swallow hard and tighten my grip on my camera.

"I've told you, I don't have them," I reply. Then, with the boldness of age and a confidence I don't feel, I riposte, "Show me *your* papers." If he really is an undercover cop, he could well be dressed like this. And maybe this is exactly how they operate, mingling with the crowds, on the lookout for pickpockets which Angela had warned us to be on our guard against. But here, in just about the quietest part of town? He looks tough enough to be a cop, yet there was something about the way he told that he was working undercover that jarred somehow.

He is still studying Mapman's passport, or appears to be. "Show me *your* papers," I repeat, more boldly. More than ever I have a feeling something is not right.

He ignores me. Instead, he hands Mapman back his passport. "Come with me," he tells him and they turn round and head in single file towards the Ponte Vecchio – Cop first, then Mapman, followed by his companion in the straw hat whom I'd actually forgotten about. I cross the road, unscrew my bottle of water and watch them until they reach a corner.

Cop turns and looks back at me then they disappear from sight.

I stand and stare at the spot where I had just been, scarcely believing it had really happened. Is Mapman under arrest? Why give him back his passport in that case? How many crooks were there? Just one, or three? Whilst I was engaged with Mapman and Cop, had the third one, the one I couldn't see, been eyeing up my bum with a view to pickpocketing me? Or was it all about relieving me of my passport? If I'd produced it as hastily as Mapman, would they have scarpered with it?

So many questions. I don't know any of the answers but one thing's for sure – I've just had a close escape from something and only my timely challenge to the cop had prevented me from being taken for a mug or mugged. Pretty nice people, really; they might not have believed me when I said I didn't have my passport and beaten me up for it.

I resume my journey along the river bank. By now I expect to find Iona impatiently waiting at the rendezvous point, but when I get there, there is no sign of her. Strange. Nothing for it but wait. Pity there's nowhere to sit.

After a while I go the end of the Via dei Malcontenti where I expect to see her coming down the street. All I can see is a group of tourists coming and it doesn't look as if she is amongst them. The last stragglers arrive and are whisked away on a bus. Americans. Now I can see right down the Via and there is no-one in sight who looks remotely pink and perspiring. Maybe she's coming another way along the Via Tripoli or the Viale Giovine Italia. But there's no sign of her there either. Surely to God she should be here by now? Maybe she's fainted somewhere or been knocked over by a Vespa.

Where the hell could she be? I am beginning to feel like one of the Malcontenti myself. That's twice she's disappeared today.

I decide to give her five minutes more, but after three, I decide to go back to the hotel as there is still no sign of her coming from any of the possible directions. Hopefully what's happened is she has got fed up waiting for me in the heat and with nowhere to sit in the shade, is waiting for me there with a rolling pin, asking *me* where the hell *I* have been. Yes, that must be it.

I set off up the Viale Giovine Italia, hoping I may catch up with her on the way, but I reach the hotel still without any sign of her. My last hope is when I ask for the key at reception they'll say it's not there which means she will be in the room lying on the bed with her feet up. But the receptionist hands me the key without demur.

"Have you seen my wife?"

As soon as I utter the words, I realise what a stupid thing that was to say. He wouldn't know Iona from Eve. I should have asked, "Has a pink blob been here and dripped a pool of sweat on the floor?" Hastily I rephrase my question, "I mean has anyone else asked for the key?" Alas, the receptionist shakes his head sadly.

I decide to go up anyway to see if there have been any signs of recent occupancy but there are none. Where on earth can she be? What could possibly have happened to her?

21

A Surprisingly Sumptuous Restaurant

SOME way to celebrate your wedding anniversary this! There's nothing else for it – I am going to have to trail all the way back and hope I'll meet the other celebrant before I get there. If only we had taken our mobile phones! Except mine might have been pinched anyway by the "cop" behind me, who had probably been looking for a pocket to pick like one of Fagin's urchins.

But back at the Piazza Piave there is still no sign of her. I wait for ten minutes and when she still doesn't show up, I decide there's nothing else for it but to go back to the hotel and see if there have been any developments. I curse myself for not having taken a taxi from the Boboli. How ironic I didn't in case I was ripped off, and because I hadn't, I nearly was! I suppress thoughts that at this very moment I could be having a nice cold beer in the hotel bar letting the pain drain from my feet instead of pounding them to a pulp on these un-forgiving pavements.

As I enter the foyer, I pray the key will not be at reception. I will go up to the room and Iona will scream: *Where the bloody hell have you been?* as well as other choice words of endearment at the joy of being rejoined with her underling again. My ordeal will be at an end, once the pain has gone from where she has stomped on my feet, her favourite method of administering correction for my misdeeds. But a greater fear by far is she will not be there at all.

The receptionist hands me the key and my heart sinks. Where the hell *can* she be? I take the lift to the room, collapse on the bed and slip off my 50p shoes from Lidl's. Ah, the relief! After a while, I decide I may as well have a shower and if she *still* hasn't come back by then, at least I'll be a bit more refreshed in order to resume the search. The problem with this strategy is she might try to get in the room whilst I'm in the shower; or she'll think I've been relaxing all this time without sparing her as much as a solitary thought. Pompeii in 79AD would have been a safer place to be. Then, I could have taken my chances.

Swathed in a towel like a Roman senator, I am lying on the bed again, feeling the rhythmic ebb and flow of the throb in my feet, feeling the soreness drain out of them, feeling soothed, when the telephone startles me into alertness.

"Pronto." (When in Italy.)

"Oh, you're there!" It's a familiar voice. She sounds more relieved than furious. "I just wanted to make sure. I'm coming right up. Don't go away!"

As if I would! Before she gets a chance to say anything, I get in first and explain I waited for ages and had already been back to look for her. She says she had been waiting for *me* and had even chased after some poor innocent man whom she thought looked like me. Isn't that an incredible thing! Out of the millions of people in Florence there's someone as green about dress sense as me and, what's more, she had happened to see him!

"Where were you waiting?" she asks irritably.

"Where we agreed – at the gate where the Malcontenti were executed." I think I know how they must have felt.

"I might have known it! I told you the *third* road on the left."

"That's where I was. I counted them."

"Well you can't count!"

Crippled feet notwithstanding, she gets up off the bed and produces the map from her rucksack.

"Look: one, two, three. I always knew you were arithmetically challenged, but I didn't realise you were this bad!"

"Just a minute," I protest, putting my finger on the Piazza dei Cavalleggeri. "What about this?"

"Well, what about it? It's a piazza, not a street."

"Well, there's a street leading to it," I point out, reasonably.

So it's all my fault. I always knew it would be.

She rakes in her bag, pops a pill out of a silver-foil bubble and slugs it down with some water.

"What are you doing?"

"Taking a Migraleve."

"Have you got a headache?"

"No. My feet are killing me."

"So you are taking a headache pill for your feet?"

She's flipped. Maybe she's got sunstroke.

"It's a painkiller, isn't it?"

"You think I'm a pain but I bet it doesn't make me disappear."

"Huh!"

This evening we are all going out for a meal to the Palazzo Borghese, the former residence of Napoleon's younger sister, Pauline, who was married to Camillo Borghese, the 6th Prince of Sulmona (wherever that is). As we walk along, I regale Angela with my recent strange encounter.

"I know a crime was attempted," I ask her, "but how many crooks were there?"

"Well," she replies after some thought, "it's true the police do work undercover and it's also true they have the right to stop people and ask to see their papers, so they *might* have been cops. But probably they were after your passport. There's a big demand for passports from the likes of Bosnia and Croatia. That's why we say to people to leave them in the hotel. If there's a problem, we can always sort it out afterwards."

I wonder what a Bosnian or Croatian passport looks like. Was that what Mapman had flashed?

I change the subject. "By the way, Angela, it so happens that today is our wedding anniversary."

"Oh, is it really? That's nice."

"Yes. And I just wondered if you mentioned it to the waiters, if perhaps they could arrange something..." My voice trails off. I have a bit of a cheek really. I must have been mad to suggest it. I feel covered in confusion while Angela waits for me to dig a bigger hole for myself. "It's not for me, you understand – just something to make the night more special and memorable for Iona. She likes that sort of thing." Actually, I am lying through my teeth. She does nothing of the kind but I hoped there might be a free bottle of wine in it for me.

"Just leave it with me, I'll see what I can do."

I have been so busy chatting I haven't noticed where we have been walking and now we find ourselves at the restaurant.

Right from the start, I can see this is going to be a really special occasion. A couple of flambeau are flickering on either side of the entrance while a red carpet leads through imposing doors to where a guard with a double-headed axe is standing sentry. He is wearing purple-and-white striped pantaloons, a tunic with puffy sleeves and body armour on top. The effect is completed by a red-and-white plumed helmet.

Palazzo Borghese
(Image Credit: Saliko, licensed under the Creative Commons Attribution-Share Alike 3.0 Unported license.)

We are permitted to pass into a long corridor with statues in alcoves. It is illuminated by real flames burning in bowls set on tripods and at last we come to a tastefully-decorated vestibule with arches with greenery in them and more statues, one of a semi-nude, semi-reclining lady. Angela tells us it's a copy of Canova's *Venus Victrix* and the model is none other that Pauline herself.

"She was once asked how she could pose for the artist like that," Angela tells us. "'Oh, it wasn't a problem', Pauline is said to have replied. The fire was on."

We pass through a heavy gold curtain and mount some stairs where the strains of medieval music come wafting down to us. At the top of the stairs, a man is dressed as I imagine a Medici might have been. He has black boots, white tights and a gold-coloured tunic flared out at the bottom with a ruff at the neck. Over that, a white jacket-sort-of-thing with puffy sleeves edged in black. The crowning glory is what looks very much like a nightcap with the point dangling over his right shoulder. The things some people do to earn a crust!

We progress into an elegant room where we are greeted by a quartet of ladies dressed in medieval costume. One is playing the harp, another the flute, while the talents of the other two will presumably be revealed later. The music makes me think of Henry VIII and *Greensleeves*, although this is meant to suggest medieval Italy. If all we have seen so far is anything to go by, our meal is going to consist of fourteen courses which will include swan and wild boar.

We leave the ladies to their music and move to another room, then an antechamber lit by a massive chandelier (electric), with candles on the walls and tables. I may be mistaken but the furniture looks Louis XIV in style, disgustingly fussy bow-legged monstrosities including a sofa with three gilded panels on the back. I bet it's not the last word in comfort but there is no mistaking the opulence of the room.

All this combines to make me feel as if I've been transported back to the past. But what's a scruff like me doing in a place like this?

And it's not over yet by any means as we pass through yet another room with expensive-looking red wallpaper, heavy brocade gold curtains, more bow-legged chairs upholstered in gold material and some hideous gilt mirrors hanging above equally hideous gilt tables. At the far end of the room, to the left, one half of a pair of double doors has been left open. But doors the like of which I have never seen before! White, divided into three panels, the bottom and top with crescents of gold leaf, the middle a green oval in a white frame but most impressive of all, in the centre, a golden face in high relief with golden rays radiating from it like some Aztec god. This is the portal to our dining room.

This is sheer elegance. None of that heavy gilt furniture here, but four round tables set for our feast; an enormous chandelier (probably *papier mâché* as otherwise it would be so heavy it would drag the ceiling down); electric candelabra on the walls; a pale blue wallpaper with gold stripes and motifs; a big gilt mirror and four more of those amazing doors.

But before we settle down, Angela asks us if we'd like to see Pauline Borghese's bedroom. Being permitted into the inner sanctum of ladies' bedrooms is an experience in which my life has been sadly lacking. I don't need to be asked twice.

It was a rhetorical question anyway. Off we troop in Angela's wake to see where Napoleon's sister wakened up after a good night's sleep. She was a famous beauty of her day but, by reputation, beauty sleep was not something she got a lot of.

Party Time at
Pauline Bonaparte's

UNBELIEVABLE! What a room! It sparkles like a jewel. Gold wherever you look – gold on the walls, gold on the ceiling, gold on the candelabra, gold on the chandeliers, gold on the mirrors, gold on the doors. And light – light glistening and winking like diamonds from a myriad of electric candles, reflected as the points of stars in the mirrors. It's breathtaking.

"So unlike our own little love-nest at home, dear," I remark *sotto voce* to Iona.

"This was the bedroom of Pauline Bonaparte, Napoleon's sister," Angela is saying. "She married into the Borghese family. Up there is the minstrels' gallery." She indicates it high on the gilded wall at the far end of the room. "That's where the musicians used to come every morning to waken her up. But the curtains on the bed were always drawn, so they couldn't see who she was waking up with!" (Laughter.) "Her marriage did not last long. She was very good at public relations however, especially with men, and a bit of a diplomat. All her receiving rooms and her bedroom had at least four doors, so that none of her visitors could tell who was coming or going!" (More laughter.)

It's true. There are five doors here, as ornate as the one leading into the dining room, but maybe I am deceived (like the lovers) and one is really a reflection. I look in one of the mirrors and reflect myself. Perhaps this very mirror has also reflected Pauline doing triple X stuff with her lovers. Now there's a thought.

"Would you like to see Pauline's party room now?" Angela asks redundantly.

Would I heck! If this is what her bedroom is like, her party room must be something to behold. Forget the food. Why not take over Pauline's party room and have a party *à la Pauline*? On second thoughts, maybe not.

As is so typical of life in my experience, anything you look forward to too much turns out to be a disappointment. And so it is with Pauline's party room. It's nowhere near as exciting as her bedroom. It also has a minstrels' gallery, a bit more ornate than the one in the bedroom – I suppose a lot more people would see it – and it also has a painted ceiling and mirrors, two chandeliers and innumerable candelabra on the walls. It doesn't sparkle quite the same as the bedroom: the gilt is more muted, making the room more tasteful and elegant, an impression further enhanced by the classical statues in alcoves around the room. It's smaller too, though you could still hold a ball in it, and set out with tables draped in white crisp linen. Angela tells us it is let out for special occasions like weddings and anniversaries (note!). If we had been a bigger tour, this is where we would have been. Instead we have to slum it in the blue room, to which we now retrace our steps.

Bottles of wine have been set out, as well as the water antidote, as is the Italian custom. We find ourselves at the same table as Bill and Pat, and Tom, Dick and Harriet, to which you can add a vacant chair. This is good news, as apart from that, Dick is too young to partake of the wine. All the more for us. Soon Banquo's place is occupied by Angela. Not to worry. Since she is working, she may not pose too serious a threat.

It's a set menu. The antipasto consists of *crostini* – pieces of toast with puréed tomato and liver pâté and two others in two shades of green; one pale like sludge, the other so dark it is almost black. Angela says it's anchovy and olive. Iona and I swap – my pâté for her anchovy. I am hesitant about pouring myself another glass of wine. No-one else seems to have touched much of theirs at all. God knows how long it will be before they empty them and I can top them up again and help myself to some more.

The second course is called the *primo*, according to the rules of Italian logic. It's a ravioli dish. Empty or not, it's time for my companions to have their glasses replenished. I attentively pour some wine into Harriet's glass and am gratified to see Bill pouring some into Pat's.

Now we have *il secondo*, the main event, which is pork. By this time we are getting into our stride and tongues are a little loosened. It turns out we are all going to be staying in Sorrento next week and we all agree it would be a great idea to hire a minibus and visit Herculaneum, Vesuvius, the Amalfi Coast and such like. Angela says she can fix it for us with a reliable company with English-speaking guides and we all feel very happy.

There's just one problem: we are out of wine. Bill and I agree to get another bottle between us. Surely he meant *each*?

But anyway, it's a start. The waiter brings it and goes away again. I notice the other tables are also being rebottled.

"Is the wine free?" I ask Angela with sudden insight, though *included* would have been more semantically accurate.

She nods. Why on earth did she not tell us this at the start? And if I had only known there was to be unlimited "free" wine I need never have embarrassed myself by asking for the anniversary surprise. Water under the bridge now. This puts the seal on our new friendships. We raise our glasses to the holiday, and next week.

The *dolce* is a long time in coming, which is fine – time for more wine. The waiter brings two more bottles, red and white. It's not great wine, but it's good enough and getting better all the time. When the sweet does come, it turns out to be a pastry shell filled with strawberries and confectioner's custard. It's a pale blue which perfectly matches the blue in Iona's dress.

The maître d' comes round to tell us about it. "This was created by our chef," he says, "especially for tonight. He was inspired by –"

My thoughts are racing ahead. This must be the anniversary surprise, a sauce made to compliment Iona's dress. It will catch on and be known hereafter as *Iona Sauce*, celebrated the world over like Peach Melba. But then the maître d' spoils the fantasy by continuing, "– the Italian sky and the wallpaper in this room."

How prosaic and how disappointing! The wallpaper and the sauce *are* the same shade of light blue but as a foodstuff, to be honest, I find the colour somewhat off-putting. Besides, I know the wine will taste terrible after it.

Interior of the Palazzo Borghese
(Image Credit: Saliko, licensed under the Creative Commons Attribution-Share Alike 3.0 Unported license.)

But now a diversion. The lady minstrels, who had welcomed us, and whom I'd completely forgotten about, now reappear. Angela catches my eye: *This is it!*

She must have pointed Iona out to them: *The woman with the blue bits in her dress like the sauce,* for they look over and nod at us and smile before going into their routine. They play some sort of melody and although I can't see it from where I am sitting, what sounds like two bits of wood being clapped together. Presently they segue into Mendelssohn's *Here Comes the Bride,* to much laughter and applause. Angela must have gone round the tables and told the others what to expect as Iona seems to be the only person in the room who is puzzled by this musical frog-leap through the centuries and goes as pink as a prawn – not for the first time today.

When it is over, I thank Angela profusely. The surprise apart, it has been a good meal in the most sumptuous of surroundings any of us are ever likely to dine in again anytime soon, or ever again, for that matter. Meanwhile, there is still some wine left in the bottles and I hate waste, even although the others don't seem to mind. All the more for me.

The conversation and laughter continue, louder and more freely than before. The wine tastes better than ever.

As we get up to leave, after the coffees, I look longingly at the half-full bottle of white looking lost amongst all its dead companions. Surely it would be a kindness to put it out of its misery? Iona gives me one of her Gorgon stares: *No. Don't even think about it! Just leave it!* However, as we file out the door, I notice Gordon is cradling a bottle.

Outside, I stop and look back at the building. I still don't know what street it's on, but the number on the wall is 110. The flames, the guard and the red carpet, are of course, long gone, as are my companions. I hurry after them and catch up with Gordon.

"Your wife is way ahead somewhere," he says.

"Oh, is she? Damn! I've lost her twice today already. I thought maybe third time lucky."

His teeth gleam whitely in the velvety darkness as he chuckles at my feeble joke.

I tell him I admire him for sneaking out the bottle of wine and he says we can share it when we get back to the hotel. That's what I like to hear. I've heard the chimes at midnight, many, many times. I am hopeless in the mornings but I've never missed a chance to stay up all night and party.

Back at the hotel, Gordon and Blondie and the couple from Yorkshire, who it turns out, have also liberated a bottle, are rearranging the furniture and getting glasses when La Belle Dame Sans Merci waylays me.

"I've been invited to join them for a drink," I tell her, knowing even as I say it, it's hopeless.

"Oh no you're not! You've had quite enough already. And you've to get up at half-past six tomorrow. You know what you're like in the mornings."

As we pass the party group on our way to the lift, Gordon nods towards a seat he has prepared for me. It will have to be for Banquo. I will be with them in spirit only. I shake my head sadly, and behind Iona's back make the face: *I've got to go to bed. Anniversary, you know. Wink! Wink!*

Gordon looks back knowingly. I hope he believes me. It would be too humiliating to be unmasked as the underling I really am after only three days' acquaintanceship.

We step into the lift and it takes us heavenward. Well, as far as the third floor anyway.

Pisa

23
The Perils of Pisa

A
S we draw into Pisa, the sun is streaming through
the window of the bus. Giancarlo pulls into the car
park and I begin gathering my stuff together. Prematurely, it turns out. It seems this is only the car park for the
car park, where it takes a quarter of an hour while Giancarlo
gets the necessary documentation to park somewhere else.

At last we pull into a vast, practically empty, bus park.
That's a good sign. Maybe the Campo dei Miracoli, the Field
of Miracles, will be relatively quiet. That *would* be a miracle!
We make our way across a field of asphalt to a bus stop to
wait for a shuttle bus.

No guide here. We are on our own. Angela tells us we
have to be back at the shuttle stop at 9:45. She repeats the
time, like a primary schoolteacher instructing a particularly
obtuse class on an obscure point. Is it my imagination, or is she
looking at me in particular? We haven't time, she says, to
climb the Tower: you have to queue for tickets and then are
given a time for the ascent.

Before we reach the Campo, we are obliged to run a
gauntlet of souvenir stalls. Pisa appears to have been entered

into a Who-Can-Sell-the-Tackiest-Souvenirs-of-the-Year Contest. Resisting the temptation to buy garish Leaning Tower table lamps and iridescent Field of Miracles plates, we arrive at an ancient crenellated wall. We pass through an arch and – lo! – the Campo dei Miracoli, like a banquet of architectural delights, is spread out before us on a tablecloth of green.

The Leaning Tower is arguably the most famous icon of a city, or indeed a country, in the world but one rarely sees it with the other buildings on the site. Here it is now, at the far end of a vast green sward, teetering precariously, or so it seems, but after years of stabilisation work, it is now quite safe from toppling over. Angela had told us they could have made it perfectly straight, but the tourist board, quite rightly, insisted it still retained a lean, so now it is restored to the an-

gle it had in Galileo's day, from where, as every schoolboy knows, he conducted his experiments on gravity and to which tourists have been gravitating ever since.

The lean is best seen in conjunction with the Duomo where the Tower looks as if it is trying to peer over its shoulder to catch a glimpse of the Baptistery, like a child playing hide-and-seek but giving the game away by peeking out,

The Baptistery

unable to resist checking to see if the finder is coming yet. It's really rather comical.

For us the Baptistery is the first structure in the Campo and the second oldest, taking more than two centuries to build. That's dedication. It was completed in 1363 and from what I can see of the two other buildings, on first impressions, I have to agree with Angela who had told us she prefers it to the Tower and the Duomo. Designed by Diotisalvi, it's very pleasing indeed. Circular, it's capped by a dome that looks like a lemon-squeezer. It seems perfectly proportioned and although it is rather fussy in the middle with rather too many columns and Gothic arches, that is counterbalanced with a bottom section composed of elegant columns and Romanesque windows set in a plain marble wall. The third tier, also rather

Façade of the Duomo and Tower Playing Peek-a-Boo

plain, has echoes of both. And, unless my eyes deceive me, like the Tower, the whole thing seems to have a bit of a lean also.

The trouble with the buildings on the Campo is they are built on sandy soil and when we go round to the rear of the Duomo, we can see that it too is sinking, that the top two stripes of grey marble are not running parallel. With its curves and columns, the apse echoes the Tower and – if you stand in a certain position – you can get the two to touch, as if the Tower is lazily leaning against it.

The façade of the Duomo is a bit too fussy for my taste, nevertheless it knocks the others we have seen into a cocked hat. The most noticeable feature is the forest of four tiers of slim columns, the top two of which, narrower than those below, could be a building in its own right. It's like a Roman temple, except the arches are distinctly Moorish. As a matter of fact, the building of the Duomo was funded in 1063 from the spoils of war against the Muslims in Sicily. Incredibly, it took only thirty years to build, although Buscheto's original building was extended in the 12th century by Rainaldo, who also designed the façade.

It's closed and, anyway, you have to pay for admittance. A bit much isn't it, if all you want to do is come in for a bit of a pray? I suppose there must be times when the faithful can get in for free, but if the idea is to raise revenue for its upkeep, it seems mad to shut it now with all these tourists swarming about. Happily, they have left the massive brass carved doors in the centre open and when those scores of irritating tourists, having had their fill, at long last move out of the way, like a voyeur peeping through a keyhole, I can at least see where I may not go.

The nave looks impressive with its sturdy Corinthian columns holding up the coffered ceiling but it's a bit of a disappointment to see below that, the grey stripes, which had been scarcely noticeable from the outside, seem much more obvious here. And there's the lamp on high (not the original and at the moment as steady as a rock) whose regular swinging to and fro inspired Galileo to think a pendulum would be a handy device to regulate a clock. However he didn't pursue the notion until later in his life and it was Huygens, fifteen years after Galileo's death, who produced the first reliable clock based upon his original idea.

Further down the nave is Giovanni Pisano's Carrara marble pulpit, not to be confused with Nicola Pisano's in the Baptistery. Despite what it may seem, Nicola was a bloke and Giovanni was his son, a chip off the old block. After the fire of 1595, the pulpit was dismantled and boxed up, and that's how it stayed until 1926. But like Humpty Dumpty, they couldn't put it together again, or at least not quite in the right order. And guess what – its stairs have never been found! But perhaps the more probable, more prosaic truth is Giovanni never made them in the first place. When you see the amount of detail on the pulpit you shouldn't be surprised if that was indeed the case.

In the distance, the very far distance, in the dome of the apse, is the mosaic of *Christ enthroned between the Virgin and Saint John*, the curve of the dome making Christ appear to be looking down from heaven upon this place beneath. Unfortunately I can't see it, but the face of Saint John on His left is by Cimabue. It was painted in 1302 and it's his last work. Miraculously, it survived the fire of 1595.

Having seen as much as we can see, we stroll back to the Tower. No need to describe that. Its cotton-reel marble drums are constructed of Carrara marble, and unlike the other *campaniles* we have seen, completely devoid of those horrendous pyjama stripes. In fact if they *were* pyjamas, you would go to bed each night praying there would not be a fire in the night and people would see you in them.

We are lucky to see it as it is. If we had been here just a few years previously, we wouldn't have been able to see the Tower for unsightly cables and lead weights which they used to correct the lean, which – by the 1990s – was precarious. Restoration is still going on as some screens have been stretched over some scaffolding on the topmost tier, the belfry. But wait a minute! It *is* restoration work, isn't it? From this angle the screens look shiny, like mirrors, making it look extraordinarily like Telstar. The Tower is one of the highest buildings in Pisa. Surely they wouldn't use it as a communication tower would they? Surely those screens don't hide half a dinner-set of satellite dishes, do they?

Whilst I am contemplating the enormity of this, a man interrupts my musings to ask me to take his photograph and, horror upon fresh horror, before I can stop him, he skips over the chain railing onto the emerald-green sward and positions himself bang in front of the Tower.

"Hey, you can't do that! You're not meant to walk on the grass!" No one, but absolutely no-one is committing such a sacrilege. It's that broad expanse that adds enormously to the appeal of this place, the magnificent buildings arising out of the green instead of grey paving stones. It's the perfect antidote to the cramped and squashed cluster of buildings in Florence. Besides, there's probably security people on the prowl who would probably leap to the conclusion that I had told him to stand there in order to get a better picture and I would get the bollocking, not him.

Even if he doesn't understand English, the panic in my voice must have been clear enough to convey my meaning as my subject skips back over the chain without hesitation. I kneel down, not in thanks to God, but so I can get the whole of the Tower in. I motion to him to take a few steps to the side so he is standing beside it, not growing out of the top of his head like a chimney.

Despite me not letting him stand on the grass he thanks me warmly when he sees the result. Little does he know that if the tourist police had started yelling at us I would have grassed him up like a shot.

The Tower (with Telstar on the Top)

24

Souvenirs and a Supplication

I T'S a splendid view, standing here with the Tower to our left and the apse of the Duomo ahead of us. Running parallel with the side of the Duomo is a sparklingly-white marble wall with no fewer than forty-three blind arches and an intriguing little Gothic tower over the doorway to the right. This is the Camposanto or Cemetery. According to legend, on the fourth crusade of 1203, a cargo of soil from the hill of Golgotha was brought back so the great and the good of Pisa could be buried in holy ground, where it is said, their flesh would melt clean away into the ground within twenty-four hours. Hamlet might liked to have known that; how *they* did, heaven alone knows.

I stand under the mini Gothic tower, marvelling at the delicate tracery of the stonework which forms the overhanging base of the tower. Four gargoyles are leaning over, looking down at me, looking up. If we want to go in, we have to retrace our steps to an adjacent building where they sell tickets, just as we had to do at the Pitti Palace. It's a pity we haven't time to pay a visit, because apart from the Roman sarcophagi and sculptures and those frescoes that have been restored after the Allied air raid of 1944, in the Capella dal Pozzo are relics from eleven of the twelve apostles, two pieces from the True Cross, a thorn from the Crown of Thorns and a piece of fabric from Mary's dress! Isn't that an incredibly impressive collection of relics!

Butting onto the pristine-looking cemetery wall are the much older-looking crenellated city walls, randomly sprouting vegetation. There is nothing I like better than walking along medieval ramparts but I don't see anybody else up there, which probably means they are not open. In any case, if friendly fire was the enemy of the Camposanto, time is ours here.

We walk over to have another, closer look at the Baptistery. The carving on it really is fantastic. This doorway, for instance – just look at the detail! So much going on! Christ and the apostles over the door, each with distinctly individual

The Camposanto, Pisa (Image Credit: Pixabay)

faces and flowing garments and on the arches, smaller figures, like individual frames on a roll of film, running between them. Utterly amazing!

I walk round the building in increasing wonder and admiration until I come to an open door. A hefty security girl with a radio clipped to her waist is standing with her back to me just inside. I take the chance to squeeze past her plump posterior and slip inside. I know it's the exit but it's time to play the tourist idiot, my aim being to catch a glimpse of the interior to see if it's as magnificent as the outside.

My eyes have not even had time to adjust from the fierce sunlight to the gloom of the interior before the lady, by some sixth sense, spots me.

"Ticket?"

"Ticket?" I play for time, trying to look past her bulk but all I can see is a vast empty space.

"Yes. You have to buy a ticket."

I let a look of comprehension dawn on my stupid, red, tourist face. I hope she thinks the redness is due to embarrassment. I ask her where I can buy a ticket to add substance to the deception and thank her as I back out. Not really a successful mission, but I think I've seen enough to decide this is the converse of the Santa Croce, much more interesting on the outside than the inside. The beauty lies without.

On the other side of the field is a phalanx of tourist stalls. There is only one gap in their ranks, a banner which proclaims this is the entrance to the Museo delle Sinopie. The *sinopie* are the preliminary sketches, what were discovered beneath, and all that remained of the frescoes that were damaged in the fire of 1944. It has another of those enigmatic one-handed clocks high on the wall, topped with a monumental arch. If I read it correctly, it says we don't have time to go in, so we turn our attention to the souvenir stalls instead.

They are all a variation on a theme. There are enough leaning towers to fill the Baptistery. You can have them in any colour, in any shade, in any size. You can have them as lamps, as ashtrays, as toilet-brush holders. No, not really. They don't have the last two, only they should, as that would be a very appropriate purpose for their dreadful tackiness. We are incredulous at the extent of the variety – and the awful-ness.

"Look, look! Here is a really nice one!" I point at a tower two feet tall, a lurid purple, dusted with glitter. "And it says it changes colour *and* glows in the dark! What more could you ask for?"

Nearby is a tray with scores of smaller imitations piled on top of each other. "Let's get one for Hélène! We've *got* to get one for Hélène!" Iona is practically dancing with excitement. Hélène is our daughter.

I look at her in horror. "You're joking! You've *got* to be kidding! What? Waste €2 on rubbish like that!"

But once La Belle Dame Sans Merci has made up her mind, there's no changing it. Thankfully our purchase is wrapped in a brown paper bag, the same that the cormorant lays its eggs in, or like the package in a plain envelope that the postman delivers and which you don't want your wife to see.

There are further delights in store. You can have a minia-ture of the whole of the Field of Miracles, all the buildings crushed together in the same lurid colours. Or what about a mug with a picture of the Tower and wittily sloping away from the handle so you can miss your mouth and slop your boiling coffee into your lap? Or perhaps the discerning tourist would prefer a tasteful plate depicting the Tower which you

can hang on the wall: *Instructions. To get maximum enjoy-
ment from your plate, please hang at an angle.*

We come across Bill and Pat buying a miniature tower.

"Hah! Hah! Caught you! We won't tell on *you*, if you
don't tell on *us*!" I waggle our discreetly-wrapped package
before their eyes like Galileo's pendulum.

"I know, they're so awful, they're irresistible aren't they?
It's a pity we don't smoke – we could use the tall one as an
ashtray," says Pat.

Great minds! "Worth taking it up just to have one, I
would have thought."

We move on to another stall. The Yorkies are buying a
two-inch brass tower.

"Hah! Hah! Caught you! I won't tell on you, if you don't
tell on me!" Once I've thought of a good line, I don't let go of
it readily. I never seem to learn the lesson to stop when I'm
ahead, let alone when I'm not.

Mr Yorkie fixes me with one eye; the other is looking over
my right shoulder. "What d'ya mean?" he asks ingenuously,
without a mote of hostility.

Oh God! What *do* I mean? He obviously *likes* his purchase. There is something about his appearance, his casual but
non-conformist attire, the battered hat on his head, the length
of his unkempt hair spilling out from beneath it that makes
Sherlock Addison deduce he is a lecturer in art. Only those in
his *métier* could possibly see any merit in the abominations on
display here, recognising in them something we artistic igno-
ramuses are too stupid to appreciate. Quick thinking is required.

"Oh... er... shopping, instead of using the time to go into
the Baptistery or the Museo."

He nods. "Yeah, right!" Does he believe me? It's hard to read his eyes. As long as he thinks I'm just some sort of harmless nutter, I'll settle for that and count myself fortunate.

It's time to start heading back to the shuttle stop, through the gauntlet of souvenir stalls without the city walls and hopefully without buying anything else on the way, but unfortunately Iona is distracted by boxer shorts hanging like bunting from the canvas roof of a stall. The backside has a photograph of *David's* buttocks, the front, his dangly bits. They are a dusky white, just like the statue, but the shorts themselves come in a variety of colours. The ones Iona particularly likes are finished in an attractive shade of brown, dark at the seat and lightening up to the waist, as if the wearer had been afflicted with a severe case of diarrhoea. Of all the tack in all the tacky stalls of Pisa, this is the tackiest, and brown the tackiest colour. Iona *has* to have them for our son – a snip at €5. It's a onesize fits all, so the lady says, and a moment later they are ours.

As we head to the rendezvous point, Iona chortling with glee at her purchases and the anticipatory thought of how appalled our kids will be with their gifts, we see an old woman coming towards us, except "coming" is a totally inadequate word to describe how she is walking. Dressed in black from her headscarf to her shoes, she is leaning on a stick, bent double, shuffling forward on chickenwishbone legs. Probably rickets. Her free hand is held pathetically out, palm upwards. I am already feeling for a €2 coin which I press into it as we come abreast.

Then suddenly, a man to her right tries to grab it. There is a moment of sheer panic on her face and quicker than I thought it would be possible for her to move, she clutches the coin to her chest and cowers like an animal expecting to be beaten with a stick. The man disappears into the crowd. It's all over so quickly, I can scarcely believe it had really happened. Who would steal from a woman like that?

Without looking back, the crone continues her laborious journey. Where is she going? Where does she live? Does anyone look after her? Doesn't the State?

25

Feeling the Heat and the Cold

A T the shuttle stop we are not the last. In fact we appear to be in good time, for an enormous queue has already gathered. Angela is looking distinctly nervous as the Yorkies haven't turned up yet and neither have Gordon and Blondie.

We *have* to catch this shuttle, Angela impresses upon us, because where our bus awaits – surrounded I imagine by scores of others by now – we have been allocated only a limited amount of parking time. And if that doesn't tell you how many people descend on Pisa all day, every day, then I don't know what else will. Angela emphasises that when the bus comes, as it must, we must climb aboard, no matter how crowded it is – and it *will* be, she warns.

This is going to be fun. Angela isn't having any. Her eyes keep wandering back to the stalls from where she hopes she'll see the truants emerging. I sympathise. I know what it's like, having organised many school trips abroad in the past. Kids you expect to be trouble; adults you expect to be more responsible. Next week she has a full busload. There's bound to be at least one troublemaker out of that lot – as if she hasn't enough to contend with in our little group. I wouldn't be in her shoes for all the tacky towers in Pisa.

The sun is wonderfully hot even although there are two hours and more to run before the noonday sun. Thankfully a low wall provides a handy seat where I can sit and present my face to the life-giving force, basking in the relief that it's not my responsibility to make sure these grown-ups keep to the schedules and trusting them not to get lost. Sometimes they can be worse than kids.

Still no sign of Gordon and Blondie, but at last here come the Yorkies laden down with brown packages. Angela is vastly and visibly relieved, but how on earth could they have found so much to buy? Perhaps they have lots of relations they hate, or friends they want to irritate.

Whilst I am contemplating the wonder of this, a vendor comes along with a briefcase full of watches. Time to bargain. I need a replacement for my £4 "Rolex" from Penang. Someone took it to be the genuine article and nicked it. It was last seen at the gym, thereby confirming my opinion that exercise is not good for you. But there is nothing to tempt me here – big chunky timepieces with straps like the chains cyclists use to tie up their bikes.

Angela's relief was momentary. She asks the Yorkies if they have seen Gordon and Blondie. They say they saw them last at the Campo but that was ages ago. It might as well have been the Congo for all the good that did Angela.

Now here comes the bus and Angela's nerves go into hyperdrive. As if waiting for their cue, Gordon and Blondie emerge from the shade of some stalls on the other side of the road where they have been waiting all this time, out of the sun. They have been able to see us, but no-one has spotted them. It was thoughtless of them, but presumably they had no

The River Arno running through Pisa (Photo Credit: Pixabay)

idea of the knots they were creating in Angela's knickers. Or did they? Was this their idea of a prank to play on her? No time for her to berate them or even utter a single word of reprimand. It's time to fight our way onto that bus, come hell or high water.

As the bus draws up, we look at each other in utter disbelief. Angela is surely the joker now. She cannot be serious about all of us getting on this thing! It's already bursting at the seams and there are tons of people ahead of us in the queue – if you could call this mass of humanity a queue. Some are getting off, thankfully, and although the rule is alight at the rear and enter at the front, this is Italy where rules are rarely given the time of day at the best of times, never mind a time like this. A mighty struggle ensues as those trying to get off meet a tsunami of people shoving each other to climb on. You could be forgiven for thinking the bus was a lifeboat and it was get aboard or drown. But then these other would-be passengers will also have been told they must get on at any cost.

It's sheer mayhem, but at last we are all aboard, or so I believe. It's impossible to pick out my companions amongst this sea of faces. I have to face the way I am standing, my head the only part of me that I can move, my arms pinned to my sides like a little toy soldier. Chance places me into the sort of full-frontal intimacy with an attractive young lady that could only happen in my dreams. Is this heaven or is it hell? It's feels like the latter – fiendishly hot, no air conditioning and even before we move off, I can feel sweat leaking out all over.

We lurch round a corner and I teeter forward into an even closer encounter with the young lady. I apologise profusely. She doesn't say anything but at least I haven't used my hands to steady myself. The bus careers round another corner and I lurch into her again. If I have to lurch into someone, then let it be her, for she is extremely lurchable. As for her, it wouldn't surprise me at all if I made her think of Lurch from *The Addams Family*.

It's a relief when we get to the terminus. It's a double relief to Angela to find we are all present and correct. Pity no-one from the Guinness Book of Records was there to count us to see if we had broken the record for the greatest number of people you can squeeze onto a single-decker shuttle bus.

So that was Pisa. We didn't see a lot really, but it was a darn sight more than we did the last time we were here, which was just the airport – probably the only people ever to come to Pisa and not see the Tower. And there's a lot more to Pisa than the Campo dei Miracoli and there's a lot more to that than we saw this time. We'll just have to come back.

When travelling, you should always leave something to come back for – and I don't mean a personal possession.

We board our bus which whisks us away towards Siena. About an hour afterwards we stop somewhere along the motorway with red and white oleander growing in the central reservation and with palm trees in the car park. The moment I leave the bus the heat hits me with the force of a blast furnace. The air seems to vibrate with heat. Incredibly, it surprises me every time: it just doesn't look that hot from inside our air-conditioned cocoon.

It's just a short step to the air-conditioned shop in the service station. As usual, sitting near the front, we are the first to alight and that's why I am first in the queue at the big chiller cabinet in the corner stocked with soft drinks and water. I grasp the handle and pull. I pull again, harder this time, but it doesn't budge a centimetre. Gordon and Blondie are standing behind me and I sense rather than see their impatience, wondering why I'm taking so long. I don't like to show I'm such an idiot that I don't even know how to open the door of a see-through fridge, so I pretend I've changed my mind and don't like the look of the cans and bottles in there, that I prefer the identical ones in the cabinet next door.

I move across to let Gordon have a shot. Let's see if he can do any better. This door opens readily enough, but to my consternation, I find it is between me and the contents. On the other side of the glass Gordon is holding his purchases with a *You're a bit old to be playing peek-a-boo aren't you?* sort of look on his face. Dying of shame, I close the door and cross over to the other side.

Harriet is beside me now at the troublesome cabinet. Let's see how she gets on. I confess to some *Schadenfreude* when I see her give it a tug, then another and a look of consternation crossing her countenance as still the door refuses to open. She's a big strong woman, Harriet, or looks it. I wouldn't care to be at the receiving end of her left hook anyway.

"I can't get it to open," she says in her soft, south-western burr.

Cometh the hour, cometh the man. Motioning for Harriet to step aside, I manfully seize the handle. Channelling every ounce of my strength into the effort, I begin to pull. I feel the suck of the seal beginning to give way and then with a sound like Elastoplast being ripped off a hairy leg by a sadistic nurse, only minus the scream, the door swings obediently open. Harriet gives me a look of gratitude, or perhaps it's admiration at my manly strength. I give a weak smile and the slightest of shrugs as if it were nothing, as if the perils of Italian chiller cabinets hold no fears for me. They'll never make a fool out of me.

Siena

26

The Panther and the Sculptor

A S Siena draws nearer, the landscape and names on the signposts become familiar from our visit at Easter: Empoli, Volterra, San Gimignano and the magnificent medieval Monteriggioni dominating its hilltop. The vines, which were knobbly sticks between thin lines of wire then, are now in a state of leafy levitation, preparing to bring forth my favourite fruit, though I prefer not to take them in pill form but after they've been squashed to death, fermented and bottled.

In Siena, we undergo the same ritual as in Pisa, going to one car park to get a ticket so we can park in another. Oh, well. When in Italy. We are disgorged at the Porta San Marco and make our way up the slope of the Via di San Marco. We are to meet our guide at the Panther, one of the signs which denotes which district of Siena you are in. There are 17 such *contrade,* ten of whom compete in the world famous Palio in the Piazza del Campo. As you stroll through the town, if you are observant and look up, you can see carvings of animals on the walls which lets you know you have entered another district.

Here we are at the Contrada della Pantera. We know because there is an iron plaque on the wall which says so and a panther, rampant, as they say in heraldry. He appears to be at a Christmas party, wearing one of those paper crowns on his head and doing the hokey cokey. He's had a bit too much to drink apparently as he is putting both his left leg and left arm in at the same time.

We are given some free time to get some lunch before meeting our guide, and Iona and I finally track down a couple of pastries in a baker's shop so she will not drop down dizzy like she nearly did in the Boboli gardens. Angela dismisses us with the caveat that we don't have time to sit down in a restaurant; nevertheless, I see the Yorkies disobey orders and go into one.

We make our way back to the Panther and sit on the wall of a fountain, which has a bronze crouching panther on the top as if bending to drink. May as well rest our legs whilst we can before the walking trail ahead. Our guide has already turned up. She's dressed in white with her jet-black hair tied back in a ponytail.

Everyone seems to be here apart from the Yorkies. Time passes and still there is no sign of them. The Guttings are sitting side by side on the wall, he staring dejectedly at a point three feet from his feet, she, a little more animated, her head raised a bit more but still looking glum. Having sat down for so long, the rest of us are tired of that and are standing around in small groups, chatting.

Angela is alternately looking at her watch and down the street where she hopes to see the Yorkies materialise.

"Has anyone seen the Yorkshire couple?" she asks.

What to do? Do I rat on a fellow tourist or, understanding how Angela feels, do I tell her as it may help her to decide what's to be done? I am a party animal like the panther and La Belle Dame Sans Merci often calls me a pig. I don't know what year it is according to the Chinese calendar, but I decide that today is the Day of the Rat.

"Well, I saw them go into a restaurant. But that was some time ago," I add in mitigation, the inference being they might turn up at any moment.

Angela makes a little growling noise in her throat like Marge Simpson. "I *told* them there wouldn't be time for that. We've got to meet the bus at the gate on time as there is only limited waiting time there." *Plus ça change, plus c'est la même chose.* But hey, don't shoot me! I'm only the dirty rat who *clyped.* Still, my sympathies lie with Angela. Who would be a travel rep?

At last the Yorkies come striding up the street, their speed telling us they know they have sinned. If that had been me, Iona would have crucified me. I wonder what Angela will say to them but before they get to the panther fountain, Angela marshals her troops and we set off at a brisk pace. Thus without a word having been said, the Yorkies are humiliated. Masterly, Angela.

There are colourful flags on the streets which weren't here on our first visit – left over from the first Palio on July 2nd, or in anticipation of the second on August 16th in less than a month's time. Here is the *chiocciola* (snail) flag (surely it never wins – but remember the hare and the tortoise) – red and yellow checks with a blue border and a white shield with a snail at the centre.

Someone wrote a song *I'm in love with Vienna* and last time I was here, I sang under my breath and in my own inimitable style *I'm in love with Siena* – and that despite the Duomo and its horrendous *campanile*, a black and white striped tower of horror, its only redeeming feature being the arched windows which increase in size and number as it gets higher. The worst of the lot, by a long shot.

Claudia is our guide and she tells us the cathedral was begun in 1136. Does she really like it I wonder? If you are Sienese, out of loyalty, do you think your Duomo is better than Pisa's or Florence's – your traditional rivals? I suppose the façade *might* be better than Florence's, all pink and white Gothic icing on its upper two-thirds, but spoiled by the repulsive zebra stripes on the bottom third.

To show I'm interested, or perhaps to disguise my distaste, I ask Claudia who the architect was and she tells me it was a joint effort. A bit like the camel then, which someone described as an animal designed by a committee. That might help explain it. Camels are not the most handsome of beasts it

Siena Cathedral (Image Credit: Pixabay)

has to be admitted, and it's another of the animals in Iona's bestiary to which she has compared me, because of my capacity to do without toilet stops. Well, I think that's the reason.

Just inside the cathedral some people are handing out green ponchos. They are intended for the scandalous women who are showing bare shoulders and calves, but I want one too because

The Campanile of Siena Cathedral

it's the sort of material that would be ideal for polishing the car.

God, this place is ghastly with its black and white stripes! Dark and gloomy, it's perfect camouflage for zebras. No wonder the row of pope's heads near the ceiling are looking down in such disapprobation.

We march straight past the Piccolomini Library where Pinturicchio's frescoes of the life of Pius II had captivated me and which had made me doubt, before I saw them, if Giotto's could compete with them for colour or sheer artistry. I was right to be sceptical. They didn't. But then of course he was standing on his shoulders, so to speak. Which he would have needed to have done to see over the heads in a crowd. That's what Pinturicchio means: "little painter". It's a pity my fellow tourists are not being taken to see these masterpieces; probably they will never realise what they have missed. There may be some comfort in that.

Claudia has taken us to an octagonal stone pulpit, supported on pillars on the backs of lions. She points out how realistic they look. They are snarling: *What's that on my back? Get off! What a bloody weight!* She puts a coin in a machine and a light illuminates a densely-carved scene of figures in high relief. This pulpit was carved, she tells us, by Nicola Pisano in 1265, the same who carved the pulpit in the Baptistery in Pisa. Nicola was his name and carving pulpits was his game.

The carvings depict scenes from the life of Christ and are very skilfully executed – each figure, as Claudia points out, having a unique expression. But it's not so much the quality of the carving which impresses me so much as the sheer number and complexity of the figures. In this panel for instance, there are horses, full of vigour and movement which nobody seems to notice, trampling some animal to death. It's probably a dog but its head is obscured by a tangle of legs, so it's impossible to tell. And there are what look like a couple of mounted camels and behind them a host of figures, who, from the viewer's perspective, should have been invisible.

I don't know what scene from the Bible this is meant to represent, and it's certainly impressive, but to be honest, perspectives apart, I think it is just too full of figures. It certainly must have kept old Nicola busy and out of mischief. Maybe that's why his mother gave him a girl's name – so he would stick in at his sculpture and not go chasing after women. Imagine him trying to pull a girl at his *contrada* dance and the object of his desire says: *What do you do then, handsome?... Oh, really? And what's your name then?... Oh, right!* No self-respecting girl is going to entrust her genes to a bloke called Nicola, so there he was, carving out a name for himself as a sculptor instead.

Well done, Mrs Pisano! You were right.

27

The Slaughter and the Bell Ringer

WE follow Claudia over to an area of floor which has been roped off. I had already noticed that parts of it had been covered with plywood and taped down. She feeds another coin into a meter and an area of floor is illuminated. It's meant to be for us, but by the time I join the group, I can't get near for the press of tourists who already have ringside seats. In fact it would have been better if they *had* been sitting down. I am no giant but I know how Pinturicchio felt. I can't see a thing. Not only that: they are getting a free talk into the bargain.

Claudia is describing a marble inlaid picture. She says that makes Siena unique, the only cathedral that has such decorations: *Hah! That's one in the eye for you, you revolting Pisans*! I can just about hear what she is saying, but I want to see *what* she is talking about, so I move further away where the crowd is less dense and if I stand on my tippy-toes, I can just about get a glimpse of floor over the heads and shoulders of those in front, only now I can't hear a word she is saying.

When the money runs out and the light goes off, everyone moves away and I can see at last what all the fuss was about. It is a bloodthirsty scene, executed in white, yellow and that reddish-purple marble known as porphyry, revered for its rarity, but detested by me for its hideous colour which reminds me of raw liver, the sight, smell and taste of which is anathema to me. Soldiers with raised swords are raining blows upon their helpless victims. One soldier, with sword ready to strike, has his hand on the leg of a naked baby who is clinging to his mother's breast. Another is held aloft, snatched from his mother's despairing arms, while the bodies of other babies lie strewn upon the floor and piled in a heap. It is certainly a powerful image and sends shivers up my spine although I am sweating under my car polisher of Lincoln green. It's *The Slaughter of the Innocents* by Matteo di Giovanni, executed in 1481 – the picture, not the man, Iona explains, when I catch up with the group.

We are going outside by a side door where a couple of men are standing by to receive the ponchos. Do they recycle them or are they a form of human dustbin? Because I want mine to start a new career as a car polisher, I saunter past them as if I'd forgotten all about it despite it being as hot as Hades. On second thoughts, I might keep it as a winter coat instead.

It's a case of out of the frying pan and into the fire as I emerge blinking like a mole from the dim interior of that gloomy, sepulchral place into the dazzling heat of the Sienese afternoon.

Claudia is showing us where the ambitious Sienese had planned to expand the cathedral. If constructed, it would have been the largest Christian church in all of Christendom. The existing nave – and *that* is huge – would have become a transept, while a new nave was to be built out to the south. Work was begun and there were some stability problems, but more than anything, the impediment was the Black Death which struck in 1348 and both money and people ran short, a third of the population falling victim to the plague. There are markers on the piazza, now a handy car park, to show where the massive pillars would have stood.

The other side, which did get as far as having the pillars and arches completed, has been blocked in with red brick to create the Museo dell'Opera del Duomo. At the far end, in white marble and rather reminiscent of the roofless ruins of the old Coventry cathedral after it had been blitzed, is what would have been the new façade featuring an immense door and above it, two empty spaces, one above the other, which had been destined for windows. It would have been a wonder to behold, certainly, and even better, the *campanile* would have had to go, or rather, would never have been built, at least not where it is now, as it is a century younger than the Duomo.

We walk down the steps adjacent to the Duomo and arrive at the Piazza San Giovanni. There is something about a huge flight of steps that appeals to me and even the Duomo looks good, looking up at it in profile from the bottom. This is where the Baptistery is. As expected, it is built in the same style and colours as the façade of the Duomo, if not quite as ornate. Between the stripes are diamond lozenges, presumably considered to be an attractive embellishment, but actually the points are like arrows pointing up and down, like arrows, to the black stripes. The Baptistery at Pisa it most certainly is not.

We turn right down the Via dei Pellegrini, an attractive street with huge barred windows and huge iron rings on the walls, which I presume were for tethering horses. I know if we were to walk through this arch to our left and take this little street off to our left, the Via di Beccheria, we could look across to the bulk of San Domenico which contains the head of that celebrated mystic, Catherine of Siena, but Claudia doesn't think it worthy of mention. Isn't that an astonishing thing! It never ceases to amaze me how many bits of saints' body parts are scattered around various parts of Europe. Years ago, we went out of our way to a church in Brittany called St Jean du Doigt on the strength of it proudly boasting to have the index finger of John the Baptist. When we got there however, we discovered the foremost digit was bricked up in a wall. Our journey, you could say, was pointless.

Although San Domenico had looked tantalisingly close, Siena is built on three hills and so it was actually much further away for us than crows can fly. The car park was eating up a euro an hour and we might have climbed up hill and down dale just to have another wasted journey at the end of it, so in the end we didn't bother to hunt down Catherine's head and we're not going there this time either it seems. But then I don't expect everyone to be as interested in shrivelled-up body parts as I am.

To walk down the Via dei Pellegrini, without deviating, without being lured from the ultimate destination, requires a strong effort of self-denial. There are many entrancing alleyways with the louvred windows of the houses open invitingly, quaint street lamps on brackets high on the brown warm walls and most appealing of all, arches upon arches, some with slim white pillars and Corinthian pedestals, still more, like flying buttresses, spanning the narrow space between the houses. These are some of the reasons why I'm in love with Siena.

But the main reason I'm in love with Siena is now before us. It's the square known as Piazza del Campo where the world-famous Il Palio horserace takes place, only it is shaped more like a scallop shell, gently sloping down to the Palazzo Pubblico or Town Hall. I love the gently-curving, scooped shape and how it dictates

District Banners on the way to Il Palio

the shape of the Palazzo as it follows the curve of the piazza and bends in a shallow arc. Pairs of slim Moorish-style pillars form two tiers of arched windows, standing out startlingly white against the warm, brown stone. Soaring above them in the centre, is a stocky tower looking as if it had been drafted in from *Beau Geste*.

The bottom part of the building is constructed of white marble with huge arched windows and to the left, above an ornate white marble portico, rises the stunning tall and slender bell tower with its white marble tip. It's the Torre del Mangia, at 289 feet, Italy's third highest *campanile*. It was built to match the height of the Duomo's to symbolise the equal importance of church and state. Actually, it's ten metres taller to account for the higher elevation of the latter so they would appear to be the same on the skyline.

This beautiful tower, as opposed to the black and white monstrosity, is named after its first slothful bell ringer, who "tolled the knell of parting day", Giovanni di Balduccio, nick-named *Mangiaguadagni* – literally "Earnings eater". It's meant to be a derogatory term, criticising the way he spent his wages as soon as he earned them. So he was regarded by his contemporaries, but I have some sympathy for him. As the proverb pithily puts it: "Shrouds have no pockets." And he can hardly have enjoyed his job. Well, how would you like to have to climb more than 500 steps every day just to get to your work? *Every day, bloody steps! Steps! Steps! Steps!* I bet he wasn't slothful so much as worn out.

On the other side of the piazza, the buildings mirror the Town Hall's architectural style, creating a pleasing harmonious balance to the whole. The area in the middle, which at Easter had been black with people, is surprisingly empty now, so it is easy to pick out the grey lines on the salmon pink and which divide the piazza into nine segments, a reminder of the Council of Nine, the *Noveschi*, who got together to design the piazza in 1293. Well done, boys!

One example of a committee that did design something much better than a camel – or a cathedral for that matter.

28

The Palio and the Sopranos

AT the top of the central segment in the piazza is a rectangular white marble fountain – the Fonte Gaia, so called because people were overjoyed to see it. It's not really a fountain; more a basin formed by sculptured panels by Jacobo della Quercia between 1414 and 1419. It depicts Biblical scenes, though what we see are copies from 1858 and even they are showing their age. The water comes trickling into the basin out of the mouths of what I took at first to be crouched and extremely skinny lionesses, but actually are she-wolves. According to legend, Siena was founded by Senius, the son of Remus, who, as every schoolboy knows, was suckled by a she-wolf before he went on, with his brother, to found Rome.

Now, the pigeon population, in all their feathery flocks, come to savour the life-giving water which comes from the source fifteen miles away by a system of underground aqueducts known as *bottini* (barrel-vaults), just as it did in the 14th century. The present-day urban rats are not ungrateful. They give heartfelt thanks from their bottoms.

Piazza del Campo (Image Credit: Pixabay)

Claudia lets us drink in the scene and tells us about the Palio. "You stay with your district all your life," she says. "Sometimes a woman will come back to her district, just to give birth, especially if it's to avoid her baby being born in a rival district."

I wonder which district the maternity hospital is in. That must surely swell the number of supporters, despite what Claudia has just told us. I remember at Easter seeing some flowers on a door and a card announcing the birth of a baby.

"Do you get mixed marriages?" I ask.

"Oh yes," says Claudia, "but it can divide families, especially when it comes time for a baby to be born. You know, we Sienese, we're *pazzo*. You'll sometimes see fighting in the streets between districts and in the race, there are no rules – you can do anything you like to win, or make your rival district lose. Each district has its own special rival and making it lose can be just as important as winning the race. It's the horse that wins, not the rider, so a riderless horse can win. Cheating is all part of the fun!"

My God! I thought the rivalry between Celtic and Rang-
ers in Glasgow was bad but it seems they are just beginners, if
you please, compared to the Sienese.

"If you want to go to the race," Claudia continues,
"You've got to be there early." She unfurls a poster she has
taken from her shoulder bag. It shows Il Campo and the
whole shell, except for the Fonte Gaia, dense with motley-
coloured pins which are actually the heads of spectators.
There are massed ranks of people around the perimeter too,
and a wide track, covered in sand, has been created between
them. "The race begins at 7:45 but you need to get there by 2
pm if you want to get near the front."

Imagine that! Standing there for nearly six hours and then
what do you do if you need to go to the toilet, as you will
certainly have brought some beer with you? Well, there's always the Fonte Gaia, if you're close enough.

"The race lasts about 90 seconds." What! Did I hear her
correctly? "Yes," says Claudia obviously pleased at our astonished reactions. "But you won't be able to leave the Campo
till about 8:30." Right enough, with all those people, it's going
to take some time to empty. And there could be fights between rival groups of supporters with the crowd swaying and
people being trampled underfoot as they try to avoid the fra-
cas. "I told you we were *pazzo!* We're more *pazzo* than the
French! " Claudia adds with conviction.

She's *pazzo* and proud of it. But why did she say more
pazzo than the French? It's true they have some bizarre ideas
like their way of doing things is the best in the universe – so
much so that they had to invent a term for it after the geezer
who first dreamed up the notion, Chauvinism – but mad?

Of course, in her desire to be considered a complete *pazzo,*
Claudia has been rather economical with the facts. She hasn't

told us the race is only one small part of the proceedings; that it's really a spectacle of medieval costume and pageantry, with amongst many other things, flag-twirling and throwing. Then there's all the excitement and atmosphere before and after the race and the attendant partying. All the same, I am glad I am not Sienese, even if it is free to see the Palio, unless of course you want to pay a pension to get a view from one of the houses or the Town Hall. The Mangia should have remembered *that* when he climbed his daily stairs – he's got the best seat in the house.

"And what's the prize?" I ask Claudia, knowing as soon as I do so that it will be something ridiculous.

"A banner. That's what *palio* means."

Well, why not? We indulge in the same sort of thing, except to a far lesser extent, for a silver cup. I'm thinking particularly of football matches.

Claudia is just about to roll up her poster when Gordon steps forward and points at one of the pinheads. "That's you," he says and everyone laughs. Why didn't I think of that?

That's it then, that's all we're going to see of Siena, at least as far as Claudia is concerned. We've some free time now and Angela and she stride off in the direction of one of the cafés on the piazza. We've to meet again at the panther in forty minutes. I am really glad I've been here before as, like Pisa, this has just been the merest of introductions to this fabulous city (apart from the Duomo and its *campanile*).

There's not much time to do anything apart from buy our daily *gelati* and sit on the long wall at the front of the Fonte and take in the atmosphere. At last, we make our way up the Via di Città and as we do so, I am struck by another beautiful building, one which I had not noticed before, but how can that be, since this street is one of the main thoroughfares and we must surely have come this way before?

It's built in the same style as the Town Hall, with the same elegant arched windows and crenellated battlements and a tower at the left-hand side. It also bends in the middle, following the gradual curve of the street. Quite magnificent! Pity the street is so narrow – you can't step back to admire it all the better. But what is it? A brass plaque provides the answer: Accademia Musicale Chigiana, and it goes on to say in no fewer than four languages that it cannot be visited. Not to worry, I tend to prefer the outside of such buildings rather than the inside, but we can at least go into the courtyard.

It's a little gem of a place, one of these occasional serendipitous discoveries that make it all the more worthwhile as no doubt hundreds of people walk past it every day and don't realise what they have missed just yards from the bustling street. There is a stone bench running the full length of the back wall and down one side. Two orange trees in massive terracotta pots at each corner provide some greenery and the illusion of being in a garden. There is an ornate well in front of a colonnade lining the back wall. It's a perfect place for restoring the soul of sole-weary shoppers but hardly any people are here and no sound permeates, even through the wide arch which gives on to the street. Above the colonnade is a painting like a patchwork quilt, executed in vibrant but harmonious colours. Imagine having missed this before!

It's with a sense of reluctance that we leave and head up the street again. We've not gone far, however, when at the other side of the street, we come upon a trio of naked figures rolling about on the floor of an open doorway. Yes, they really are, except they are at least twice life-size and made of some white inflatable material. They are moving languidly in response to erratic currents of air and it's not in the least erotic. It's the Palazzo delle Papesse, the Centre for Contemporary Art. Well, what else did you expect?

As we head to our rendezvous with the bus at the Porta San Marco, I in the sun and the rest of the group at the other side of the street in the shade minding my own business when suddenly a louvred window high above my head is flung open, releasing the sound of a female voice screeching in agony as if someone had just plunged a bread-knife into her. Then, from the open window next door comes the sound as of cats having their tails pulled, the two now combining to form the sort of ear-splitting shrillness that could reduce crystal glasses to splinters and any sane person to a degree of madness beyond the ken of anyone in Siena, or France for that matter.

Have I somehow suddenly died unaware and gone straight to hell and these are souls crying in torment? No, it's merely sopranos limbering up their tonsils, practising their scales. If there's one thing I hate (apart from porphyry and liver), it's those practitioners of the operatic art with their proud voices raised at full pitch.

To think they call that sort of thing "art"! Give me blown-up bare people any day.

Rome

29

The Trattoria and
the Talcum Powder

WE'RE well on the road to Rome now. Since all roads lead there, you would think that Giancarlo could not go wrong, but somewhere along the road he has, because the sun, which was on my side of the bus, is no longer there and Angela has gone to stand beside him, scanning the road signs. It looks as if we are heading towards Perugia, in the opposite direction. My suspicions are confirmed when we come off the motorway, cross a flyover, and the sun reappears on my side of the bus. I suppose all roads lead *from* Rome too.

It's incredible how dry the earth is. The parched land is desperately crying out for water. Not a drop for months now. The colour of burnt sienna, it is amazing to think how anything could possibly grow here. Further north, the sunflowers, *girasole* in Italian (so much more evocative and musical than the English word), were holding their golden heads up to the sun but here, on wrinkled stalks, some burnt black, they are hanging heavy, parched, like alcoholics desperate for a drink, only in their case, they crave the life-sustaining *aqua,* not the *aqua vitae.*

On the other hand, those grapes, plumping on the vines with all that sunshine, must surely make for a vintage crop. In a year or so from now, as I pour myself a second glass of sunshine in a bottle, I shall say to La Belle Dame Sans Merci, and sounding rather pathetic like poor Mr Pritchard in *Under Milk Wood,* "*I'm just taking my vitamin C, dear. Only because it is good for me.*" And much good may that do me.

We pass Orvieto, spectacularly built on a cliff – the sort of place we would have stopped and explored if we had been independent travellers. Angela tells us that from Roman times until recently it was famous for its sweet white wine but most of it is drier now. I am glad to hear it. I cut my wine teeth on Barsac and Sauternes but would regard them as undrinkable now. A dry, full-bodied red is much more to my taste now. It matches my body-type and ruddy complexion. We were obviously meant for each other.

We have a break at the ugliest service station I have ever seen in my life. I am loitering in the sunshine by the bus, making the most of it, waiting for the stragglers to arrive, when last of all, along comes Harriet, munching the last of her *panino.* She knows it's sinful to eat on the bus and must finish it before she gets on if she doesn't want to face the wrath of Angela.

"Isn't it awful?" she says, nodding in the direction of the concrete and iron-pillared monstrosity. No doubt, like me, the splendours of Siena are still fresh in her mind.

"Well, it was never designed by Michelangelo anyway."

Harriet laughs. "More like a student."

"First year, failed."

Harriet laughs again. We're getting on like a house on fire. I'm sure she hasn't forgotten the incident with the chiller-cabine at the last motorway service station we stopped at.

* * *

Our room in Rome is on the first floor, directly above the main entrance. I can see multi-coloured flags of European nations through the brown gauze that serves as a curtain over the brown-tinted windows. It makes the outside look dull and gloomy when in actual fact, it is swelteringly hot and humid.

We have to find our own food this evening. Angela says we have a choice: we can either turn right out of the hotel and go straight on and we'll come to a posh place, or we can turn left, then left again and we'll come to a good, but cheap *trattoria*. It's not much of a contest for a Scotsman of slender means.

It would be nice to sit outside but all those tables are occupied, so here we are inside, at the back, squashed in at a table that appears to be on the flight path to the kitchen, waiters hurrying to and fro, rushed off their feet. An aeon ago we dispatched the *coperto* which had been put on our table by a passing waiter but no-one has bothered to come back and take our order. Fortunately the wine has arrived and I am making steady progress through it, judging from what I can see darkly of the remains through the green glass. It seems to me it's evaporating faster than my wife will let me drink it.

Phew! It's stiflingly hot and there's no air-conditioning. Iona is turning a pinker shade of cooked prawn by the minute.

We have a general rule, in a restaurant, if there is a seat which faces a wall or very few other diners, I sit in the less sterile environment so I can observe what's going on. I call

Rome, The Eternal City (Image Credit: Pixabay)

myself an observer of human nature; she calls me plain bloody nosy. That's why I am able to see Angela arrive and sit at a table near the door. Timing is everything. Had we waited half-an-hour, that could have been ours with air wafting in, cooling the beaded brow. It may well be warm air, but at least it would be fresh, not this recycled Turkish-bath moisture we are sitting in at present. Trust Angela to know. But what's to be done? We can't invite her to join us as our table is only for two, but maybe we should invite ourselves over to *her* table. Iona, however, vetoes this modest proposal.

"No, it's her time off. Leave her alone. She doesn't want to listen to your jokes and weird sense of humour. Give her a break."

It's all right for her as she has her back to Angela but I keep catching her eye and it seems a bit rude to let someone you know strangle themselves by eating on their own, as the Italian proverb has it. Then she lights up a cigarette and in an instant, I decide she's better off without my scintillating conversation after all.

The service is so slow, in order to save a couple of hours, we decide to miss a course and restrict ourselves to *primos.* In the romantic Eternal City, Iona wants to get back to our air-conditioned room as soon as possible. The hair at the nape of her neck is soaking and I don't know about her, but I can feel a rivulet of sweat trickling its way down between my 36Bs.

"I'll just order another bottle of wine shall I?"

"No, you will not! You don't need it!"

"But I *do* need it! I've got hardly any left to have with my food."

"Well, you shouldn't have drunk it all before it arrived."

"I needed something to do. The service is so bloody slow. If it hadn't been so slow, I wouldn't –"

"Oh, all right! Have some of mine!" She splashes a thimbleful into my glass. "But you're not getting any more!" She knits her brows and glowers balefully at me across the table, my German wife, Frau Ning.

The heat has made her irritable and apart from anything else, she doesn't want to prolong the dining experience with another bottle. It would only make matters worse if I were to tell her I could polish it off pretty fast.

Now I can see, but she can't, that a very fat man is making some sort of *sotte voce* request to a waiter he has somehow managed to stop in his tracks. In a few moments, the waiter comes back and gives the customer something that looks very much like a tin of baby powder. I can't see exactly, but it looks as if he is opening up his shirt and dusting himself down with it. Right enough, if the sweat is running in tiny rivulets between my bosoms, there could be a stream between his. But just to open your shirt up and do it in public like that! Even I, whom Iona calls a boor, wouldn't do such a thing. But what boggles my mind even more is the restaurant just happening to have a tin of such a thing ready to hand! Presumably customers must ask for it all the time as the waiter had fetched it as if he'd asked for nothing more extraordinary than another bottle of wine – considerably easier than bringing one to this table, that's for sure. What will he do next? Will he open up his flies and dust in there? Perhaps it's really a pesticide and he's exterminating little creepy-crawlies.

But he doesn't and the waiter picks up the tin of powder, casually in the passing, on his flight path back to the kitchen. Maybe I should ask for it too. When in Rome... it's not often you can say that and literally mean it. I could certainly use it to mop up my sweat and Iona looks as if she could soak up a whole tin by herself.

We have to pass Angela's table as we leave. She would have been in a perfect position to see what was going on. Besides, it makes a suitable topic of conversation as I still feel we should have asked if she minded if we joined her. But how would we have known if she was merely being polite or not? She probably would have said yes out of politeness when she really meant: *Look! I'm with you lot practically the whole bloody day, so just sod off and leave me alone to have a fag in peace!*

After the niceties, after how hot and humid it is, I pose the burning question. "Did you see that man with the talcum powder? What was he doing with it?"

"It's a stain-remover. He spilt his wine. The powder soaks it up."

"Ah, yes, I thought so."

As we stroll back to the hotel in this muggy Roman evening, I am very glad I hadn't told Angela what I really thought he had been doing.

So, this will be our first night in Rome. The hub of the Roman Empire. The city for lovers. Or is that Paris? Anyway, tomorrow will be an exciting day, but best of all, I won't have to get up until 8am. It's still fiendishly early, but bliss compared to some of the starts we've had on this trip, regardless of whatever happens in what's left of this sweltering, sultry evening.

30

Transports of Undelight

THE brown gauze curtains and tinted-brown windows make the weather look decidedly gloomy. Wait a minute though – it really *is* gloomy. I don't see any blue skies and yes, surely the cars have their wipers working and the road looks damp. I wrestle with the gauze to get at the handle of the window and when I open it I see why we had such a quiet night, not a single Vespa or a tooting horn disturbing our slumbers: the double-glazing must be three inches thick. The sound of traffic floods into the room. And it *is* raining! For the first time in months, it is actually raining in Italy! There will be rejoicing all over the land or at least where the rain falls. The drought is at an end at last.

"Would you just look at this," I call over my shoulder to Iona who is busy at the mirror. "The weather's exactly how I feel in the mornings."

"What? Bloody miserable?"

"Precisely!"

But by the time we have finished breakfast in the basement and gathered in the foyer, the rain has stopped. Before going down I had gone outside to gauge how hard it was. Not hard, slanting Scottish rain, but soft, warm, gentle Italian rain which "droppeth upon the place beneath" as Portia put it, though that of course was in another place. But can we trust it to stay off? Probably not. It may be gentle, but would nevertheless still soak us through to the skin if we were to be out in it all day, as is the intention. Can't afford to take the risk, which means we're going to be lumbered with humping our raingear about all day in what may turn out to be broiling heat, if the gods have any part in it. And I know very well how they love to toy with us for their sport.

I am suddenly struck by an idea which is rather unusual for me, the brain being slow to get into first gear in the mornings, never mind at this hellishly early hour. I roll up my cagoule as tightly as I can and stealing up behind Iona who is engaged in conversation with Pat, I unzip her little rucksack which has the zips conveniently placed for pickpockets.

She swings round. Obviously I am in need of practice, though my plan is the reverse of the pickpockets, putting something *in*, rather than taking it *out*. "What do you think you're doing?" she snaps.

"Just putting my cagoule in your bag, love of my life. It doesn't weigh a thing."

She doesn't want to make a fuss in front of Pat and the others. I'm a burden to her, but today she can be *my* beast of burden.

Angela is counting us. Gordon, who is near a pillar, slips out of sight behind it. Angela looks perplexed. Someone is missing, but who is it? I feel sorry for her. Gordon thinks he's clowning but he knows not what he does. I, on the other hand, know what it's like to organize a bunch of brats and have one of them go missing, so I shout out in pantomime style: "He's behind you!" and some others take up the refrain.

Gordon puts on an act like a scolded schoolboy and breaks cover. He's appointed himself as group clown apparently. It also puts beyond any reasonable doubt that he had deliberately been hiding from Angela at Pisa just to get her knickers in a twist. Not funny at all.

We had given Angela money last night and now she hands out tickets for the bus and metro. She explains they last for two days and we must validate them when we board the bus or we could be given a fine. Like a general, she marches us past the *trattoria* where we were last night, to the bus stop. As at Pisa, we must all get on the bus, no matter how crowded it is. Not for the first time, I wonder how she will possibly manage next week with forty-two. That's a busload on its own. Maybe that's what will happen – a bus to themselves. This is far more exciting.

I'm not so lucky this time. When at last I manage to struggle aboard, I find I'm wedged hard up against a man who looks as if he's about to give birth to twins imminently and worse, has had something horrendously garlicky for his tea last night. The sweat is running down his sideboards and his armpits are a dark pool of colour. Thank God there is no smell from them – at least not that I notice. But maybe that's thanks to the knock-out garlic.

It's impossible to move, so we pass our tickets like a chain of fire-fighters passing a bucket, up and down the line to Donald, the male half of the other Scottish couple who happens to have landed next to the validating machine. To those who can't actually see what we are doing, it must look like Houdini struggling to free himself from handcuffs.

At long last we arrive at the terminus where I am released from bondage from my garlic-eating companion (I'd like to have seen Houdini wriggle out of that one) and we scuttle in

The Metro, Rome
(Image Credit: Daniele, licensed under the Creative Commons Attribution 2.0 Generic license.)

Angela's wake through ranks of buses before burrowing into the Metro. It's a lot less complicated than London or Paris as it has only two lines – A and B. We're taking the B. If we were in New York, I would undoubtedly have preferred to take the A train, but we're not.

As everywhere else, you put your ticket in a slot then push against the arms of the stile, which is meant to turn a notch to let you through. But not for me. It refuses to budge in response to the pressure from my stomach. What's worse, to my horror, my ticket has been swallowed up and has not been regurgitated. What's the matter with the damned thing? Everyone else before me with far lesser stomachs than mine had passed through effortlessly.

Iona, who was in a different queue, has already passed on the other side, like the Levite. I can feel the hostile stares and impatience of commuters behind me. I feel tempted to jump over the turnstile but like Macbeth, I prevaricate. If only o'er-leaping this barrier were all, but there is the hereafter, in this case the fine, to say nothing of Iona's ire. Cameras will certainly be trained on this spot and they will certainly be able to track me down, thanks to my trademark Panama hat.

Then, to my enormous relief, my ticket pops out of the machine again. I snatch it up and abandon the queue with an expression which I hope others will interpret as a "there's-something-wrong-with-this machine" sort of look. I get into the queue for the turnstile on my right and this time there is no problem as the machine accepts my ticket and I pass through without hindrance.

"What on earth were you playing about at?" snaps La Belle Dame Sans Merci who has been loitering with intent to murder me if only there were time enough. "Come on, get a move on! The others are far ahead."

"Bloody machine wouldn't work," I manage to blurt out after her as we scamper after them.

"Did you put your ticket in the right way?"

"What do you mean – right way?"

"With the magnetic strip down."

What magnetic strip? I'd never bothered to look at it. "Course I did! Bloody machine just didn't like me."

I probably haven't fooled her for a minute but at this moment, she's more concerned with horsing after the others and shortly, and in even shorter breath, we catch up with them. If we don't all make it aboard the train, Angela is saying, we are to get off at "Colosseo".

"Colosseo," she says again, making it sound like New York, New York and we are mentally-challenged Neanderthals. Or maybe it's just for my benefit. Anyone who can't work a turnstile is a liability. What we're meant to do when we get there and if we do get separated, especially me from my minder, she doesn't say.

We all squeeze onto the blue train when it arrives and make our way, on arrival, through labyrinthine passages until we emerge into the open air beneath woolly white clouds and blue skies. Whilst we have been moleing it down below, the grey skies have been banished and it is already very warm and humid. I doubt we'll need the rainwear today after all. Thank God for Iona's backpack.

Even at this time in the morning, the area round the Colosseum is throbbing with noise and heaving with people. Some men, dressed as Roman soldiers with sandals, swords and leather breastplates and helmets with bright red plumes on the top are standing by to pose for photographs, at a price. They are already sweating under their gear and the heat from the young-day sun. It is still hours to high noon.

There are other ways of parting tourists from their money – touts selling postcards in sealed cellophane packets. A good deal: only €1 for 24. There is a red pack and a blue pack. At that price I might even blow the bank and buy one of each. There's certain to be enough acceptable ones amongst that lot that I could send to the half-dozen people I have still to send one to. I wish I hadn't bought so many in Florence at 45 cents each. Hindsight is a wonderful thing.

Ah, here is Angela waiting for us with our guide who is carrying a car aerial with a bit of material tied to the end of it, no doubt so we can receive her better. Yole is her name and she will be our guide today and tomorrow. She takes us over to the shade beneath a broken wall of the Colosseum where a man selling books like the ones we saw in Pompeii with the transparent overlays, hands her one and retreats into the background whilst she introduces us to the Colosseum. They have obviously done this before. He will certainly pounce when she is finished.

He doesn't know it yet but it's his lucky day. On the strength of the Pompeii book – mad, impetuous fool that I am, I decide I'm going to buy one even before I have seen it, even before Yole has finished her exposition.

Contrary to popular belief, a Scotsman and his money are soon parted.

31

Funny Happenings on the Way to the Forum

YOLE gives us the lowdown on the Colosseum – after the Leaning Tower of Pisa, I imagine Italy's next best-known icon and certainly Rome's best-known. Although it's undeniably big, the largest amphitheatre in the world in fact, it's not called the Colosseum because of its size: it's because of a colossal statue of that fiddle-playing megalomaniac, Nero, which used to stand near the site.

Originally known as the Flavian ampitheatre, it stands on the site of a lake which was in the grounds of Nero's palace. It was begun by the Emperor Vespasian in AD 72 and amazingly, took only eight years to build. It was inaugurated by his son, Titus, the next emperor, with 100 days of non-stop "games" during which 9,000 animals laid down their lives to satisfy the Roman bloodlust. In its lifetime it's estimated that 400,000 people were killed and a million animals.

Yole invites us to look at the architecture. Constructed of brick and tufa with an outer skin of travertine, three storeys of tall arches – Tuscan columns at the bottom, Ionic in the middle and Corinthian at the top. It's an impressive building, even today, although it has been knocked about a bit by the ravages of time and earthquakes, but more particularly by subsequent generations who found it a handy source of build-ing material.

The stadium could seat 50,000 people, Yole tells us, and they could enter and clear it in minutes through the 80 arched entrances. "If you look carefully," she says, "you can see the number above each arch. The spectators had wooden tags which told them which entrance to use and which seat they were in."

Just like theatre tickets today. And right enough, we can just make out the numbers over the arches – XL is just behind us.

"Is that for the extra large people?" I ask before Gordon gets a chance to come out with it.

The Colosseum (Image Credit: Pixabay)

Yole freezes me with a Gorgon stare. Oops! I've done it again. Yole is big: not so fat that if she had a caravan, she'd have to go in sideways, but she has enough flesh to make one of Raphael's cherubs look anorexic. I never meant to suggest that that would have been *her* door if she had been around in those days.

"That was *my* joke," she says in the sort of tone which means I can't tell if she's joking or not.

"Oh, er... oops! Sorry!"

"The spectators were ranked according to class," she continues, unfixing her stare, and I can breathe again. "Naturally the emperor had the best seat in the house and the commoners, women and slaves were furthest away from the action. And of course, entrance was free."

If I had attended the games, and I would only have done so reluctantly, my mates mocking me: "Come on you miserable little wimp! Christians versus lions today. Should be a good laugh! What's the matter with you?" If I *had* gone, I'd want to be as far removed from the action as possible. I'd probably have been a commoner anyway, if I weren't a slave, but that would suit me down to the ground as I have read Ovid's erotic verse and he's always banging on about what a good place the games are for picking up women. That's what I'd be doing: eyeing up the talent and avoiding as much of the blood-bath as possible.

Alas the Romans have handed down a legacy of this mass spectator cruelty to us today in the form of bullfights in Spain. Should I ever be given the choice of attending one or having my toenails pulled out one by one, or being strung up by my gonads, then that's when, and only when, you'll see me there. I'll be sitting in the cheapest seat in the *Sol*, not because I'm one mean hombre but because I'd rather be in the *Sol* than the *Ombre*.

The clever Romans, however, conjured up an ingenious system whereby *all* the spectators were kept in the shade and to this day, no-one knows for sure how they did it.

"There was an awning called the *velarium* which they used to keep the sun off the spectators," Yole says. "You can see the holes where the poles used to be, up there." I knew about this before as I'd seen a TV programme about it, but try as I can, I can't make them out.

It comes as a disappointment to some of us to learn we are not going into the arena. But not to us, as being Roman junkies, we have been to the amphitheatres in Nîmes and Arles and El Djem in Tunisia, to name but three. Like God with people, they are all variations on a theme.

Instead, Yole is going to take us to the Forum, along the Via Sacra. "On the way," she says, "we will pass that arch over there."

It's the Arch of Constantine, the first Christian emperor. The main central arch is flanked by two smaller ones and was dedicated in 315 AD to commemorate the tenth anniversary of Constantine's victory over his predecessor, Maxentius. Yole tells us that the medallions and statues are pillaged from other monuments and the whole thing is a bit of a hotchpotch, earning itself the derogatory nickname, *Aesop's Crow*. What that quite has to do with the fable involving it and the fox and the cheese, Yole doesn't say and I am too scared to ask. All the same, it looks pretty impressive to me. The stylistic differences of the architecture which bother the purists so much don't bother me one whit.

"In the film, *Cleopatra*," Yole does tell us, "Elizabeth Taylor made her entry into Rome through that arch, though it wasn't there then. But of course, the film makers do not bother about that sort of thing."

Well, that's very true. I wonder how many Scots believe William Wallace painted woad on his face and take everything else in *Braveheart* as gospel besides. Constantine lived in the 4th century AD and Cleopatra at the end of the 1st century BC. It's as if Columbus, arriving in America, found the Civil War over, Lincoln assassinated, and Alaska had been bought and paid for from Russia and had joined the Union.

Now we are on the Via Sacra, on the original Roman road that leads from the Colosseum at the bottom, to the Arch of Titus at the top, which in its turn, stands at one end of the Forum. On our left is the Palatine, where it is said, the she-wolf suckled Romulus and Remus. While that may just be the stuff of legend, archaeologists have found traces of an Iron Age settlement there, so it's probably historically true to say this is indeed where Rome started.

In Augustus' day the Palatine was the snobby part of town. Indeed, the word gives us our word "palace". Amongst the famous residents were Cicero and the poet, Catullus. Augustus was born here and lived in a relatively modest house, compared to his successors at least, and so did his awfully wedded wife, Livia, who had a separate wing all to herself. From

The Arch of Titus

what I know of her, that still would have been a bit too close for comfort. Her son, and Augustus' successor, Tiberius, also lived here but he built a massive palace rendering tons of togaed toffs homeless.

We've been standing in the shade of some trees near the Arch of Titus, Vespasian's son, whilst Yole has been telling us this, and about the arch, and the Forum, which we are about to start exploring. Some lucky people have found some ruins to sit on. Others, like me, are shifting weight from foot to foot in the hot sun and I can see their eyes beginning to glaze over.

At the top of Titus' arch I can read the first line of the legend, SENATVS, and beneath it, POPVLVSQUEROMANVS. Despite the letters all being run together like that and a V being used instead of a U, it gives me a slight *frisson* as I am able to read it without Yole's help: *The Senate and the People of Rome.* How many times had I read that in my Latin grammar and history textbook and how many ancient Romans had actually read the very same words I am reading now! To my surprise, Yole tells us that these words, or rather the initials SPQR, can still be seen all over modern Rome today on all sorts of things from manhole covers to bus timetables on bus shelters.

The arch was built in AD 81 by the Emperor Domitian, Titus' brother, to commemorate his sibling's apotheosis. I suppose being the son of a god, there must have a good chance of your being a god yourself one day. As he lay dying, his father Vespasian, the founder of the Flavian dynasty, is said to have aspirated: "I think I shall be a god soon." Ironic having to die before you can be immortal. I suppose, like teenagers, it's just a stage you have to go though.

Being a god now, Titus could look down on his arch and see that it was good. Well, I think he would anyway, not a hotchpotch like Constantine's – but then, Constantine was a mere Christian. It's only a single arch and the exterior is not plastered with statues and medallions like Constantine's, but there are a couple of panels on each side of the interior celebrating Titus' successful Siege of Jerusalem in 71 AD and the ceiling is coffered with rosettes and a big central panel depicting Titus being carried off to heaven.

Down at the bottom, there are deep grooves on the insides of the arch where generations of drivers have scraped their carts. The earth has been tramped down to expose the foundations to a depth of five feet or so, up to my shoulders in fact. Obviously a well-used thoroughfare to and from the Forum.

I feel the feet of history on my shoulder.

32

Gods and Virgins

L OOKING through the Arch of Titus in the direction
we have just come, the Colosseum rises like a broken
giant cotton reel at the bottom of the Via Sacra. Now
turning our backs on both it and the Arch, Yole leads us to a
vantage point, where spread out below us, is the Forum
Romanus. We've been all over Europe, Iona and I, visited
Roman temples and monuments, aqueducts and viaducts, and
here, at last, for the very first time, we are gazing at the hub
of the empire.

It's one great, big, messy confusing disappointment. Here a
broken wall, there another even more dilapidated; here a column, there a cluster of them; an arch to the left of us, another
to the right; a modern-looking building without pillars over
there, another, nearer, with columns looking the way a Roman temple *should*. But just how do you begin to make sense
of it all?

The trouble is history doesn't stand still, which undeniable
truth is reflected in the Forum. Rome wasn't built in a day, as
everyone knows, but it looks as if Yole could talk for a day
and a half on it as she attempts to explain the hotchpotch of

ruins spread out before us. It was continually being recon-structed and added to, to commemorate some victory or other, so what with that and its ruinous state, it makes it very hard indeed to visualise what it might have looked like at any given period of time.

Judging by the expression on the faces of my companions, they are suffering from a surfeit of information in this energy-sapping heat. Some have wandered out of earshot, perching on nearby pieces of ruins, even if they are not in the shade. The sun is blistering now and the air seems to thrum to the beat of the cicadas' wings or back legs, whatever they use to produce that evocative sound which always makes the tem-perature seem hotter. You never would have thought it had been overcast and raining less than two hours ago when I had stowed my raingear in Iona's backpack.

We are not going to be exploring all the ruins; that would take hours. We are merely going to be walking down the Via Sacra. Not to worry: I'm sure we'll come back with our guidebook and explore at our own pace.

To our right is the Basilica of Constantine. It looks as if a complete side has been removed, like a doll's house, to reveal three monumental arches, through which I can see, on the other side, three more arches perfectly framed in the absolute immensity of the outer ones. Three seems to be the order of the day as Yole tells us that in the 4th century it was three times bigger than it appears now. At the time of its construc-tion it was the largest building in the world. It must have been mind-blowing then because it takes the breath away now. It *had* to be huge because the apse accommodated a thir-ty-foot-high statue of Constantine of which the eight-foot-high head has survived, along with a gigantic foot and a hand with a forefinger pointing to heaven. These parts had to be huge to

The Temple of Castor and Pollux

be in proportion with his swollen head. They can be seen in the Courtyard of the Palazzo dei Conservatori of the Musei Capitolini.

Next is the circular 4th Century Tempio di Romolo, reinvented in 527 as the church of Santi Cosma e Damiano, two saintly brothers, a sort of antidote to the nearby pagan temple of the twin brothers, Castor and Pollux. The big green bronze doors framed by pillars of porphyry, high above the present pavement, are firmly shut.

The Church of San Lorenzo in Miranda was formerly the Temple of Antoninus and Faustina. He was the Emperor Antoninus Pius, and a holy man was he. He was preceded in deity by his wife, Faustina, who joined the immortals in AD 141. It took twenty years for him to shuffle off the mortal coil before he could join her in heaven.

The Temple of Antoninus and Faustina

As for the temple, before it was converted to Catholicism, it survived an attempt to pull it down – see the grooves cut into the tops of the columns where they fitted the ropes. A massive flight of steps (which show just how extensive the excavations are) lead up to a portico of six columns with a further two on each side. The scale truly is amazing but what's even more astonishing is the way the upper part of the façade of the Renaissance church towers over them. It has two great horns at the top and a central window beneath. It's a surreal thought, but I can't help but think it looks like something from the fertile imagination of Picasso – a bull in its pen before it is released to die in the arena.

On the other side of the street is the Temple of Vesta. There are only a few columns remaining now, just enough to give the hint of a curve to show it was a circular building and, it seems to me, would have been one of the most interesting buildings on the Forum. I already knew from school that the duty of the Vestal Virgins was to keep the sacred flame alive and that if it went out, according to superstition, Rome would fall. So now we know. There were only six virgins at any one time, and as their name suggests, the job description required them to abstain from sex. If they sinned in this respect, they were buried alive in a specially-prepared vault and their partner flogged to death. There were ten such known cases, so Yole tells us.

The Virgins were usually of noble birth and the job lasted for thirty years. They were about ten, most of them, when they began their duties, ten years learning the job (what – keeping a fire going!), ten years in practice, and ten years teaching the new girls. They'd be over forty when they got out, Yole adds unnecessarily. You get less for murder nowadays. I expect they remained virgins after they were released. What you've never had, you never miss. Anyway, at forty, you would have been considered an old woman in those days.

Mind you, there were perks to make up for the abstinence. They lived in luxurious accommodation but since their old man was probably well-off anyway, that doesn't sound such a big deal to me. And they got the best seat in the house, next

The Temple of Vesta

to the Emperor at the Games. Even bigger deal. Best bit sounds the job – just sitting in front of the fire, giving it a bit of a poke now and again; looking after some important peoples' wills like Julius Caesar's and Mark Antony's to name but two; and fetching water from a holy well. The snag was if you let the fire go out, you were whipped before you were sacked.

Nearby is the Temple of Castor and Pollux with three restored fluted Corinthian columns which give us some idea of what it must have looked like in its prime. It commemorates the intervention of the heavenly twins at the battle of Lake Regillus in 496 BC which resulted in the Romans' victory over the last of the Tarquins, the final kings of Rome. The rest is the history of the republic.

There was an earlier temple here in 484 BC, one of the oldest in the Forum, but this dates from the time of Augustus, nearly 500 years later. That's the trouble with the Forum; it kept burning down (some Virgin asleep on the job), changing and evolving. No wonder it's so difficult to make sense of.

Diagonally across from it, on the other side of Via, is a huge building with a solitary window ridiculously high up on the side facing us. It is the Curia Julia, or Senate House, which was ordered to be rebuilt by Julius Caesar, hence its name, according to the rules of Latin grammar. If it looks very well-preserved, so it should. It was restored in 1938 on the orders of Mussolini. It's a reconstruction of the original Diocletian Senate House, destroyed by fire in the 3rd century AD, which itself was a replacement for the original Curia Hostilia. Construction was underway when Caesar was assassinated, not here, but at the Theatre of Pompeii which was acting as the Senate House in the interim. Pity. But maybe just as well as I could not have resisted the temptation to make a fool of myself by standing on the steps and declaring: *Et tu, Brute!*

At the far end of the Forum is the Arch of Septimus Severus. This was built by his sons, Caracalla and Geta, joint emperors after their father's death, to commemorate his victory over the Parthians – what we would call "Iran" today. Somehow overcoming their bashfulness, the doting sons included their names, along with their father's, on the monument. At the top there were statues of Severus and his ever-loving sons being pulled in a chariot drawn by six horses. But Caracalla had his brother assassinated and expunged his name. The holes where Geta's name once was can still be seen. Another charming, self-effacing Roman family.

And so our introduction to the Forum comes to an end. As for it itself, the beginning of the end came when Constantine relocated the capital of the empire to Constantinople in 330, followed by Theodosius I who firstly outlawed all pagan religions, then in 394, ordered the closure of all temples. After that, the Forum was plundered for building materials but the ultimate humiliation came when cows were let to graze and it became known as the *Campo Vaccino* or "Cow Pasture".

And there hath pass'd away a glory from the earth, as Wordsworth might have put it.

33

The Shopping Mall and the Wedding Cake

WE emerge from the Forum onto a broad boulevard, the Via dei Fori Imperiali. Away to our right is the Colosseum and to our left, we can just make out the top of Trajan's column. That's the direction Yole and the others take whilst I, like Wordsworth, look back down on the Forum and reflect in solitude for a few moments.

Galloping to catch up, I find the others parked under a statue of Julius Caesar where there is some shade and some seating but none for me. It's got nothing to do with sour grapes: I wouldn't have wanted the shade anyway. Here, Yole competes with the roar of the traffic to tell us about Trajan's column which we can see more clearly now further up the street. It is not on our itinerary, but, says Yole, we will get a better look at it on our way past – not close enough though, she warns us, to see the detail of the carvings which spiral round the shaft. She says that was all previous groups had wanted to see; there had been some television programme about it apparently. She looks relieved she doesn't have to shepherd us across the ferocious Via dei Fori Imperiali now the fuss about the column has apparently died down.

The carvings, on 29 Carrara marble drums, wind round the column 23 times and in 155 separate scenes, commemorate Trajan's victories over the Dacians, who lived in present-day Romania. Apparently they are a very rich source for scholars of Roman military methods. Erected in 113 AD, the column, including the plinth, is 126 feet high, the same height as the spur of the Quirinal hill, which, along with a side of the Capitoline, was excavated to make room for the new forum in which the column was situated. That's an awful lot of earth to move; but they also moved heaven for Trajan.

The story goes that when he died in AD 117, his ashes were placed in a golden urn in the base of the column, which is hollow. (It would be nice to follow in the steps of Goethe in 1787 and climb the 185 steps to the top but we can't – even if Yole would let us – as it's closed to the public.) Pope Gregory the Great (590-604), seeing a panel on the column where Trajan was comforting the mother of a son who had been killed, prayed to God to release Trajan from hell where he undoubtedly was since he was not a Christian. Strange to relate, when they disinterred his ashes, his tongue was still intact and told of his release from hell and ascent to heaven! Isn't that an amazing thing!

To tell you the truth, I find this a bit hard to swallow. Trajan was buried with his wife, Plotina, and to me it sounds much more likely it was *her* tongue that did the talking. Anyway, it's thanks to this miracle that the column survived and what's more, the surrounding ground even became holy ground. Trajan's statue took pride of place on the top until 1587 when it was replaced by one of St Peter by Pope Sixtus

V, which I consider a bit of a desecration to an ancient monument.

At the other side of the track of death from us is Trajan's Forum. We are not going to waste half-an-hour waiting for the traffic to stop at the zebra crossing to go across and have a look at it either, but, Yole tells us, the complex, as well as containing the column aforesaid which was flanked by Greek and Latin libraries, also boasted the Basilica Ulpia, a massive civic centre. From here we can see the topmost part of the ruins of a massive semi-circular building of red brick. This is Trajan's Market, a shopping mall consisting of more than 150 shops, selling goods such as fruit and flowers, oil and wine, pepper and other spices, and a whole range of exotic goods from all over the empire. So that's another thing the Romans gave us. The delights of shopping malls. Thank you very much, Trajan. Thank you very much indeed.

Trajan's Market (Image Credit: Pixabay)

On our side of the racing track is the Forum of Caesar who paid for it, or rather the defeated tribes of Gaul did. To build it, part of the Capitoline hill had to be levelled. What draws the eye most are three Corinthian columns with, on the top, a frieze and a cornice that could have come from Miss Havisham's wedding cake. Actually the columns, standing tall with the aid of some iron brackets, date from the Trajan era. But in the beginning, in Caesar's day, this was the Temple of Venus Genetrix, the goddess of motherhood, the mother of Aeneas and going back far into mists of time, his granny – or so he claimed.

In the forum was a statue of Caesar wearing a cuirass while in front of the temple was an equestrian statue of the conquering hero. Inside the temple, amongst other pieces of art, were a statue of Venus and a gilded statue of his mistress, Cleopatra. Which tells you I suppose, how much he worshipped her. To skip to the end of the story (which everybody knows thanks to a certain W. Shakespeare, Esq.), she made the fatal error of aligning herself with Mark Anthony in opposition to his former friend and colleague, Augustus, or Octavian, as he was known as then. After his victory at the battle of Actium in 31 BC, Octavian lost no time in exterminating Caesarion, Cleopatra's son with Julius, and annexing Egypt.

As far as Caesar's end was concerned, he was the author of his own destruction. He was getting just too big for his boots. Already believing himself to be of divine descent, his megalomania was turning him into an absolute dictator. On one occasion, he actually received the Senate in the temple and persuaded them that their meeting-house, the Curia, should be relocated in the southern corner of the forum. His come-uppance came in 44 BC, just two years after the temple was consecrated.

The Forum of Augustus

In 80 AD it burned down, was rebuilt by Trajan in 113 AD and in 283 AD, after another fire, was rebuilt again by Diocletian. The stumps of some other columns can be seen poking through the burnt grass (due to the long, hot summer) along with some other sundry stones – all that remain of the shops which flanked the temple in the Augustan era. *Sic transit gloria mundi.*

Just as that temple dominated Caesar's Forum, the most prominent building in the Forum of Augustus was the temple to Mars Ultor (the Avenger). During the battle of Philippi in 42 BC, the climax of his war of revenge on his benefactor and mentor's assassins, Brutus and Cassius, Octavian had vowed to erect a temple should he be victorious. Today only four columns remain. Pliny declared it to be the most beautiful forum in the world. As Augustus modestly put it on his deathbed, "I found a Rome of bricks; I leave to you one of marble". He was the first to use Carrara marble, by the way.

How he must have gnashed his teeth wherever the Roman gods live, to see most of his forum disappear under the Via dei Fori Imperiali. Is nothing sacred? Mussolini bulldozed this road through and over the ruins, trampling centuries of civilisation underfoot, so he could hold military parades in order to stamp *his* authority on the past. "I am the master now", he was saying; this was his Via Sacra, built for his glorification, just as the emperors of old basked in the glory of another military triumph. *Plus ça change...*

The statue of Augustus, and Trajan's Market on the other side of the Via, are only intermittently visible, blocked out by an incessant stream of tourist buses and heavy lorries. But for this road, where would all the traffic go? Maybe *Il Duce's* claim to fame should really be as a forward-thinking traffic planner. Sod the archaeologists and the past.

The others have moved off, leaving me to ponder these imponderables once more in Wordsworth mode, as I look down at what's left of Caesar's Forum, trying as best I can to imagine the scene as it was in those days. My thoughts are interrupted as I become aware of a couple behind me.

"Gee, honey, here's a statue of Mr Caesar!"

I don't need the accent to tell me where they come from – the words do it. I wonder what their conception of ancient Roman history is like. Maybe because they have a Senate like the Romans and the office of a President who, being Commander-in-chief of the armed forces, approximates to the role of a Roman emperor, they assume the Romans went about putting Mr in front of the word, when they are speaking to him, especially when they are being deferential, or like Marilyn Monroe, singing "Happy Birthday" to him.

Unfortunately I can't hear what else they are saying because just then a shiny black 1960s limousine, with fins bigger than a shark's, sweeps by with horn blaring. I catch a glimpse of a white, veiled figure in the back. The horn is saying: *Get out of my way. I've got to get this bride-to-be to the church in time.* Thanks to Mussolini, she might just make it.

Whilst we had been looking at Caesar's Forum with Yole, it had been impossible not to be distracted by the striking white marble building rearing up behind it. It's so white, so well-proportioned, it looks like a set of new dentures gleaming against the brown of the burnt grass and terracotta buildings over which it towers. It's the Victor Emmanuel Monument. Appropriately enough, considering what had just passed by, it's not-so-fondly dubbed *The Wedding Cake.*

The Wedding Cake

The Arch of Severus, The Wedding Cake and The Curia

When we come round to the front of the building on the Piazza Venezia, where the Via dei Fori Imperiali terminates, it's easy to see why it's so-called. I can see why they also call it *The Typewriter* – a curved colonnade of columns above a solid base which, if I were looking at a photographic negative, would remind me very much of my father's black 1942 *Royale*, which my mother bought for him in Egypt. It is built of Brescian marble which has the quality of never fading, of never weathering, of never mellowing and blending in with the surrounding buildings, so it will, despite the best efforts of the pollution from the Roman traffic, remain pristinely white and dazzling like an advert for denture cleaner.

Completed in 1925, it was built to celebrate the unification of Italy in 1861 under the first King of all Italy, Vittorio Emanuele II. It also houses the tomb of the Unknown Soldier. In the foreground, like the diminutive figure of the groom you

256

see on the top tier of a wedding cake, is the mounted figure of the king. You get the idea he would like to ride off into the sunset: *You didn't tell me when I became king of you all I'd have to marry the country too – far less that you were going to bake a cake.*

The view from the top of the colonnade is supposed to be spectacular. I can believe it probably *is* one of the best views in Rome because, when you are standing on it, you wouldn't be able to see the monument.

You *can* have your cake and not heed it.

Augustus and Trajan's Market

34

Three Coins for the Fountain

FACING the Wedding Cake, though not its façade, is a much more modest building – the Palazzo Venezia. Three storeys high, it appeals to me immediately because of its windows: arched on the bottom, rectangular and larger in the middle, small and square on the top. All are picked out in white which is very effective against the subdued burnt ochre, a contrast to the in-your-face-whiteness of its neighbour. There is a three-storey tower and battlements to complete the overall harmony and rhythm of the building. I like it and it may not even be its best side!

In the fifteenth century, it became the residence of Cardinal Pietro Barbo who continued to live in it when he became Pope Paul II. Later it became the Venetian embassy and in the nineteenth century, the seat of Austrian Ambassador to the Vatican but more recently and interestingly, it was Mussolini's headquarters. There in the centre of the middle storey is a green door with a balcony so small, it hardly seems to be worth the bother, but it was from this tiny place that *Il Duce*, who must have completely filled it, whipped up the masses in the Piazza Venezia below.

It is through it that we are making our way now. At the far end, on the left of the Via del Corso, is the Palazzo Doria Pamphilj and on that building, a green-covered balcony on the first floor which extends round the corner. There are louvred shutters, all closed. Apparently this is where Napoleon's mother used to sit and, when she heard of her son's death in 1821, the shutters were closed and have never been opened again since. I notice however, it's a handy perch for one of those increasingly ubiquitous Orwellian cameras. Napoleon's mum may be gone, but there's someone else watching now.

On the Via delle Vergini, Yole stops us in the shade of an arcade and tells us we are approaching the Trevi Fountain. There's no shade there so she's telling us about it now. The name Trevi comes from *tre via* or three roads, which meet here. It was designed by Nicola Salvi and completed in 1762. The water comes from the Aqua Vergine and there's a panel on the fountain of the Virgin herself showing some Romans the source of the spring.

It is a huge baroque affair, like a theatre set, using the back wall of the Palazzo Poli as a backdrop. I am prepared not to like it, having seen it most recently on a postcard from a friend and thought it hideous. It was said if you drank the water, you would return to Rome, but someone, probably from the Tourist Board, had the bright idea that you should throw in a coin instead. I knew that already, but Yole says if you throw two coins in, you will get a lover and if you throw in three, you will get a divorce. I am looking for two coins, but as I rake in my pockets, I happen to find I have three single cents. It is a sign, as they usually don't bother with anything smaller than a five. Normally I don't have any money at all. I fish them out and wordlessly hand them to Iona, who unsuspecting, takes them.

Gordon is creased up with laughter. "Might as well get *her* to divorce me, then she can pay the costs," I say *sotto voce.*

La Belle Dame Sans Merci draws me a look that says: *Shut up!* I can't be sure if it's my joke she's annoyed at because she thinks it's not in the least amusing; or I'm so mean I won't pay more than three cents for a divorce; or because she can't hear what Yole is saying; or because I am not paying due attention. Enough reasons to start proceedings, but I shut up anyway or my life wouldn't be worth tuppence.

At a corner of the piazza, now we can see the fountain, Yole describes the details we should look out for. Neptune is in the middle, riding a seashell drawn by two sea horses. They're not like seahorses as we understand them, more like real horses with horrible bat-like wings growing out of their shoulders. The one on the left is rearing up and being difficult, whilst the other is tame and docile. This represents the two moods of the sea, apparently. They are being led by a couple of Tritons, splashing through puddles amidst some very rough rocks over which the streams tumble in cascades into a basin of ultramarine water.

It's the roughness of the rocks, I think, that gets my attention the most, rather than the carved figures. On each side of the alcove from which Neptune is apparently emerging, are two figures that represent Abundance and Health and above them, two panels depicting the discovery of the source. And all this in a wall that could have been a sandblasted Buckingham Palace. Towering over the centre is a fussy armorial shield supported by a couple of angels and below that a panel with some writing in block capitals of which I can only read the first line: CLEMENT XII PONT MAX. The rest of the

writing is too small to read, but it probably says what a great Pope he was to give us this splendid fountain.

Funnily enough, now I have actually seen it, I find it less offensive than I had thought I would. The colour of the water is very nice and the sound of the rushing water, apart from invoking the need for some to visit the toilet, is rather pleasant. Although every tourist in Rome seems to be here, there is plenty of room for people to sit on steps or benches. Yole says we have half an hour to recover before we move on to the next part of the tour. I've been in a lot worse places than this for a pit stop.

The Trevi Fountain

I am despatched for *gelati*, but what I really want to do is sit down and get the weight off my legs. I also want to throw a couple of coins in the fountain. It could be money well-spent. Hopefully I will get some small coins in change from the *gelati.* I don't want one of those expensive lovers – a nice cheap one will do me fine. It's my lucky day. I get some small change and secrete them in the pockets of my swimming trunks.

The trick with eating *gelati* in Italy is to eat them faster than they melt in this sweltering heat, especially if you are like me and want to sit in the sun at the same time. So there I am perched on the rim of the basin in full sun, whilst Iona is on a stone bench in front of me, in the shade. No matter how fast I lick, the ice cream is running down my elbow and my hands are stickier than an interrogation from La Belle Dame Sans Merci after she's discovered I've had a whole bottle of wine to myself. No problem with all that water behind me. I rinse my hand and arm in it and scoop out a couple of handfuls to wipe over my face. Lovely! How cool! How refreshing!

It's then it occurs to me how lovely it would be to dangle my feet over the edge. I had already slipped them out of my dusty plimsolls to give them an airing and to let the fresh air dilute the aroma, by now of Gorgonzola proportions. No-one else seems to have thought of this and no-one else seems to be cooling off in that oh! so refreshing water. On the other hand, so to speak, I can't see any notices prohibiting it. If Anita Ekberg can go paddling about in it, at least I can give my poor aching feet an immersion. It's the work of a moment to swing round and dabble my feet.

Bloody hell! What was that? It sounded like someone right behind me, blowing a whistle in my ear. It's enough to give anyone of a nervous disposition a heart attack. I swivel round, my feet still in the invigorating water, to see a couple of policemen dressed in white gesticulating at me, one blowing a whistle fit enough to crack his cheeks. There is no mistaking what they want me to do. I get my feet out of the water as if it were scalding. Oh, God, I am thinking, what if they come down and give me a fine? I'll not throw any money into the fountain as a penance. That will pay a couple of cents of it. How much will the fine be?

But to my relief, they just move off. I am off the hook except everyone is looking at me, or it feels that way, but Iona certainly is and glaring is more the *mot juste*. I know she is longing to come and stomp on my offending feet as this crime is of such public-shaming magnitude that I deserve no less. But for the moment I am safe. She can't do that without blowing her cover.

She is sitting beside Bill and Pat, so they know, but there are so many other people, it's impossible to tell if anyone else who knows us has witnessed this public humiliation. It's impossible to tell what Bill and Pat think, but their impassive faces suggest they don't wish to know me either.

I feel in my pockets for the coins. Maybe I should invest more than a couple of cents. I may need to find a new Mrs Addison before this holiday is over. There is still more than a week to go.

The Trevi Fountain by night (Image Credit: Pixabay)

35

The Oculus and the Sarcophagus

AS we gather at the corner of the Piazza where we are to meet Yole, I keep a respectful distance between me and Mrs Addison, at least for the present. "Respectful" because I respect her wish to not be identified with me. As we troop out of the square, I walk alone along the Via delle Muratte.

Presently we come to the Piazza di Pietra, where, stone me, we are awed and amazed by eleven massive Corinthian pillars, nearly 50 feet high, part of what once formed the Temple of Hadrian. Originally there were thirty-eight. *Sic transit gloria mundi.* It has certainly seen better days. Pigeon guano lies thick at the base of the columns, black with age and pockmarked with pollution. It was built to mark Hadrian's deification. Oh, God, not another one! It's beginning to look that being a god is part of a Roman's emperor's job description.

It was dedicated by Hadrian's son, Antoninus Pius, in AD 145. (Ah, yes, he's the one with the temple/church that looks like a Picasso painting of a cow in a pen we had seen in the Forum, and a godly man he was too.) So this is where they once worshipped his father, though he couldn't have been that great a god if he couldn't hammer the Caledonian savages, so-called, having to build a wall to hold the empire's northern frontier to keep them out. Now it's part of La Borsa, the stock exchange, where Mammon is the new god. Is it just me, or has it occurred to anyone else that this might be the very reason why the Italian economy has gone to the wall?

Emerging from the Via del Seminario, we arrive at the Pantheon, the imitation of which we had seen in Naples, albeit in the distance, through a web of scaffolding. On first impressions, I have to say, the imitation is better than the original. This looks very tired and grey. It is entitled to be so since it dates from about 125 AD, the oldest most-complete structure in the Roman world.

On the pediment is written: M. AGRIPPA. L.F. COS-TERTIVM. FECIT which despite the last word looking and sounding like an Irish expletive, actually translates as *Marcus Agrippa, son of Lucius, in his third consulate, made it.* He was Augustus' son-in-law and general and to whom, in fact, Augustus owed much of his success and power. The original building was built about 23 BC but after a series of fires it was rebuilt to the original plan by Hadrian who obviously fancied himself as a bit of a builder.

To enter the portico is to venture into a petrified forest. The 16 massive Corinthinian columns completely dwarf and overwhelm, reducing me to a pigmy (as if I didn't suffer enough from shortness of stature already) in a land of giants. Incredibly, they are monoliths and came all the way from

The Pantheon (Image Credit: Pixabay)

Egypt. There used to be a bronze roof here, but what was left of it after an earlier pillaging, was stripped off in the early 17th century to make the *baldacchino* which covers the altar in St Peter's and which we are going to see tomorrow, as it happens. Having said that, like many other buildings in the Roman Empire, it is thanks to the Christian Church that the Pantheon itself survived. It was consecrated as a Christian church as early as 609 AD – the church of Santa Maria ad Martyres.

However impressive the portico is, however, it is the circular interior of the Pantheon which makes it the remarkable building it is. Someone once said it's not the breaths you take that you should measure your life by, but the things you see that take your breath away. This is one of these moments. To enter the Pantheon for the first time is an experience, which by definition, can never be repeated and for which you can never be prepared, like seeing *Hamlet* for the first time for example. You feel as if you are in a globe and the reason for this is the symmetry of the proportions. The height is precisely the same as the diameter – 142 feet. The dome is the largest non-reinforced concrete dome ever constructed, even bigger than St Peter's, and is coffered to reduce the weight, but what immediately draws the eye is the great hole at the top – the *oculus* which is open to the elements. The floor is gently cambered and there are channels which lead any rainwater into brass holes in the marble floor. I don't suppose a lot of water comes in anyway. At the moment, a broad shaft of sunlight is striking the floor like a spotlight on a stage. It's incredibly light in here and it shouldn't be, not with the oculus the only source of light, but the remarkable thing is – it is! There are pillars and niches around the whole circumference, and yet the dome is entirely self-supporting. Amazing!

We are free to roam at will and meet in the portico in twenty minutes. Great stuff: there must be some famous graves here, surely! That massive semi-circular niche over to my right for example, with the two rose-coloured pillars and what looks like the largest candleholders in Christendom, more than twice the size of the guards standing like sentries beneath them, *has* to be someone important. I can't wait to be unleashed and find out who it is. It just *has* to be one for my collection.

There is a big black sarcophagus on which is written in gold lettering: *VITTORIO EMANVELE II* and below *PADRE DELLA PATRIA*. So this is where he ended up and to think I had never even heard of him this morning!

Right, bagged him. Now what about the niche over at the other side, if a circular building can be said to have sides? A person of great importance evidently as they have planted the poor bugger in porphyry, which is considered a great honour. It is the tomb of Umberto I. Ah! Right! I visited your shopping mall in Naples. I hadn't heard of him either before I came to Naples, but he is the son of Vittorio and as far as I'm concerned, never mind being less famous than his father – is less famous than his wife. She is Margherita, of pizza fame, and it really is my lucky day, for written on the wall behind the hideous sarcophagus, is: *Margherita, Regina d'Italia.* Two graves of the famous for the price of one. For free actually.

Now, who else is there? Not far away is a real find. There is a statue of the Madonna and child and set below this, in the black-and-white marble base of the statue, is a pane of glass which is illuminated from within, so it's rather like looking into an aquarium. No fish here of course. It contains a sandstone sarcophagus on which are carved wreaths and scrolls and on a plaque at the bottom, his name in Latin: *SEPUL-CHRVM RAPHAELIS SANCTII.* I have stumbled upon

the tomb of Raphael. He died on his birthday, possibly, which happened to be Good Friday, April 6th 1520. According to Vasari in his *Lives of the Great Artists*, he died from an excess of sex with a baker's daughter after which he fell into a fever. Not wanting to admit the real reason for it, he was given a "cure" for something else and from which he subsequently died.

Interior of the Pantheon
(Image Credit: Pixabay)

He was only thirty-seven, poor devil.

Not a bad haul, I reflect, as failing to find any other graves, I head out into the shimmering heat of the mid-day sun. I don't see any of my fellow travellers in the portico yet, and after a glimpse at my watch and with still some time left, I hurry out into the Piazza della Rotonda. It has a fountain which has an Egyptian obelisk at the centre of its elaborate marble basin into which mythical beasts are spewing water. I want to get a view of the building from a distance because, from the direction we approached it, we saw nothing but the massive portico and I'd like to see if any of the rotunda is visible, or, if from straight on, the portico conceals it completely.

I have just set out on this quest, have got only as far as the fountain from where all I can see is the portico, when my eye is attracted by some movement. Iona is waving at me furiously while some others are merely waving, as if to say: *Not that way! This way! Over here, moron!*"

I trot towards them as fast as dignity and fear will allow. I am really for it now, this coming on the heels, so to speak, of my transgression at the Trevi.

"Where the hell do you think you were going?" La Belle Dame Sans Merci hisses. "You were told to be back for twenty past!"

"I thought twenty-five past. She said we'd twenty minutes inside."

"She said we'd to be back *outside* at twenty past. You weren't listening as usual. Where the hell did you think you were going to anyway? You walked straight past us."

Could it really be possible I had walked past them and not noticed them? It is dark in the portico and they *could* have been behind those enormous pillars. Besides I was in too much of a hurry to look properly, not expecting them to be there anyway.

"Thought I'd save everyone any more trouble and drown myself in that fountain," I mutter darkly.

"Oh, shut up and give me some water, before I turn into a god." She's referring to Vespasian's immortal words as he lay dying.

"You would be a goddess, darling. You know I have always worshipped you."

"Shut up! Don't call me 'darling' and don't try my patience any more than you have already, right? Just give me that water, for God's sake!"

She's never in the best of moods when she's hot and bothered.

36

Statues of Stone and Flesh and Blood

A T the corner of the Corsa Agonale, Yole tells us our tour is nearly over. She's going to tell us about the Piazza Navona and then the rest of the day is ours to do with as we please, like go back to the hotel and collapse. We must have tramped for miles on these unforgiving Roman pavements.

Typically, the square is not square at all, but rectangular with curved ends, just like a racetrack – which, as it happens, is what it used to be. In a previous existence, it was the Stadium of Domitian where they used to hold athletic and chariot races. The floor of the piazza was concave then and flooded so they could hold mock naval battles, or *naumachiae*. Their descendants also made use of this facility up until the 19th century when it was flooded in the summer to cool the feet of the horses pulling the carriages of the clergy and the rich, and the Shanks's ponies of the poor. In the winter, if it were cold enough, it was turned into an ice rink.

But no paddling for this poor person in the sweltering heat of this Roman afternoon. I'm not so forgetful that the *faux pas* in the Trevi is not still fresh in the mind but in any case, the focal point, the fountain in the middle, the Fontana dei Quattro Fiumi, by Bernini, is barred with heavy metal fences. It's another bit of propaganda. Commissioned by Pope Innocent X, the four gigantic figures represent the great rivers of the continents where the Pope held sway: the Nile, the Danube, the Ganges and the Plate.

The River Plate has his arm outstretched as if to prop up the façade of the church opposite, the Sant'Agnese in Agone by Borromini; The Nile has his hand raised, covering his face, apparently in horror at the façade of the church. Towering over them is an Egyptian obelisk but on top of that is the Pope's coat of arms – the dove and the olive branch. In other words he's saying, just like the Roman emperors before him: *I am the boss of the world. And now that I am – peace to you all.* It was paid for by taxing bread which is where the Pope departed from his Roman predecessors, for whilst the emperors kept the people happy by giving bread away, Innocent, eponymously and erroneously, supposed they wouldn't mind. Not a popular move.

It seems Bernini and Borromini were rivals to get the commission for the fountain which, it was said, Bernini only won by bribing the Pope's alleged mistress – his brother's widow, as it happens. I will refrain from making any comment about keeping it in the family but can't resist pointing out that the Pope's soubriquet of "Innocent" was ironic to say the least and that it should really be *her* coat of arms on the fountain as below every Pope (at least in those days) was a woman.

Whatever the truth of that may be, alas there is absolutely no truth behind the story of the Nile's hidden face. The church was not even begun when Bernini's fountain was completed. The reason is symbolic. At that time, its source was unknown.

The façade of the church is also hidden, shrouded in scaffolding. It is built on the site of a former brothel, where in 304 AD, the thirteen-year old Agnes, daughter of a patrician Roman Christian family, was stripped naked in front of the crowds and dragged here because she refused to marry any of her many suitors, preferring to devote her life to Christianity, a proscribed sect in those days. Unfortunately for her, less than a decade later, by the Edict of Milan, Constantine I decreed freedom of worship, not just for Christians, but for worshippers of all gods.

Someone was watching over her. Miraculously, her hair grew amazingly long, just like that, and with which she covered herself up. Presumably she was a very well-developed girl for her age. Sadly, although her modesty was preserved, her life was not. On this spot, they tried to burn her at the stake but in another miracle, the flames refused to touch her. They beheaded her instead.

The *Agone* of the church's name does not refer to Aggie's pain as one might suppose. It's one of those false friends, a translation trap for those students of foreign languages. Actually it refers to the athletic contests, *the agones,* which were held here and which in the fullness of time became *in avone*, then glided into *navone*. The rest you know and we know, thanks to Yole.

Adjacent to the church is the Palazzo Pamphilj, designed for Innocent X by Borromini aforesaid. It's too far away to see clearly and we can't go in anyway, as it's now the Brazilian embassy. It's a wonder the piazza is not called the Piazza Innocent X, because as well as the palace and the Fontana dei

Quattro Fiumi, he was responsible for restoring the two other fountains in the piazza, the Fontana del Moro and the Fontana del Nettuno. There's nothing more satisfying than spending other people's money for them, especially if you spend it on yourself, building your dream house and your own memorial.

With that Yole is finished with us, at least for the moment. We'll see her tomorrow in another place at another time – another country, in fact, at the Vatican. But for now it is time to sit down and partake of some refreshment. We head for the nearest café. I don't know about anyone else, but my feet are in agony and if I don't rest soon, I think I'll soon become a god like my nearest and dearest was feeling like not so long ago at the Pantheon.

Ah, the relief, just to sit down and take the weight off our feet! Bill and Pat are with us, so I am outnumbered and have to make do with a seat in the shade. Out there, in the heat of the piazza, a young man standing completely motionless on a gold box is dressed head to toe in a close-fitting gold Lycra costume and wearing a mask of Tutankhamen. I can tell it is a male because the costume is really tight. I hope he doesn't fall in love with any skimpily clad tourist who catches his eye. I suppose he is inspired by the obelisk on the Fontana dei Quattro Fiumi – but hopefully not too much. At the other side of the Fontana is yet another still figure, by accident or design, gussied up completely in silver, including his face.

To complete this trio of odd personages, a Roman soldier with a helmet crested with a bright pink plume is waving his *gladius* about in a limp sort of fashion at pedestrians passing through the piazza: *Come hither you Caledonian bastards, I'm going to give you a jolly good thrashing!* Thank God it's only his *gladius* he's waving about, not his weapon of mass repro-duction, though in his case, probably it isn't.

I order a beer, a *grande*. I don't care how much it costs, probably a fortune in this location. Whilst I pour that down my throat, the others pore over the map. Iona knows what I want to do which is to go to the Spanish Steps and visit the Keats-Shelley Memorial House and since she doesn't have any better ideas, that's what we're going to do. From the map, it looks as if we can walk there and on the way, we can take in Augustus' mausoleum. And I'd like to have a look at the Ti-ber too. Bill and Pat say they'll come as well.

Iona goes down to the toilet and reports you can see the original pillars of Domitian's stadium down there. Unfortu-nately, she doesn't tell me this until we are making our way out of the piazza, towards the Fontana del Nettuno. If only I hadn't been so bladder-retentive, I could have seen them too.

I suppose we should have gone down to the other end of the piazza first and looked at the Fontana del Moro and the façade of Innocent's palazzo, but it's in the opposite direction

Fontana del Nettuno (Image Credit: Pixabay)

to our route. No-one seems to have thought of it and besides we have many steps ahead of us in this baking heat, so here we are at the Fontana del Nettuno instead. Neptune is about to stick his spear into some snaky monster octopus of the deep which has wrapped itself around his godly thighs.

I really like this – almost as much as Giambologna's *Rape of the Sabine Women*. While the thrust of that had been un-relentingly upward, the movement here, by contrast, is defi-nitely downward. There is real power in the thrust of Nep-tune's shoulders as he is about to drive his spear home. Better be careful though as he is nude and we wouldn't want any accidents. Still, he'd be dead unlucky to hit *that*! What's the point of being a god if you can't be better endowed? Michel-angelo's *David*, the giant killer, was meant to be small, but for the god of the sea you would expect a bigger muscle than something that could curl up in a mussel shell.

There are sea horses and all sorts of other figures on the periphery. I like the overall effect and this fountain appeals to me a whole lot better than Bernini's *Quattro Fiumi* which is meant to be the outstanding work of art in the piazza. But I would of course. It comes from being a crab. Cancerians like to be in the minority, apparently.

I should probably trek to the other end of the piazza to see the Fontana del Moro as the central figure was also designed by Bernini and which gets an even bigger write-up in our guidebook than this one, but I decide to conserve my energy. It says that *Neptune* was sculpted by Antonio della Bitta. I think you deserve more credit, Antonio, if you're reading this in heaven.

37

Mausoleums and
Mirror Churches

W E turn right out of the Piazza Navona and presently come to the Via della Scrofa which in due course changes its name to the Via di Ripetta for no good reason, apart from obeying the rules of Italian logic. On our right is the Palazzo Borghese. (Yes – another one.) It was bought by Camillo Borghese round about 1604 when he was a mere cardinal, but when he became Pope Paul V the following year, he extended it as befitting his new station in life. The guidebook says there's a beautiful porticoed courtyard which we might be able to get a glimpse of.

The palazzo was called *il Cembaio* or "Harpsichord" because of its shape. The concave façade to our right must be the keyboard or *la tastiera*. It looks a tasty enough building, however when Pauline Borghese came here, she didn't like it and refused to live there, saying it was too cold and damp and complained about the lack of sanitation. I bet it was really her bedroom that was giving her the hump: *My bedroom's only got two doors. How do you expect me to strike the right chord with my clients in this dump?*

The bit we're looking at forms the junction of three streets and must be the narrow end of the harpsichord. There's a balcony at the top with climbing geraniums spilling between the balustrades and dangling into space, whilst below that is another balcony which has been enclosed entirely in glass. I don't suppose that was there in Pauline's day though, just like the Spanish flag fluttering from the uppermost balcony. That's because it's the Spanish embassy. From there, there should be a good view over the tops of the trees to the river.

The Tiber is just behind us. We cross the road to have a look at it. The water seems very green. To our right is the Ponte Cavour, named after Vittorio Emanuele II's right-hand man, and to our left, the Ponte Umberto I. We're nor far, as the crow flies, from the Castel Sant'Angelo, another of Hadrian's building projects, designed by him as his mausoleum, but over the centuries it saw service for other emperors and their families, as a papal refuge, as a prison, as a garrison during the Napoleon era and finally, what it is today, a museum. It is so-named because according to legend, that warlike archangel, Michael, was seen sheathing his sword to signal the end of the plague in 590.

We retrace our steps and on the ochre wall of the Palazzo we see a little plaque of a boat on top of wavy lines. On the top it says: *2 FEBR V 1805* and below the boat, *FL VMEN.* If Pauline were here then, no wonder she thought the house was damp, because the wavy lines come up to my shoulder.

As we make our way down the back of the harpsichord, down the Via dell'Arancio, we look in vain for the fabled courtyard. You probably have to be inside it to see it and

The Castel Sant'Angelo (Image Credit: Pixabay)

that's not possible as it's closed to the public. (Why do they put it in the guidebook then?)

What we do stumble across though is a cylindrical water fountain like the upright barrel of a cannon with a red beret on the top. It looks as if it is made of lead, but what's of interest to me is that above the spout it bears the letters SPQR just as Yole said we'd see if we kept our eyes open: *Come and get your lead poisoning here, folks.*

At last we have arrived at the first of our two goals – the Mausoleum of Augustus. What a disaster! It's like a bowl sitting in a saucer and has been allowed to fall into a terrible state of disrepair – little more than a weed-strewn mound. You can see the entrance and an arched window above, but the saucer, or outer wall of grey stone, has a pair of locked iron gates. Clearly, we are not going in here either.

A noticeboard shows what it would have looked like in its glory days and tells something of its history. It was circular with four concentric passageways, linked by corridors and two obelisks at the entrance which have been removed to grace two piazzas elsewhere. Augustus built it for himself in 28 BC but he was not the first resident. That dubious honour went to Marcellus, his nephew and the husband of Julia, his daughter, who may have been poisoned by Augustus' wife, Livia, who, with mad matriarchal misguidedness, thought her son, that arch-lecher, Tiberius, would make a better emperor than Marcellus. Augustus did end up here in AD 14 however, and was succeeded by Tiberius who rapidly saw that Augustus had some company.

As a thanatourist, the collection of famous dead people to whom I have paid my respects would have been augmented considerably by bagging the remains of all those famous Romans, the great and the good, not forgetting the downright bad and evil. But alas, in the 5th century, the mausoleum was pillaged by the Visigoths who were only interested in the golden urns, couldn't care less about the contents, and disrespectfully spilled them on the ground.

To our left, between us and the Tiber is the Ara Pacis, the Altar of Peace. The whole thing is covered not only in scaffolding but in canvas as well, but there is a representation on the canvas of what lies behind it. It was commissioned by the Senate in 13 BC after the defeat of Gaul and Spain and which brought peace to the Mediterranean, hence its name. Four walls surround the altar, two of which depict a procession of the Imperial family in Carrara marble, like a family portrait. It's a real pain that the restoration isn't finished yet: another reason to come again, I suppose.

It's still a bit early, so instead of walking due east to the Piazza di Spagna, we take the Via del Corso towards the Piazza del Popolo. The other direction would take us back to the Wedding Cake. All the roads in this area seem to funnel towards the Piazza del Popolo. In fact, it is known as "The Trident", with the Via del Corso forming the middle prong, thrusting into the very heart of Rome.

If this is the heart of Rome, then at the epicentre of the city is yet another Egyptian Obelisk. Rome seems littered with them. If it had not been for the fact that I hadn't been pestered to death to buy something from street traders, I might have begun to think I *was* in Egypt. In actual fact there are (only) thirteen. This one was erected during the reign of Rameses II, more than 3000 years ago and brought back as spoils of war by that peace-loving first Roman emperor, whose Ara Pacis have we just not seen, after his conquest of Egypt. But apart from that it has special significance as it used to be in the Circus Maximus, one of those in the *spina*, the dividing line in the stadium where the charioteers raced to entertain the crowds.

We are sitting on the steps of the Santa Maria dei Miracoli on the Via del Corso. Across the street to our right is its mirror image, the Santa Maria di Montesanto. The architect was Carlo Rainaldi (1611-1692). Actually, if you look closely, they are not quite identical twins. Because the space occupied by the latter was smaller, clever old Carlo came up with an ingenious solution: he gave the Montesanto an oval dome and the Miracoli a circular one. Ingenious, eh? How identical they are on the inside I couldn't possibly say as both are closed, presumably because it is siesta time. I'm beginning to think it will be a bit of a miracle if we find anything open today at all. Knowing my luck, I bet when we get to the Piazza di Spagna, the Keats-Shelley House will be closed too.

On the other side of the elliptical piazza, is a monumental arch – the Porta del Popolo which leads to the Via Flaminia, one of the ancient Roman roads which connected Rome to the Adriatic.

Being guideless, we are relying now on our guidebooks. One says the Porta del Popolo was designed by Nanni di Baccio Bigio; the other says it was Bernini. I prefer to think it was the nanny of Big Baccio who dunnit, as they say in crime novels. I can just see him sitting on her lap, though he was a bit big for that sort of thing: "Draw me a triumphal arch, nanny."

"Tell us all about it, David."

"Er... what?"

Bill is nodding at the guidebooks. "Tell us about what we're looking at."

I stand to face my three companions sitting like the three monkeys on the steps of the church and give them the benefit of what I've just read, like a real guide. It was supposed to be for their ears only but the monkeys' neighbours, for want of anything better to do, have tuned in.

Suddenly my exposition is drowned out by an almighty amplified voice as if from heaven above: *Allo! Allo!* It seems God is speaking Italian these days, but then He would here, wouldn't He? Actually it sounds just like His representative in this place beneath, the Pope. It can't really be he, can it? Whatever, I regard it as a sort of divine intervention and sit down on the steps beside the monkeys.

The voice has now been replaced by someone on a keyboard. It's coming from a stage in the centre of the piazza. If I had not been so rudely interrupted, I was going to tell my audience this was once a place of execution (and entertainment for the masses), one method being to bang people on the temples until their brains ran out. Incredibly, it remained a place of execution until 1826. (Famously, twenty years later, in 1846, Dickens witnessed a public guillotining near the church of the Beheaded John the Baptist. Someone with a grim sense of humour.)

I would have also told them the greenery they can see is the Pincio gardens designed by Giuseppe Valadier, who – as it happens – also redesigned the piazza, giving it its present oval shape. (So more pleasing to the eye than a square.) I make the suggestion we could walk through the gardens to our goal, the Piazza di Spagna, but this modest proposal is vetoed by my companions as it looks such a steep climb. They have a point. The gardens are on the Pincian Hill.

Thus we miss seeing another obelisk as there is another one there. Not Egyptian this time, but a copy, erected by Hadrian in the second century AD, as a memorial to his slave and lover, Antinous. Serendipitously, however, on the Corso, we stumble across number 18, the Casa di Goethe. This is where the great man stayed for two years while he wrote his *Italian Journey*.

"Why don't *you* write a book about *our* trip?" Iona suggests. "Give you something to do now you are retired." It annoys her, who has so many hobbies, that I have none, apart from alcohol and admiring other ladies. Except she doesn't know about the last one (I hope) and doesn't think the former qualifies, so that's why she thinks I haven't any.

The rest, as they say, is history.

38

In Search of Keats and Others

THE Piazza di Spagna is an essential destination for the modern Grand Tourist. Out of the entire trip, my goal (which comes only second in importance after Pompeii), is to visit the Keats-Shelley House, which my guidebook says is the pink one on the right-hand side at the bottom of the steps. Here I will have the opportunity to visit the room in which the poet died, carried off at the tragically early age of 25 by the same consumption which afflicted poor Emily Bronte.

Keats was only one of the many writers and artists who lived in the vicinity. Hans Christian Anderson, Balzac, Berlioz, Elizabeth Browning, Byron, Henry James, Rubens, Shelley, Tennyson, Wagner, to name but a few and, to complete this otherwise alphabetical list, Liszt. Not forgetting Goethe of course, but unlike Keats, they survived – at least for the time being.

I am mildly surprised to find the House is not pink, like my guidebook shows, but a much more tasteful two-tone affair in apricot and cream and looking good enough to eat, if I liked cream, which I don't. I am, however, not in the least surprised to find it is closed. Just my luck, but it should open, according to the notice on the door, at 4 o'clock which is in half-an-hour's time. Well, we'll see. It'll be Italian time anyway, so if it opens at all, it won't be when it says it will, so there's plenty of time to explore the piazza first.

The obvious thing to do, weaving one's way through the crowds squatting on the steps, is to climb to the church at the top, the twin-towered Trinità dei Monti, from which there should be a good view of the entire piazza, not to mention the Steps, but there's further rebellion in the ranks. Iona and Pat protest it's more than a step too far. They are too tired and

The Trinità dei Monti
(Image Credit: Pixabay)

too hot to make the ascent. But Bill is made of sterner stuff and says he'll accompany me.

It's not a difficult climb. The stairs, which would not be out of place in some grand baronial mansion, sweep down in an elegant cascade, flanked by villas of pink, ochre and yellow. Half-way up, there is a handy balcony with balustrades from which you can pretend you have stopped to admire the view while actually you are getting your breath back, especially if you're packing what Iona calls a *puku*. It's a Maori word for the thing that normal middle-aged men carry about their waists like a back-to-front back-pack.

I pause for a moment, looking in particular at Keats's house, pondering if he had the puff and energy, before his last few consumptive

The Spanish Steps

months, to climb the Steps, even as far as this. And when I emerge from my reverie and look around, Bill has gone. I thought he had stopped too, but perhaps he hadn't. After all he doesn't spread out in the middle like me and is certainly not as Keats-fixated. Perhaps he had said he was going on and would see me at the top. If he had, I hadn't heard him, but no matter; I'm bound see him at the summit.

Only when I get there he is nowhere to be seen. Not to worry. There are more steps to be climbed for the asking, those up to the door of the Trinità dei Monti itself. It is closed, but nevertheless, there should be an even better view from there. These steps are a lot steeper but mercifully fewer than the grand Spanish Steps – quite enough after 137 of them in this blistering heat.

What should have been a good view and photographic point down the entire length of the steps, as well as to the piazza and the city beyond, is obscured by a pedestal on which yet another Egyptian obelisk has been plonked.

Having climbed to the top, there's nothing to do but, like the Duke of York and his men, come down again. For the sake of variety, I take the right side down the steps, keeping an eye open for Bill, but without success. What's more, when I go back to where I had left the ladies, there is no sign of them either. I am lost again. Well, not exactly. I know precisely where I am, but where could they have got to? If I am not reunited with them somehow or other, then I really am in trouble, for not only do I not have any money, but I haven't the foggiest idea of how to get back to the hotel. In the meantime, at least I have the guidebook for company. Let's see what else there is to see.

At the bottom of the steps is a fountain, so the guidebook says. Ah, yes, I believe I can just about make it out through all the people swarming around it. It is called *the Fontana della Barcaccia*, designed by Bernini Senior and a bit of a joke, apparently. It's a half-sunken barge, the water supplied by the Aqua Vergine, the same which feeds the Trevi Fountain. If I could get close enough to see, maybe some of the silt from my feet will have arrived here by now. Anyway, there was not enough pressure to have spouting jets of water as intended, so we have this half-sunken wreck instead. In the middle is something that looks like a bird-bath, from the centre of which spouts a feeble stream of water, similar in volume to the drinking fountains which used to grace the streets of my youth, but which now seem to have disappeared entirely.

The inspiration for the fountain is said to have come from such a barge which was stranded in the Piazza after the Tiber flooded in 1598. If that is true, then that was some flood and Pauline Borghese should have been around then to see just what a *really* damp house was like.

I stroll off towards the left, towards the Piazza Mignanelli, keeping my eyes skinned for my companions. I want to have a look at the column in the square. It's a Corinthian column, and on the top is the Virgin with a halo of stars hovering round her head, like a cartoon character who has just received a severe blow to the head and who is reeling from the blow. Or it could be she has been elected patron saint of the European Union.

In actual fact it dates from 1857 and commemorates the Doctrine of Immaculate Conception, an idea thought up by Pope Pius IX, namely that Mary was the only person ever to be born without original sin. Well, I didn't know that before and neither did anyone else until a century-and-a-half ago. I wonder how many of my Catholic friends know what a recent idea this is and how old Pius himself found out about it. Perhaps it came to him in a dream. Like Martin Luther King, I too have a dream, but unlike his, mine is not very noble. Maybe that's why it hasn't come true and I have to go around stroking boars' noses and throwing money away in fountains to make it happen.

There's no time left to speculate any further about such matters. If I am to catch the opening of the Keats-Shelley House, it's time I was heading back to it, although the way my luck is going, I am prepared for it not to be. On the way, however, my attention is captured by a department store on my right. If the obelisks make me think of Thebes, this makes me think of Amsterdam, for the whole frontage, all three storeys, is given up to little illuminated windows just big enough to take one person, in which women are displaying their wares. I am, however, impervious to these weapons of mass seduction. Apart from my having no money, they are only mannequins modelling clothes.

At the other side of the street, at number 66, is another store with a very tasteful ornamental archway over the door and of interest to me as it once was the residence of Byron. And there, like the three monkeys, squatting on the pavement in front of it, licking *gelati,* are my lost companions. I prolong their happiness by pretending not to see them and head down the street to see if the museum is open yet. It is not despite being past the opening hour.

I look at it sternly. "Open sesame!" I command, like Aladdin, and would you believe it, there is the sound of a bolt being drawn back and the door swings open to reveal a slim girl in her early twenties who could be the identical twin of my son's ex-girlfriend's sister. I don't know what surprises me more – that, or the door opening just then like it did. I am overcome with confusion. Did she hear me or not? I can't tell from her face, as to cover my embarrassment, I turn away and semaphore across the piazza to the others that the house is now open. They, however, are concentrating on their *gelati,* not at all concerned about my whereabouts. After flapping and waving my arms around as if I were beating an invisible bluebottle to death, I realise there is nothing else for it, but to go over and tell them the good news. When I turn back to explain this to the girl, however, she has already gone.

When my companions notice the return of the prodigal, there is no weeping tears of great joy, far less the killing of the fatted calf, though it has to be said not any visible signs of disappointment either. Since my reappearance seems to be an event of supreme indifference, I don't bother to ask Bill what had happened to *him.*

"The Keats House is now open," I content myself by saying. "If you're interested."

39

In the Society of Dead Poets

W E are requested to leave our bags under the table in the room where we purchase our tickets. I have no bag, but I stow my Panama in homage. We are given an information sheet and we step into a long room with books and paintings from floor to ceiling. One is Louis Édouard Fournier's famous 1889 *Funeral of Shelley* which shows the poet's body being cremated on the beach at Viareggio with three mourners standing near the pyre: Leigh Hunt, Byron and Edward Trelawny, their friend and future biographer of Shelley and Keats.

Actually the painting is not historically accurate: Hunt stayed in his carriage and Byron left the scene after Shelley's brains "seethed, bubbled and boiled", his skull having been accidentally punctured by a mattock when it was being disinterred from the sand where it had been buried for nearly a month while arrangements were being made. His face had already been eaten by the fishes. That said, judging by the state of the smoke from the pyre, that melting moment looks some time away and it also has to be said Shelley's body looks as if he was dressed-up to pay his respects at someone else's funeral rather than be burned to cinders. But that's Romanticism for you. Always looking on the bright side of death.

His wife, Mary, of *Frankenstein* fame, is kneeling on the left, practically out of the picture, whereas in actual fact, she was completely out of the picture. By convention, women in those days did not attend funerals. The Shelleys were by no means a conventional couple and Trelawny does not mention her as being present, and he should know.

The reason the cremation took place – and in that location – was because Italian quarantine laws decreed if a vessel in distress was rescued, or a shipwrecked sailor was saved from the deep, all concerned had to remain in quarantine for at least two weeks once safe harbour was reached. This had the unfortunate and unintended consequence that a blind eye was turned towards those in peril on the seas.

Trelawny spares us no details in his description of both the state of Shelley's corpse and the cremation. Strange to relate, Shelley's entire heart survived the incineration and Trelawny tells us that when retrieving it from the ashes he severely burned his hand. The skull also survived but Trelawny did not snatch it from the ashes as Byron had requested, suspecting he wanted it as a companion piece to the one he already had seeing service as a wine goblet. (The heart eventually ended up being buried with Shelley's son, Percy.)

It all began a few days previously, on 8th July 1822, when the twenty-nine-year-old Shelley was drowned in the Gulf of La Spezia. As well as being a poet, he was also a political activist and there are a number of conspiracy theories surrounding his death. It was alleged it was not the result of a storm or bad seamanship that he drowned, but because he was depressed and committed suicide. Considering there were two others with him, including his friend and ex-naval man, Edward Williams, the theory that he had been murdered, however far-fetched that may seem, would appear to be a more likely scenario. In fact, almost a decade previously, when living in Wales, Shelley claimed to have been attacked by an intruder in the night and fled the country, leaving multiple debts behind him. Make of that what you will.

Trelawny claims to have heard a deathbed confession from a fisherman who admitted to ramming Shelley's boat with the intention of robbing him and his companions, but made too good a job of it and the boat sank before he could carry out his nefarious plan. And indeed, to support Trelawny's story, at the time of the boat's recovery, one side did show signs of damage as if it had been struck by a larger vessel. On the other hand, if Trewlany's other literary effort, his autobiography *Adventures of a Younger Son*, is any barometer, he did not spoil a good story by sticking strictly to the facts. But perhaps the most amazing thing of all is the fact that he wrote anything at all, once you know he was dyslexic.

The room to the right, formerly the bedroom of Joseph Severn, the painter and friend of Keats, has a display cabinet which contains various artefacts, especially of the hairy sort. There is some belonging to Keats, naturally, and also Shelley, unnaturally prematurely grey, and intriguingly, in a scallop-shell locket which apparently once belonged to Pope Pius V (who excommunicated Elizabeth I), strands of hair which once were attached to the heads of two unlikely bedfellows, not least because they lived a century apart – John Milton and Elizabeth Barrett Browning. This lock of Milton's hair, apparently, after Milton was finished with it, became the property of my illustrious namesake, Joseph Addison.

Next door is *the* room – the room where Keats drew his last breath. There is a bronze plaque on the wall which tells us this is where he died on February 23rd 1821. It's an austere little room, smaller that Severn's, but on the other hand, Keats had a great view of the Steps from here.

I am looking at them now, the window open and the shutters flung back as I imagine he would have had them each morning and standing where he would have stood, all 5 foot 1 inch of him. From here he would have had a good view, over the heads of the throng surrounding the *Fontana della Barcaccia* at the bottom of the Steps, which, now I can see it from this elevation, looks more like a gravy boat than a sunken barge. (So that's why the dish you pour gravy from is called a "boat"!) Was this what inspired the epitaph on his tombstone in the Protestant cemetery which famously does not bear his name, but merely tells the visitor *Here lies One/Whose Name was writ in Water*? Ironic really. It must have seemed to him that that was indeed the case, the last published work in his lifetime being *Endymion* which received very bad reviews. No wonder he was depressed, coughing up blood every day, from the colour of which, as a medic, he knew the end was nigh.

There's no bed, nor any other original furniture left, it all having been taken out on Keats's death and burnt in the street, by papal orders. There is however, a glass case containing two plaster casts of Keats's face. The one on the right, we are told, is a life mask, the one on the left, a death mask. I am hard pressed to find any difference between them – he doesn't look very well in either of them. Perhaps they did it just before he died: *Say, John, we're just going to make a plaster cast of your face. Try not to cough will you, till the plaster dries.*

It's only fitting I should have my photograph taken with the great poet, by one who is named after one of his most famous and enigmatic characters, La Belle Dame Sans Merci. Because of the reflection from the glass of the case, it's not very good, or maybe it has more to do with the subject matter. I

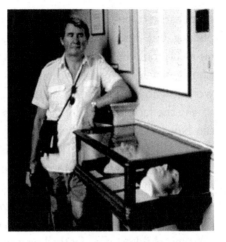

The Author, pictured with Life and Death Masks of Keats

would never have made it in Hollywood. One of my eyes is shut and I look far from happy to be there, when in actual fact this is one of the most interesting little museums I have been to since the Writers' Museum in Lady Stair's House in Edinburgh which houses artefacts belonging to Robert Burns, Sir Walter Scott and Robert Louis Stevenson.

"You look the worst," says my Belle Dame Sans Merci without malice, as if judging a sculpture for a competition.

I couldn't argue with that.

At the other side of the house, in another little room, there is, amongst a display of books and other objects, another mask. This was worn by Byron at the Carnival of Ravenna in 1820. He looks a bit of a ruffian with short-cropped hair and a week's stubble on his chin with a broad nose that looks as if it had been flattened by countless pugilistic encounters. It looks infinitely more scary than Keats dead, or Keats alive, or me, for that matter. A masked ball obviously would have been my best chance of pulling a bird, especially if I picked a handsome phizzog, but Byron picked an ugly one, hoping to scare women off so he could have a night off. Knowing his luck and reputation however, he probably ended up being lumbered with a woman who liked a bit of rough.

At the far end of the long room is a bookshop where you can buy some of Keats, Shelley and Byron's poetry, as well as that of some other Romantics. There is also a visitors' book.

As I stoop to write my name, I can't help but read the entry above. It's by an American from Pennsylvania who had written: *I teach Keats and I love him so much that I even called my son "Keats"!* How sad is that! I know some people call their children after football players, sometimes after whole teams which I think extremely pitiful, especially in the transient world of football. But to be called *Keats*! If you're saddled with that as a moniker, you have every chance of being bullied in the playground once the other boys find out you have been named after cissy poet. If there is anything more calculated to make the lad grow up to have a hatred of poetry, and Keats in particular, then I don't know what is.

I look around to see who the perpetrator of this crime might be, but there is no-one here expect for a young couple looking at Byron's mask. I sign my name and in the space for comments, I'd like to write: *Poor kid!* with an arrow pointing to the offending comment above, but I don't. After all, he could be heartily grateful his dad's not Nicola Pisano's greatest fan.

40

The Trouble with
Italian Public Transport

WE are footsore and weary, so it is time to head back to the hotel. We make our way to the nearby Piazza San Silvestro where we can catch a 53 bus. According to the timetable, there will be one in a few minutes. Just enough time, if we are quick, to get a bottle of water at the little shop on the corner. Bill and I dash across the piazza. We are just about to pay when Iona appears at the shop door for an instant, frantically flapping her hands at us before disappearing just as suddenly. Bill and I abandon the bottles on the counter and set off in pursuit, scattering pigeons in a flurry of flustered feathers.

We make it. Oh, we make it all right. The bus driver has abandoned his post; presumably he's one of those in that bunch by the kiosk in the shade, chatting and laughing like schoolgirls. Twenty minutes later we are still there. There would have been time enough to have carted a Trevi Fountainful of bottled water by now, but we dare not leave. The woman on my right, on a seat on her own, is starting to get a bit annoyed. She turns round to give the woman behind her a torrent of irate Italian. I wonder if she knows her or is just getting it off her chest to whoever's nearest, actually me, but she knows she wouldn't get a sensible answer from someone dressed like me.

I'd love to know what she is saying. The cry is taken up by someone at the back of the bus and Mrs Barrett's husband, Browning, comes to mind as the whispering grew to a murmuring and the murmuring grew to a rumbling and the rumbling grew to a sudden eruption. The woman is out of the bus and across the piazza faster than a lava flow but with a temper just as hot.

I watch in appreciation as she tears into the group of bus drivers and a moment later she comes back with two captives. One of them disappears into the safety of his cab while the other, a lugubrious, bespectacled, fat, freely-perspiring man (fear or heat?) whom I would judge to be in his thirties, follows her inside where she reclaims her seat. The passengers who have had to stand have been too scared in her absence to pinch it. From this throne, she continues to harangue him. It's a bit like a spectator sport at the Colosseum – a cruel combat. I don't know what possible defence he can have. He speaks in a calm, measured voice, flaps fat flippers of arms from desultory shoulders but which are worse-than-useless flails against the barrage of words spitting from her lips like bullets from a machine-gun. Even I feel like ducking, and I'm on her side, but I feel I could easily be caught by a ricochet. It seems a bit obscene to be watching this unequal contest, confirmation to me that I would never have enjoyed being a spectator at the Colosseum. Frankly I am relieved when he abandons valour in favour of discretion and, just before the door closes in that hiss which would have mimicked his deflated ego and utter public humiliation, he skips off the bus and into freedom as we eventually move off.

It's unbelievable! She who was so irate just a nanosecond ago, is now turning round and laughing and joking with her friend or acquaintance as if nothing had happened. How can she change her mood so utterly and so completely in such a short space of time? I feel she should deserve some applause. How long would we have sat there I wonder, had she not taken the driver to his task? What sort of public transportation system is this, where the drivers just park the bus and chat with their mates, ignoring such trivia as timetables? If the Government has never heard of EU regulations, why should a bus driver have heard of timetables? It all makes sense, once you understand the Italian psyche.

On the journey, I have time to study this shaker and mover. She's probably forty-something, perhaps a well-preserved

Rome by bus (Image Credit: Pixabay)

fifty-something and, I notice in confirmation of my suspicions, not wearing a wedding ring. She'd scare the pants off any man who came near her. A surreal vision springs to mind of them fleeing, hobbled, with their trousers round their ankles with her in pursuit: *Stop! I command you to make love to me!* She's wearing a dress in patrician purple and which no doubt explains why she is unafraid to attack those plebs of drivers in their den. She also carries the badge of her office – a matching purple handbag which, no doubt, she uses a cosh in the rare event of the purple prose of her invective being ineffective.

Travelling by public transport certainly gives you an insight into daily modern Roman life I reflect. And so does getting off one stop too early, or otherwise we would not have seen the Smart Car parked across the zebra crossing – which shows it's not that smart after all. Actually, being an Italian Smart Car, it is probably smarter than it looks as it knows it will not get a ticket, the law about not parking on those black-and-white stripy things being completely disregarded here. Probably it is smarter than us who got off at the wrong stop.

* * *

Iona has put feet plasters on her feet and taken a Hedex to relieve the pain. I lie on the bed and let my feet throb, and stoically refuse the medication. It's enough just to have the weight taken off them. Idly I pick up the literature at the side of the bed. It's about room service and suchlike, including a laundry list. One item reads: *Mens' panties €2*. Fat chance! I didn't get to my present state of impecuniousness by paying other people to wash and iron my panties. For a start I'd be too embarrassed and secondly, I've never ironed my panties in my life as no-one ever sees them and if I'm run down by a bus, I probably wouldn't care anyway.

Inspired, I tell Iona I am going to have a shower and do some washing at the same time. I may as well, as I'm not going to need my shorts for a couple of days and this will give them time to dry. I have also been told by She Who Must Be Obeyed that as we are going out for a meal tonight, I must wear my long trousers. This morning she had spotted, in a lane off the Via Corso, a restaurant which had tables outside advertising meals for €10. She knows I like to eat *alfresco* but she also knows I like the sound of the price even better. Furthermore, we are going to the Vatican tomorrow and if we want to get into St Peter's we must wear trousers as they are extremely strict about the dress code.

I strip off my lemon shirt and anything-but-mellow-yellow shorts and chuck in my ensemble of Lincoln green for good measure, put the plug in the bath, pour shampoo over the clothes, turn on the shower and as I wash me, I trample the clothes underfoot. When I look down, I see the water is black. I don't know if it's primarily from me or from the clothes, but on reflection, it would have been a good idea to have washed my feet first.

I wring the clothes out and pull the cord across the bath to hang them up to dry. That's when I notice the hard lump in the breast pocket of my yellow shirt. What the hell is that? I pull out a squidgy mess of paper, just barely recognisable from the green writing on it that is my bus, tram and metro pass.

I dry myself and wrap myself in protective folds of fluffy towel before I go to confess to Iona. I show her the sodden mass lying in the palm of my hand. It looks like something the cat sicked up.

"What's that? It's horrible! Keep it away from me!"

For a moment I thought my towel had slipped. "It's my travel ticket. I'm afraid I've laundered it!"

After the tide of insults to my intelligence has abated, I suggest in melioration, "Perhaps for tonight, I could borrow a ticket from someone else, someone who's not going out tonight. Maybe the Guttings. Don't expect they'll be wandering very far."

"Huh! And what makes you think that they'd trust you with their ticket? Don't you dare embarrass me by asking anyone for their ticket. Is that clear?"

I have little chance of resuscitating that squelchy mass that is my travel pass for today and tomorrow, but I squeeze the water out of it anyway and put it on the radiator to dry. Since it isn't on, I don't expect it to do much good. La Belle Dame Sans Merci watches my performance with complete and utter contempt.

When it is time to go, I think about taking the still sodden mass with me and explaining what has happened, but realising how pathetic an excuse that is, like pupils who say the dog ate their homework, I just chuck it in the bin.

Naturally, Iona moans to Bill and Pat about my accident, while for my part, I am more than a little put out to see that Pat has not made Bill wear long trousers in this steamy heat. On the other hand, he doesn't embarrass her by wearing swimming trunks instead of shorts.

As the bus lurches us towards our destination, I am on the alert for anyone who looks like an inspector and stand as close to the exit as other passengers permit. If an inspector gets on, I'm getting off.

Pat is rummaging in her bag and produces a little phrase book. "I wonder what the Italian for *I washed my ticket* is?"

We all laugh merrily, even me, but I am on tenterhooks the entire journey.

41

Roaming in the Gloaming

WE alight at the Piazza San Silvestro without incident and as we walk up the Via Poli, I admire the colours of the building on our left, the same apricot-and-cream of the Keats house, soft and glowing in the evening light. It is only when we emerge into the Piazza Trevi, I discover it has been the side of the Palazzo Poli whose façade forms the stage-set to the Trevi Fountain.

The piazza is as busy as ever but we do not tarry. Instead, we take the Via della Muratte out of the square and believe it or not, see another Tutankhamun statue, or it might be the same one, who, having somehow found the means of locomotion to get here, has now become as stiff as... well, a statue. His hands are in the position adopted by footballers when they are defending a free kick. Perhaps he wishes to hide how pleased he is to see us again.

Iona, feeling sorry for him, having to stand about all day doing nothing (and she berates *me* for being idle), puts some coins in his collection box and Tutankhamun bends over from the waist and straightens up again. Had it not been for this, I would not have noticed the white marble plaque on the wall of the house behind him, number 77. It tells us Donizetti lived here.

We cross the Corso and enter the Via di Pietra. Its entire length has been set out with tables laid for dinner. We choose one about halfway down to avoid any interference from traffic noise. It's all very ambient with red-and-white checked tablecloths and candles in glass globes already lit, although it is still quite light.

Our waiter wants to know where we come from. Perhaps he hopes we are American, in anticipation of a bigger tip, or maybe he just wants the excuse to tell us he is Romanian. I am able to tell him we were there in 1974 which connection, I trust, will ensure extra-special service. These pleasantries over, he asks what we would like to drink.

Pat orders a half-litre carafe of white wine. "I think that will be enough dearest, don't you?" she puts to Bill, rhetorically.

I can scarcely believe my ears. Although older than us, they have been married only half as long. Plenty of time to have stopped that sort of endearment, I would have thought. But it's not that I find so incredible, but the idea that such a thimbleful of wine would be sufficient for two. Without consulting my dearest partner in greatness, I order a litre carafe of white wine and a beer, a *grande*. It's been hot work walking in these long trousers and I long to be like Bill, in shorts. Bill thinks the beer sounds a good idea. Anything I can do, he can do smaller: trousers, wine, and beer, because he orders a *piccolo*.

The service is slow but it doesn't matter; we're not in any hurry. I'm glad of the long beer to while away the time, whilst Iona makes a start on the wine. It's not very cold and not very good, though Bill and Pat pronounce it "delicious". I give them the benefit of my opinion and I can see they think I am being fussy. I used to like wine, the cheaper the better, and resisted developing a taste for anything more expensive for as long as I could. But alas the day came when the tastebuds re-volted.

I have lasagne for my *primo*. It is only lukewarm and I beckon the waiter over and ask him to put it in the micro-wave. He doesn't look too pleased. So much for the special relationship. I don't know why he should feel insulted; it doesn't look as if it's been produced on the premises. When it comes back, it is inedibly hot: *That'll teach you, you miserable Scots haggis to complain about our frozen meal-for-one from the supermarket.*

My next course is *scallopine al limone* and I ask for it *senza fungi*. I shouldn't have done that really as I could have given the mushrooms to Iona, but I was just showing off my Italian.

When it comes, that is all it is: the escalope with a slice of lemon sitting on the top. If the plate had been blue, it would have looked like a lonely Caribbean atoll. Of course I should have known if you want vegetables, even potatoes, you have to ask for them, extra. I give Iona the lemon as it is her favour-ite fruit and my escalope looks lonelier than ever.

It's not the best meal I've had in my life and when the bill comes, it is €37, the same as last night, so that which had seemed so cheap turned out in the end to be no cheaper and not so good. There's a moral there somewhere but it was nice to sit out on the pavement in the gathering dusk of a velvet Roman evening sipping the white wine, which, although I had put it far away from the candle's heat, steadfastly refused to retain the little chill it had at the beginning.

It would be nice to see Rome by night. Well, the bits we can walk to at least, so we head back to the Trevi fountain.

Like me, it is best seen in a dim light. The upward floodlighting softens the grey stone of the palazzo and the pool shimmers in the reflected lights like an Impressionist painting. It's a place for romantics – so what am I doing here? A flower-seller offers Iona a couple of long-stemmed red roses in a cellophane wrapping but she waves him aside like an irritating insect. She's well trained. She knows I wouldn't want her wasting money on me with such romantic nonsense. She wouldn't say it with these flowers anyway because, as far as I could tell, they didn't have any thorns.

Since the Trevi looks so good lit-up, I venture the suggestion we revisit the Piazza Navona as I reckon the fountains would look very attractive illuminated and besides, we never did go down to see the Fontana del Moro. However Iona vetoes my proposal on the grounds it is too far for her plastered feet. If only she knew it, her feet are not alone. Underneath my trousers, my panties are plastered to my person. I bet I'm more uncomfortable than she is, so I am not too bothered and we head towards the Spanish Steps instead.

We approach them along the Via di Propaganda, a very pleasant street with impressive buildings sporting elegant façades with intricate mouldings. The sound of gentle music comes floating through the air from somewhere out of sight, adding to the general ambience. I would enjoy it more if I weren't waddling like a duck.

That store I saw earlier in the Piazza Mignanelli looks even better and even more like a street in Amsterdam or Hamburg than it did then, the light in each window stronger now and the mouldings round the windows making them look like illuminated paintings.

"They're only dummies, and you couldn't afford them anyway."

It's Iona interrupting my thoughts. I hadn't realised I'd been giving them such rapt attention.

The Piazza di Spagna is as crowded as I had expected, but there's a bit more room round the Fontana della Barcaccia. Now I can see it at closer range, it looks less like a gravy boat and more like a creature from the deep being landed by an invisible line with water pouring obscenely from its eyes as if weeping at its own demise.

Despite this gruesome image, it's very pleasing just sitting here on the Steps soaking in the atmosphere, watching people passing through the piazza. I'm glad to be here at this moment, when the air is soft and warm, the lights mellow and yellow. It's what I like about the continent, this evening ambience when the speed of life slackens from the frenetic to a strolling pace as if the people have picked up by some sort of osmosis, the mellowness cast by the lights. It is a privilege to be here, I reflect, following in the footsteps of the famous, seeing the sights they have seen, strolling as they once did through this piazza.

Which reminds me. I need to make another pilgrimage. In the Keats house, I had learned he had sent out to the nearby *Caffè Greco* for his meals. It was founded by a Greek in 1760, Rome's oldest café and the second oldest in all of Italy. It

The Spanish Steps by night

was patronised by all the literati and musicians of the 19th century: Byron, Stendhal, Ibsen, Hans Christian Andersen, Mendelssohn, Wagner, Bizet and Liszt, not forgetting to mention King Ludwig of Bavaria, poor man, who was mad, and Casanova, who was mad for something else. Goethe was a customer too and it seems to me if I am to write another *Italian Journey*, I should follow in the maestro's footsteps, have a drink where he had drunk. Perhaps I might gain some inspiration, somehow absorbing some of their greatness from the ether. Surely Iona can't object to that, can she? There's only one problem – where is it? We have not brought a guidebook with us.

For once the gods seem to be on my side, for just at that moment, a couple of policemen happen to come along. Actually one of them is a woman.

"Scusi, dove e Caffé Greco per favore?"

It's about the limit of my Italian, learned from a TV programme thirty years previously, and I don't even know how correct it is so I am more relieved than insulted when the female of the species replies, in perfect English: "Via dei Condotti, just down there." She points the way then delivers the *coup de grâce*: "But it is closed."

Of course it *would* be. The gods have to have the last laugh. I should have known we should have gone there straight after coming out of the Keats house.

Damn! I might never write that book now.

42

Window-Shopping
and Taxi-Riding

THE Via dei Condotti is the street you can see from the Steps pointing as straight as a dagger into the heart of Rome. It's normally the sort of street I'd avoid like the plague. It's *the* designer shopping street: Versace and Armani are represented here as well as a host of other fashionable clothes and leather outlets. If there's one thing I can't stand, it's fashion. Like jewellery, it's a mug's game. People with too much money spending it on things they don't need, to impress people who are not worth impressing in the first place.

But it *is* the street where the Caffè Greco is, and despite its being closed I prevail on my companions to have a look at it from the outside. There it is on the right-hand side, number 86. A big rectangular sign with lettering in gold block capitals over a plain arched doorway reads: ANTICO CAFFÈ GRECO. It's good to stand on the threshold through which so many famous people have passed (and many millions more, less famous). The windows upstairs are lit up but the door looks as firmly shut as one in Fort Knox. It looks like a lock-in and we've not been invited. Ah well, it probably costs a fortune anyway but I know there's more than a whiff of sour grapes in that.

Looking back up the street we have a splendid view of the Spanish Steps and the Trinità dei Monti. The whole scene is bathed in a warm yellow glow, the shiny surface of the street picking up the glow from the lamps and the shops, making it seem as if it were paved with beaten gold. Maybe it is, paid for by all the wealthy people who splash their money about here.

Here is the Versace shop. The window display features, in the background, a poster of a young man with a Chaucer's Pardoner's apology of a beard – a growth of russet hair on the point of his chin. His hair has apparently all gone to his head. He appears to have had a shock, probably at the prices, for it is sticking out in all directions like a chimney sweep's brush. In front of him stands a dummy who has lost his head, dressed entirely in black apart from a silver belt at his waist. This is the new autumn/winter collection and the price list is below: *Chiodo Pelle €807, Camicia €157, Cintura €121, Jeans €272, Scarpe €258.* Bloody hell! If I wanted to look like that (and I would rather die first), how much would it cost me? I have to ask Iona to do the sums, or else we'd be here all night.

"€1,615," she says, seconds later.

"And what's that in real money?" It sounds like a lot of euros to me.

"About £1,300."

Good grief! It sounds even worse that way. I bet I've never spent that much in fifty years of clothes shopping, and here's this peacock wearing more money than I've got in the

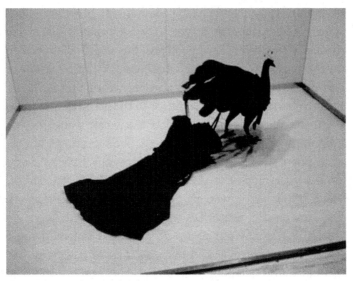

Dressing up is a drag

bank. And that doesn't include his gold medallion either, as he's bound to have one of those nestling in the rug of his manly chest.

Funny I should think of a peacock, for as we walk along the Via Bocca di Leone, I am attracted by a window display in a shop called "Moschino". It is a peacock, a midnight blue peacock and spread out behind it is a cocktail dress in the same sumptuous velvety blue material which the bird is dragging behind it. That's all it is. The rest of the window is completely bare. The floor and walls of the display are yellow, which set off the colour of the dress perfectly. There is nothing as vulgar as a price tag to offset this remarkable scene. I have to admit I am impressed. Simple but eye-catching.

Here's another shop window. I never would have believed that window-shopping could be such fun. It's on the Via Frattina and it appears to be an underwear shop. A male trunk has been placed on a revolving pedestal. He's bare-chested but wearing underpants (or maybe they are trunks?) which are opaque at the front, thank goodness, but which allow you to see the buttocks as if through the mesh of the confessional. You wouldn't want to have an accident wearing those. Think of the embarrassment when you got to the hospital.

At the other side of the window is a female trunk. She has a top in the same perforated material. She's wearing a bra beneath but I suppose you wouldn't necessarily have to if you wanted your nipples to poke through for a bit of fresh air. Down below she is wearing a thong tied with silk ribbons. These are on sale, 30% off. A snip at €8.80. Hmm! About £7 and Iona's birthday coming up very soon... I suppose I could stretch to that. Having said that, it's a lot of money for not very much material, but it is from a posh shop and it might be a good investment. It looks as if it may be fun tugging at those ribbons.

"What do you think you are doing? Come away from there before Bill and Pat think you are some kind of perv. What is it you're staring at anyway?"

"Just a thong at twilight."

Iona only has time to make a growling noise in her throat before we catch up with Bill and Pat again.

"Look out, dearest!" says Pat, alerting Bill, who jumps back on to the pavement and thus narrowly avoids being mown down by a speeding Vespa as we cross the Via del Gambero.

"Phew, he was nearly a god there!" says Iona.

"Almost the dearest departed," I add *sotto voce* and she flashes me one of her looks.

Soon we reach the Piazza San Silvestro and study the timetable to see when our bus is due to leave. Can you credit

it? In the height of summer, at the height of the tourist season, and I wouldn't mind betting, in the number one most-
visited capital city in Europe, the last bus was at 9 o'clock!
Unbelievable! There's nothing else for it – we'll have to get a
taxi. There's a whole rank of them in the square, ready, waiting. I wonder if they are bus drivers during the day.

"It shouldn't cost too much between the four of us," says
Bill.

He's probably right about that, even if his grammar isn't,
only it could never be as cheap as the bus journeys we have
stored in our passes, but at least I won't have to be on the
constant lookout for inspectors. I can relax and watch the taxi
meter instead.

The first one in the rank is one of those Fiat Uglymobiles.
There is a bit of a scramble but I end up in the front seat, beside the driver, which means I have the best view of the meter. There is something horrendously hypnotic about the way
its digital display notches up another digit with every beat of
my heart. When it stops I hope my heart doesn't stop too.

It may be ugly and by the smell of it, new, but the taxi is
roomy, at least for me. Pat, however, who is tall, has less
room in the back. She is sitting in the middle and her legs are
stretched out, one foot resting on the central console. The
driver, watching in his mirror, waggles his finger at her and
gestures her to get her foot down, like a teacher admonishing
a small child. I give Pat you-are-a-naughty-little-girl sort of
look, out of sympathy, but as I turn round again, the driver
fixes me with a steely glare. Did he see my expression, or is he
annoyed at me squirming round in my seat – or both? After
that, I am frightened to move in case I touch something and
he stops the car and throws me out. I feel I should apologise
for my buttocks wearing out the seat material. Can you be-

lieve it! A car-proud taxi driver, though how you could be proud of such an ugly vehicle, beats me. Not even a toad could love this bulbous, squat shape. An embarrassed silence descends in the cab.

It's a relief to arrive at the hotel. The figures on the meter read €8.37. That's handy as it solves the problem of how much of a tip we should give him. I have another one: *Look, mate, I think you should realise if you're going to use your Uglymobile as a taxi, people are going to come in and sit on the seats.* We give him ten euros, which means it only costs us €5 a couple. Can't complain at that, considering all the wear and tear we did to his vehicle.

I can't wait to get to my room and tear off my trousers. Maybe those underpants I saw in the Via Frattina weren't so daft after all, with all those little perforations to let the heat and sweat out, like the teabag in the advertisement.

"You needn't think you're going to be getting up to anything," says La Belle Dame Sans Merci wearily and sternly, misunderstanding my motives. "My feet are aching." Since she takes headache tablets for her feet, she is probably really telling me in time-honoured fashion that she has a headache.

"That's all right, dearest. We have another night left in Rome. Just you put your feet up, dearest."

She gives me one of those Frau Ning looks. I might have known such soft-soaping wouldn't curry any favours from her. I get her a Hedex instead.

The Vatican

43
To Hell by Metro

W E have been well warned that if we want to enter the hallowed interior of the basilica of St Peter's in the Vatican we have to be covered up. No bare legs and shoulders allowed, by papal orders, or probably from his minions. And it *is* rigorously enforced, Angela stresses.

Whilst I don't have a problem with that, the Guttings do. Their luggage never arrived with them and has never caught up with them since. In Florence, wearing only what they stood up in, Angela had taken mercy on them, or our nostrils, and had taken them on a shopping trip, at the company's expense. Or maybe it was merely a loan. Mr G hadn't bought a pair of trousers on this shopping spree, but he *would* like to visit St Peter's.

Iona offers him the loan of a sarong. He accepts it but typically doesn't show much reaction, not even one of repulsion, far alone gratitude. Iona explains when we were in Konya a few years back, visiting the home of the Whirling Dervishes, and for Turks, the tombs of some very famous mystics, a man at the entrance was doling out skirts with elasticated waists to visitors like me who were unsuitably dressed in shorts. This provided a great source of amusement for Iona who, once she had regained the power of speech, said I reminded her of the King of Tonga with my *puku* bulging over the waist. It might just work for St Peter's, she tells Guttings. Worth a try at least.

At least I didn't look like the Bearded Lady who had escaped from the circus since I was clean-shaven, but after all this time, Guttings' growth has been transformed from stubble into what could fairly be described as a beard without contravening the Trades' Description Act. He hadn't bought a razor either. (Must have been a loan.) Like Esau, he is a hairy man, long, dark tendrils sprouting from his forearms and legs. His stomach is as flat as a ruler; he could never be mistaken for the ruler of the Tongans. The sight of him gussied up in Iona's sarong has to be a sight worth seeing. I am quite looking forward to it.

Donald, my fellow Scot, is wearing shorts and so is Gordon. Perhaps they have an alternative plan to circumvent the dress code, or perhaps they are not going to bother with the basilica, as that is only part of our tour. We are going to be visiting the Vatican museum, while of course, St Peter's Square, with the curving sweep of its welcoming arms is well-worth a visit for its own sake. Shouldn't be called a "square" though: it's definitely oval.

Those delights are in store, but first we have to get there. It means another of those nightmare bus journeys followed by the delights of the metro. As we wait for the bus to come, not for the first time, I sympathise with Angela who has nearly half a hundred to take care of next week.

"Why don't they get the bus driver to take you? I mean, you've got a full bus load."

"Can't be done. Parking for one thing, and the traffic is a nightmare."

Sounds to me it would be less of a nightmare for poor Angela than travelling by public transport, but for us at this time in the morning it shouldn't be too bad, should it? The rush hour should be well and truly over, shouldn't it? Won't it?

Not by the number of people squashed onto the bus when it comes. Where are all these people going to at this time in the morning if they don't have to get up and go to work? Why not stay in bed?

"Think of me next week," Angela says as we shove our way on. I would pray for her if I thought it would do any good. I wouldn't be her next week for all the spaghetti in Italy. That descent to the Metro will surely seem like entering the first circle of hell.

The bus journey turns out to be the *hors d'oeuvres*; the main course, the assault course, is just about to begin. There is a collective groan as we see how crowded the Metro carriage is. The short bus journey from the Campo dei Miracoli in Pisa, plus the journeys we have undertaken in Rome, I realise now have been but training for this moment.

"Line A, direction Battistini. Get off at Ottaviano San Pietro. Ottaviano San Pietro," Angela repeats before we sharpen elbows and engage battle.

Sardines, in this tin can of a metro carriage, would find it positively roomy. My hands are pinned by my sides, my Panama and my camcorder clutched in one hand.

The first stop is Repubblica. Surely to God some people will get off there and relieve the pressure. But it's worse. Even *more* people crowd on and we shuffle up even closer and more intimately than before. A woman, completely unaware of how she is invading my private space, is standing on one of my feet. Fortunately she doesn't weigh very much. I try to slide my foot out, but it's no good. For as long as this journey lasts, we are bonded together. At least there is no chance of an inspector squeezing on to examine tickets.

There is no air-conditioning, or if there is, it is hopelessly ineffective against the heat from this mass of bodies. As far as I can tell, we are all *living* bodies, for the moment at least. The unwelcome thought springs unbidden to mind: *What if there's a fire or a power failure? Imagine being stuck down here, in here and in the dark with all these people for God knows how long?* It doesn't bear thinking about. I try to suppress it.

I am sweating now and not just with fear. I can feel it oozing out of my armpits and trickling down my neck. And that's just what's happening under my short-sleeved shirt. I don't

St Peter's, The Vatican

like to think what's happening under my long trousers, but I can feel the sweat trickling down my legs. I can see a dark blue stain under my pits. Is there a corresponding one down below? God, how embarrassing. What if people think I've had an accident?

Maybe it's because *we* have not had an accident, realising that however unpleasant this is, things could be a great deal worse, we turn to light-hearted banter, a way of suppressing the too-awful thoughts we are all probably thinking. Or perhaps it's just a way of making this nightmare of a journey pass more quickly:

Where's Angela?
Don't know.
Are you sure you're not standing on her?
Don't think so.
Don't worry. If we lose her, we'll just follow a nun.

Sounds like a good idea. But where are they? None to be seen; not a nun in sight. Travelling by Metro under these conditions would give any self-respecting nun a fit. Being so close to a man – too hellish a thought to contemplate.

Spagna. We must be beneath the Spanish steps. Three down, three to go. Oh, hell! We're only halfway there. And, if anything, the net gain of passengers is more. Everyone in Rome seems to be hell-bent on getting to the Vatican. By now the front of my shirt is stained dark blue and I imagine the back is the same. People are beginning to notice, especially my companions, passing the message down the line, smirking at the leak in my plumbing. Why aren't *they* sweating like me? I can see the hair at the back of Tom's neck is wet with perspiration and there are beads of sweat on his upper lip, but his shirt seems dry. Meanwhile, the natives don't even look warm.

"If this were cattle," says Usha, who is at vet school, "it would be forbidden."

Back home perhaps, but probably not in Italy.

At last we arrive and, as expected, there is a mass exodus but as we make our way to the *Uscita* it seems there is a hold-up and our nightmare is not yet over. For some reason, the platform only clears slowly and now grinds to a complete halt. What's the problem? I can't see over the heads of the hordes ahead of us.

At last, as we mount the stairs, the reason for the delay becomes obvious. Three men are resting from their labours of wrestling an enormous box down the stairs and we are forced to pass them in single file. It looks the same size and shape as a refrigerator. The Italian answer to keeping the customers cool and satisfied. Can't see it working. Can't see how they are going to manhandle it onto the train.

I am an object of mirth when we emerge into the daylight and sunshine. Apart from my breast pockets, my entire shirt is dark blue where it was a paler blue before. Fortunately, my panties must have done their job and as far as I am aware, no unmentionable stains have permeated to the outside but it feels very uncomfortable indeed. How ironic! I wear my swimming trunks as shorts and stay dry; wear underpants and soak them through.

Like a cormorant holding its wings out to dry, I extend my arms, letting the warm air percolate to my pits. Fortunately we have been reunited with Angela, but should anyone get lost now, they could follow the trail of steam as I dry off – just as long as I don't get lost myself of course. However, before I leave the station, Iona makes me stand still whilst she takes a photograph.

"Next time," but only I can hear the wife's sage advice, "use an anti-perspirant!"

Really? Does everyone do that? I never knew.

44

Hell in the Vatican

NDER a big yellow sign which reads, in lower-case lettering: *musei vaticani* and underneath that, *cappella sistina*, Yole is waiting for us with her trademark car aerial with scarf attached.

As L.P. Hartley didn't quite put it, the Vatican is another country, where they do things very religiously. It's a state within a state since the Lateran Treaty of 1929, but to enter it is more like boarding an aircraft. Once through massive revolving glass doors, we pass through a metal detector where, should we set the thing off, a guard is waiting with one of those electronic paddles to pinpoint the offending part. Meanwhile, our bags, by means of a conveyer belt, pass through X-ray machines.

When Yole comes along with our tickets, we follow her up some stairs and along a corridor. She stops us in a corner and points out the dome of St Peter's. The sun is streaming mercilessly through the window but Yole says it's the only place in the Vatican where you can see the entire dome, and we fry like eggs whilst she tells us it was designed by Michelangelo but he died in 1564 before it was completed. He nicked Brunel-

Statue of St Peter, The Vatican (Image Credit: Pixabay)

leschi's idea though, as it consists of an inner and outer skin. There was an earlier church here built by Constantine, the first Christian Roman Emperor, in the 4th century, which, in its turn, was built on the site of Nero's Circus. The dome of Constantine's church was supposedly built over St Peter's tomb who was crucified here about 64 AD. He asked to be crucified upside down because he said he wasn't worthy to be crucified like Jesus, but I suspect he reckoned the whole ghastly business might be over quicker that way.

We follow our leader outside to a courtyard where there are huge posters of *The Last Judgement* and the Sistine Chapel ceiling. It's called the Cortile della Pigna because of an enormous bronze pine cone, thirteen feet high, formerly a fountain and which now, flanked by two peacocks (copies of those which once decorated Hadrian's tomb), sits in front of a massive alcove in the Belvedere Palace which was commissioned by Innocent VIII at the end of the 15th century.

Since speaking is not allowed in the Sistine Chapel, Yole is going to tell us about the frescoes right here and now. There is a bench which we gents gallantly give to the ladies, but there is not enough room for them all. It looks as if we may be here for some time, so I squat on the ground whilst my fellow, and for the most part, younger travellers, robustly remain standing. Perhaps they think it is undignified or are worried about damaging their clothes on the dusty flagstones, but that doesn't worry me. The secret about surviving in cities is to grab a seat whenever you can.

I care more for *The Last Judgement* than the frescoes on the ceiling – at least the way that Yole tells it. It was completed in 1541, nearly thirty years after the ceiling was completed. It's an unusual subject for an altar painting apparently, the dead being torn out of their graves on the left, to be judged by an uncompassionate Christ in the centre who, with upraised left arm is casting poor souls to hell, bottom right. It makes me think of Burns's satire on Calvinist hypocrisy, *Holy Willie's Prayer* where he writes: *sends ane to Heaven and ten tae Hell/A' for Thy glory*. As a matter of fact, Paul III who became pope in 1534 and who commissioned the painting, was the instigator of the Catholic Counter-Reformation, so no doubt it's Protestants like me who are tumbling into Hades as a warning not to stray from the True Religion.

And there, presiding, is Minos, judge of the dead in the Underworld. He's an evil-looking hombre with donkey's ears (signifying stupidity) and a serpent sparing his blushes by wrapping itself around his nether regions. The joke is his face is a caricature of one of the pope's entourage, Biagio da Cesena, who harangued Michelangelo about the number of nudes in the painting. What he did not understand, the stupid fellow, is it was not nudity for nudity's sake. Michelangelo's point was, that divested of our clothes, those indicators of earthly rank, we are all equal in death.

Pope Paul died and supposed he would go to heaven for his good deeds. After Michelangelo's death, Pius IV, who was also offended by the nudity, wanted the painting destroyed and was only prevented from doing so by the intervention of Michelangelo's pupil, Daniele da Volterra, who covered-up the rude bits of the most flamboyant nudes and thus earned for himself the unenviable soubriquet of "Breeches-maker". But then maybe he preferred that to having a girl's name.

The other item of interest for me is in the centre of the painting. It depicts St Bartholomew, who was skinned alive, sitting astride a very solid-looking cloud. His own skin, grotesque and obscene, hangs limply from his left hand whilst the

The Vatican Museum (Image Credit: Pixabay)

right bears a knife aloft. The slack, empty face, like one of Sal-
vador Dali's melted clocks, looks tortured, and recalls the simi-
le *like a devil's, sick of sin* from Wilfred Owen's *Dulce et De-
corum Est*. It is said to be a portrait of Michelangelo himself.
If it is, I suspect it's another hidden message and shows his
displeasure at being forced to work on this painting instead of
getting on with his commission to complete the massive tomb
of Julius II which he had begun years ago whilst the pontiff
was still alive. First and foremost, Michelangelo considered
himself a sculptor and he resented the years spent painting
this and the chapel's ceiling – eight years in total. Still, no-one
could say they were wasted, not even the artist himself.

Yole now shifts her commentary to the ceiling, telling us it
depicts scenes from the Old Testament from the *Drunkenness
of Noah* to *God dividing Light from Darkness*. It just goes to
show you the truth of the adage "you learn something new
every day" for I never knew Noah *was* drunk, though I have
to confess I have not read the Bible from cover to cover,
though it is a Good Book. I do know however, he lived for
950 years and was spared from the Flood because he was so
good. I think he was entitled to a good *swally* after going to
the ends of the earth to gather his menagerie.

I'm sure God would have forgiven him for that little over-
indulgence but whether his missus did is another matter: *Sorry Mrs Noah, light of my life, Joan of my ark, hic!...just got a
bit fed up of drinking nothing but water. First time I've been
drunk since the boys were born when I was 500. I swear by
that rainbow I won't let it happen again, hic! Not even if I
live to be 1000.*

Or maybe he'd just been bitten by a mosquito and realised
how, with a little selective amnesia, he had missed a never-to-
be-repeated opportunity to make the world a better place

(which was God's plan after all) and was drinking to drown his sorrows. Still, he must have been bucked up to think he stopped Scotland from being quite perfect by preserving the midges.

As the scenes progress towards the altar, we are meant to see how Michelangelo got into his stride and as he loosened up, the figures become less stiff and formal. Certainly I wouldn't have argued with God in the panel where he is creating the Sun and the Moon. No Mr Nice Guy this with fluffy cotton-wool hair, but a greying, bad-tempered-looking bloke with forked beard who is not going to take any Nonsense, or No for an answer either.

I am interested to note that in the Original Sin scene, Michelangelo has chosen to depict the Serpent with the torso of a woman. Interesting idea, Michelangelo. I couldn't possibly comment.

Not an inch of ceiling has escaped the Michelangelo brush. The panels are surrounded by triangular lunettes depicting the ancestors of Christ, the Prophets and the Sybils (who foretold the coming of Christ) and in the corners, Old Testament Scenes of Salvation. Lastly there are the Ignudi, handsome naked young men with Charles Atlas torsos. No-one knows why they are there. Maybe just because Michelangelo liked them. Each scene is framed with friezes or pillars, out of which some figures seem to be stepping, which, together with the vibrant colours, creates a three-dimensional effect.

It may not have been a labour of love, and there certainly was no love lost between Michelangelo and Julius II. The maestro binned the pope's plan for the ceiling in favour of his own design and even locked him out at certain times when he came along to see how the work was progressing. It was finished not a moment too soon, for Julius lived only a few months after its completion. And, when it was, it is hard not to imagine Michelangelo looking at the finished work and even if he didn't want to do it, saw that it was good.

Incredible to think the walls barely get a mention, which – in a different setting – would be the focus of admiration themselves. It was Sixtus IV who commissioned them under the direction of none other than my hero, Pinturicchio. Here there are paintings by, amongst others: Botticelli, Perugino and Ghirlandaio. I nod sagely as if I'd heard of all these people before. I can't remember when I first heard of Botticelli since it was so long ago, but do I know my familiarity with Pinturicchio goes back only four months. As for the other two, I've never heard of them in my puff before.

But after all that's why I'm on an Italian Journey: to listen, to see and to learn. It's not as if I'm an art specialist like I suspect Mr Yorkie is and should know this already.

45

The Sarcophagus, the Goddess and the Tapestry

R IGHT! We're off! Hopefully we have learned enough to appreciate what we are going to see in the Sistine Chapel. But that is not all we are going to see. It's more like the icing on the cake, because we are going to be passing through some galleries of the mind-bogglingly exten-sive Vatican museum on the way.

First stop is the sarcophagus of St Helena, the mother of Constantine, a monstrosity in porphyry. It is supported on the backs of four lions, not so much snarling but complaining about the weight – and who can blame them? The tomb is excessively deep and very much crowded with figures on the sides: conquering Romans on horseback and the vanquished being marched off to a life of slavery. The lid boasts reclining figures at each corner, probably angels, linked by garlands of laurel. Who knows what you would see if you opened the box, but if you go down to the crypt of Trier cathedral you will be rewarded by coming face to face with her skull.

Amongst Helena's various claims to fame, she brought back from Jerusalem pieces of Christ's tunic, pieces of the True Cross (which suggests there must be many others out there) and get this, pieces of the rope which was used to tie Him to the cross! And there was me thinking all this time He was nailed to it! Anyway, the piece of the cross she brought back is encased in one of iron at the top of the obelisk that marks the centre of the St Peter's Oval as it should properly be called. It can't be much more than a splinter to fit in there but enough, I would have thought, for the scientists to subject it to radiocarbon dating tests. Wouldn't it be a fine thing if they were able to prove that the tree from which it came grew in Christ's lifetime, even if they weren't able to tell if it was an impostor or not?

We're in a long corridor now. It's the Gallery of the Candelabra, so called because, in recesses on either side of the entrance arch, are a pair of massive marble Roman candlesticks. I'd love to see the candles that burned in them, but they are not on display. What it *does* have are Greek and Roman sculptures by the score. We're on a march-through really; there isn't time to stop and stare as W.H. Davies would have us do because, for us, it is just an artery en route to the Sistine Chapel.

However we do pause in front of a statue of a well-endowed goddess, not because of the size of her bust, but the amazing number of breasts she has. In fact, they are not breasts at all, but bulls' testicles, so says Yole. I'm not an expert on them it has to be said, but to me they look more like plum tomatoes. Only the Romans never knew about tomatoes. Isn't that an extraordinary thing?

She is Artemis – but not the Greek Artemis whom we all know and love. This is Artemis of Ephesus, a fertility goddess who acquired Artemis's name. Surely these appendages are *meant* to be breasts, meant to feed all these children she has since she's so fertile? And why, for heaven's sake, would anyone want to string necklaces of bulls' testicles around their neck like the onion Johnnies from

Statue of Artemis

France who were a common sight in the days of my youth? Unless, of course, they are trophies of her suitors who were all hung like bulls and *that's* why she was so fertile! This does sound like a plausible explanation as she was a bit of a scary woman, not averse to loosing off arrows at all and sundry. And vindictive too, turning poor Actaeon into a stag to be devoured by his own hounds just because he happened to catch sight of her in the buff.

There are other busts in this gallery, but these are just heads and shoulders of blokes and of no interest to us, in Yole's view at least, nor are any of the other exhibits. However I do notice in the passing, an amusing sculpture of Pan tickling some naked guy's foot which rather tickles me but by the look on the victim's face, it looks more like torture – as tickling can be a form of sometimes.

We press on in a relentless tide and enter the next gallery, the Gallery of Tapestries. On our left are ones from Belgium

Tickling Pan

which depict the life of Christ. Here is a really amusing one. Well, it may be for us, but not for the diners. It's *The Last Supper*, and there, splayed out on a dish in front of Christ is a succulent roast suckling pig! Actually, there are two of them. One has been hacked in half and splayed out. No wonder Christ and the disciples are not amused. At the centre of the table, one has swooned away completely at the sight of the offending fare whilst Christ comforts him by stroking his luxuriant blonde locks (a common hair colour in the eastern Mediterranean).

Colourful though the tapestries may be, it's the ceiling of the Gallery which gets my admiration. It's illusionist architecture at its best. Set amongst Greek keys and laurel wreaths, the figures look three-dimensional as if in the process of stepping out of their sugar-icing frames. Of course I know they are one-dimensional and as flat as pancakes but I would love to reach up and touch them, just to make sure, the illusion is so perfect.

As we progress down the gallery, we come across a huge tapestry of the Resurrection. Christ, in a red robe and dazzlingly-white skin, also appears to be in 3D emerging from the blackness of the rock tomb. Perhaps his eyes are adjusting to the light but they seem to have an intensity which would be remarkable enough in a painting, but in a tapestry, in my opinion at least, utterly incredible. The gaze seems to hold me, and as I get closer, He appears to be returning my gaze. As I get level, then pass by, His eyes follow my progress. I retrace my steps as an experiment and sure enough, He is watching my every move, just as He does in heaven. Maybe.

From here we enter the Gallery of Maps, the brainchild of Gregory XIII, he who gave us the new calendar. One map shows all of Italy and the islands in the Mediterranean as well as the siege of Malta and the battle of Lepanto, great Christian victories over the heathen Turks. Because of our recent visit to Tuscany, Iona and I stop and look for Stigliano where we were based, and there it is, even although it is a tiny little village! And here is Sicily where we were the October before, only the cartographer, for some reason, has flipped it so that the Straits of Messina appear on the bottom left instead of top right.

Map of Sicily

If the ceiling of the Gallery of Tapestries was wonderful in its tastefulness and use of restraint, this ceiling takes the breath away in its overstated show of opulence. There are so many panels, all of different sizes, it's impossible to make sense of it, to see what the focus is. In any case, there is so much gold paint, mine eyes dazzle. Standing at one end and looking down the massive length of the corridor, it's as if I have, like Alice, fallen into a burrow, only here it is roofed with gold. It is a rest and a relief for the eyes to look out from an open window and see the verdant greenery of the Vatican gardens, though marred somewhat by the ugly skeletal pylon of the transmitting tower built by Marconi, rising above the trees. It is used by Radio Vatican to this day.

Over to the left is a good view of the dome. So Yole talked with forked tongue when she told us earlier that that was the only place where we could see the entire dome. But then, I am probably not meant to be leaning half out of the window. One little push from Iona and I would have to be scraped up like strawberry jam from the ground below. But too many witnesses for her to collect the bread from the insurance, so she doesn't.

Next stop is the Sistine Chapel. This has to be one of the highlights of the trip which has been so full of highlights already. Yole tells us before we go down the stairs that photography is expressly forbidden, even without flash, and we are not allowed to use video cameras either. But more than that, we are *not* to talk. We are allowed twenty minutes inside and we are to reconvene at the far end.

Off we go. As we descend the stairs, we pass numerous signs telling us photography is not permitted. Cameras with a dirty big red cross through it. Yes, I get the message and so must anyone whatever their native language might be.

Radio Vatican rising above the trees

However, before we enter the chapel, there is an added, unexpected attraction. It's a room dedicated to the Doctrine of the Immaculate Conception. I had seen the Colonna dell' Immacolata which commemorates this event in the piazza Mignanelli, and it had set me pondering how come they only dreamed this up some 2000 years after the event, in the 11th year of Pope Pius IX's reign. Presumably somewhere in this room of documents which are encased behind glass lies the answer, but I am on a conveyer belt of tourists and to stop would create a logjam, blocking the way to the chapel. No matter. I doubt very much if I would have understood it anyway.

I shuffle past yet another "No photography" sign and at last step I am inside the Sistine Chapel.

46

Facing the Music
in and out of the Sistine Chapel

WOW! The colours are amazing: so fresh, so clean, so new, like Pinturicchio's frescoes in Siena. These too could have been painted yesterday. I am lucky, not for the first time on this trip, to benefit from restoration works. No eggshell-cracked faces but wrinkles where wrinkles ought to be and smooth and creamy skin where that ought to be; no drab and dark garments but vibrant raiment; no lank hair in desperate need of a wash, but lustrous locks. I can see them perfectly and in close-up because I had the foresight to bring along the small pair of binoculars which has been an indispensable part of my travelling equipment for a good number of years now. I focus on possibly the most famous image of them all, the *Creation of Adam*, his outstretched arm, his fingers oh, so nearly touching those of the out-stretched arm of God, but minutely apart. You can almost feel the energy passing between the two.

There are benches round the walls so you can sit and stare at the ceiling in a bit more comfort, rather than break your back and put your neck out of joint as you stand and gaze up-wards. Better still would be to lie on the floor with my binoc-ulars but there's no chance of that without someone stumbling over me as they too look heavenward. No need to pity poor Michelangelo however, lying on his back on scaffolding for four years painting away like mad before the plaster dried. They think he stood on brackets fixed to the walls.

In any case there is precious little space for even a short person like me to find room enough on the floor to lie down. Nor is there a spare seat to be had around the walls. Those lucky enough to find a seat do a pretty good job of obscuring the paintings behind them, however. Maybe for that reason, no-one seems to be paying them the least bit of attention. Poor Boticelli *et alia*, knocking their pans in and not a single person sparing their masterpiece a glance. What a waste of paint!

Nor do many people seem to be paying attention to the "no talking" and "no photography" rules. Every so often a flash of brilliant light seems to fill the entire room and there are people unashamedly using their video cameras. Guards are ceaselessly on patrol on the lookout for the flashers and filmers. I watch as one approaches a Japanese youth who is aiming his camera at the ceiling, totally unaware he is about to be caught. What will happen? He needn't bother to plead lack of English or Italian, or any other language for that matter on account of the non-verbal signs which even the most retarded people on the planet could not fail to understand. There were no signs, at least as far I could see, in the entrance hall where I had filmed the proceedings, yet I was given a severe ticking off. I watch with interest to see what will happen here. Surely

The Ceiling of the Sistine Chapel (Image Credit: Pixabay)

he will be thrown out and the disk from his camera confiscated?

Not a bit of it. The guard taps him on the shoulder, nods at the camera, wags a cautionary forefinger, shakes his head then moves on again, scarcely pausing. Not a word of reprimand was issued, but then of course, talking is not allowed. The Japanese gentleman watches the guard's retreating back, gives a quick glance around him, and the coast apparently being clear, re-aims his camera whilst his companion adopts the role of guard. No wonder everyone is at it. I don't, despite this apparent green light, because I know I would be the one they would choose as an example *pour encourager les autres.*

Every so often a Tannoy announcement booms out, reminding us we are not to talk and not to take photographs either and, for a moment, there is a hush. But it's a hopeless task. The sound of voices coming from a multitude, however muted, is noisy and comes surging back like air rushing into a vacuum. It's impossible to maintain silence here. So many people, so awed by the spectacle, so natural to want to point out something special which has caught the eye. I hope the announcement is on a time loop for all the notice anyone is taking of it. A real person would be driven to insanity by the sheer futility of it. If they really are serious about silence here, they ought to draft in one of those fierce nuns from Assisi.

And on the absence of silence, I recall this chapel is the setting for one of my favourite pieces of music, namely Allegri's *Miserere*, his arrangement of Psalm 51, composed in 1638. If there *are* angels, then this surely must be the way they sing. Here it is performed as the culmination of the service known as *Tenebrae* in which candles are extinguished one by one until, in complete darkness, the *Miserere* is sung. That must be one of the most spine-tingling experiences ever.

The popes retained copyright of the manuscript and we only hear it today because the fourteen-year-old Mozart heard it once and wrote the whole thing down from memory! No doubt Clement IV who was pope at the time, in 1770, was fizzing and quite possibly steam came out of his ears – which reminds me this is also the place where the cardinals meet in conclave to decide who is to be the next pope. So where is the chimney then?

Outside, the chapel looks plain, non-descript, and uninspiring. Who would believe it contains such treasures within? Talk about an inner beauty! Anyway, high up, close to the pitch of the roof is the window from which the smoke comes. Yole says they bring in a portable chimney for the purpose.

No smoke today of course and therefore no fire, as the adage has it, but it feels as if we are standing next to one, as blinded by the light, we stand on the steps of the basilica.

From here we have a good view of the piazza, indeed our first. It looks surprisingly empty and nun-free. Probably there are hundreds of people there, it's just the piazza is so vast it swallows them up.

Now for the moment of truth for the underdressed! Guttings looks fetching in Iona's black-and-yellow sarong but it doesn't melt the hearts of the two men in suits at the entrance. One looks like a negative of the other, his light clothes contrasting with the dark of his companion but both have greasy, slicked-back hair, sinister shades and both mean business. Probably that's why they are wearing business suits. Had Guttings shaved off his beard, he may have passed as an underdeveloped girl, if rather an ugly one, but it's too late now. He tries again, this time pulling his shorts down from his hips and his socks up so they cover his knees. As it happens, they do practically meet, leaving just a small slit. He leans forward to cover the gaps but it's still not suitable say the suits. He's not going to be visiting St Peter's on this trip. Neither, unfortunately, is his missus who nobly stays to keep him company.

Likewise Gordon. He has his partner's wrap round his middle, and thanks to his colouring, he *could* look like the King of Tonga if he worked on his belly a bit. But his royal status cuts no ice with these cool dudes. Rejected. Bombed out.

Not so Donald, the crafty Scotsman. He pulls from his rucksack what looks like a couple of sleeves, steps into them, zips them to the bottom of his shorts and presents himself for inspection. Transformation. Pass. Smart move. Well that's all that's smart about them. My son wears this sort of baggy attire with pockets and pouches and zips in the unlikeliest of places. They would never make it in Saville Row and you'd never catch the suits wearing such things, but like my son, Donald is young enough not to worry about being seen dead in such things and, I have to admit, they *are* practical. What would I have given to have been wearing shorts on that Metro trip, which, with apologies to Apsley Cherry-Garrard, was for me, the worst journey in the world.

Yole is unsympathetic. "You *were* warned," she says, "they are very strict here". And yet they were not in the chapel. There's just no consistency. "All right, we'll meet you over there" – she indicates with a flourish of her wand some indeterminate point over to her right and with a glance at her watch – "in half an hour". I have a feeling she is not best-pleased with them.

Guttings looks glum, but then he always does. If his suitcase had not been lost, would he have had a pair of trousers which would have gained him access? Still, he knew in Florence that trousers were a necessity and hadn't bought them then. Maybe he thought his insurance wouldn't stump up.

Which reminds me. Our budget airline was on strike but we had managed to get a couple of one-way business class tickets for the princely sum of £310 – just to get to London. We had little choice really as if we had not caught that flight we would have missed our connection to Naples. We don't know if our insurance will reimburse us or not. I had forgotten all about it till now, caught up in all the wonderful things we had seen.

Thank you, Guttings, for reminding me. It's not your fault, but now I feel like you look.

47

Grave Sights in St Peter's

INSIDE the basilica, to our right, is Michelangelo's *Pietà*. Iona is confused. She is sure that when she was here before, it wasn't there, in that location. Yole confirms that her memory is like an elephant's, which I already know. It was moved to this site after some madman attacked it with a hammer, in the year of our marriage, 1972. Thanks a lot, buddy. Now it's even harder to see. Apart from the tourists who form a human shield round it anyway, there are now six inches of bullet-proof glass. Actually, I just made that last statistic up, but that's what it looks like and it sounds reasonable.

Poor Mary! She looks so young, not a wrinkle on her face. She scarcely looks old enough to have produced a son as long, as limp, as dead as He. The worst of all things must surely be to witness the death of your child. It goes against the tenets of nature. It is not right, it should not be; all of Nature cries out against such an abomination, yet Mary does not rage at his going into that good night like Dylan Thomas, but accepts the weight of her dead son in her lap with a sadness and resignation as if she is beyond grief.

La Pietà (Image Credit: Pixabay)

Apparently it was the only *pietà* Michelangelo ever finished. He was only 25 and signed his name on a sash across
Mary's chest but a combination of the glass, distance and the
heads in front of me make it impossible to see such detail. He
made Mary so youthful, Yole says, to show her innocence and
purity. Now I know why I have a face like a crumpled brown
paper bag.

It's impossible also for the eye not to be attracted to the
bronze monstrosity under the dome, in the centre of the nave.
The basilica is light and airy but this is dark, brooding and
funereal. It marks the spot, supposedly, under which St Peter
is buried and forms a canopy over the papal altar where only
the pope is allowed to perform Mass. It is Bernini's *baldacchino,* made from bronze stripped from the roof of the portico in
the Pantheon, as Yole had told us earlier. I wish they hadn't.

The four enormous pillars, twisted like barley sugar sticks, spiral upwards to support the crown of the fringed canopy. The design is bad enough, but it's the colour that offends me more than anything, so black and sombre, the gold filigree not withstanding. Imagine that lunatic with his hammer attacking the *Pietà* when he could have turned it into a weapon of Mass destruction instead.

At the bottom of the columns is the coat of arms of Pope Urban VIII, a reminder that, apart from Bernini, we have him to blame for this. It features two crossed keys, the keys to the Kingdom of Heaven, but heaven knows why they would want to destroy the effect of the dome's cupola by plonking this thing, this monstrosity, at the bottom of it.

Yes, the dome is a magnificent sight, supported on its massive four piers. Shafts of light are streaming in from the gallery of windows, illuminating the gold lettering encircling them beneath. Below them, at the top of the piers, are medallions, which – from this distance – look like paintings, but actually are mosaics. At the bottom of the four piers are depicted the relics which St Peter's supposedly has in its possession. This being the epicentre of the Roman Catholic church, you would expect them to be good ones and they are: St Veronica's handkerchief, which bears Christ's image after she used it to wipe his face; the lance of St Longinus, which pierced the side of Christ on the cross; a piece of the True Cross (another); and get this, the head of our patron saint, St Andrew – whom a 5th generation Scottish American of my acquaintance once referred to as "the greatest Scotsman who ever lived". Only apparently Paul VI gave it back to the Eastern Church in 1966. Not that it makes any difference. You never get to see any of these relics anyway. Which is a bit of a shame. A bit like locking away the best silver somewhere where it is never seen again.

Through the dismal frame of the *baldacchino*, and glowing all the more intensely perhaps because of it, is a golden light in the apse. It is the image of the Holy Spirit, shown as a white dove in the centre of an elliptical window, from which radiate golden rays which turn to red at the outer edges, so the impression is of a diamond flashing fingers of fire. To the right of this is the tomb of Urban VIII who gets a position of honour here, in the apse, instead of down below in the crypt.

Also in the main body of the church, intriguingly, is the body of Pope John XXIII. I can recall the television broadcast of his funeral in 1963 maybe because television was still something of a novelty for our impoverished family in those days, but who could forget that great aquiline nose as he lay in his open coffin? Yole waves her hand to indicate he lies somewhere over on the right, as if it's only a matter of slight significance. He's on his way to sainthood. Apparently, when they examined his body in the crypt (as you do), there were no signs of deterioration – one of the signs you may destined for sainthood. There are other tests besides, but in the meantime, until they make their minds up, they have brought him up here and put him in a glass coffin for all to see.

I can scarcely believe my luck. This is better than any relic. Imagine not including him in the tour! Just as well we have the afternoon free and I can come back and see him for myself. A grave is one thing, but the real dead body of a famous pope is something else.

We pass the entry to the crypt. Must go there too this afternoon; there must be popes galore down there. To be honest, I don't know much about popes or one from another, but I'd like to find John Paul I if I could, the one who died suddenly in mysterious circumstances. And down there too, must be the graves of the Stuart would-be-kings of Scotland, Bonnie Price Charlie, the Young Pretender and his father, who, oddly enough, they styled the "Old Pretender". They died in Rome and I know there is a memorial to them in here, somewhere. No doubt I could find it on my own later, but it might save a bit of time if I ask Yole where it is. She says we're on our way there now.

I think the Stuarts would be pretty chuffed with it. There are two pretty glum-looking angels with bent heads and drooping wings standing on either side of a door, presumably the gates of death, but just like the sort of door you would expect to see on a stately home with panels and a couple of brass knockers. Above the door is the legend: BEATI MORTVI QUI IN DOMINO MORIVNTVR. In the pan-

el above that is a whole lot more Latin. Not for the first time, I regret not paying more attention to my Latin, but I recognise IABACO III and underneath that IABACO II MAG-NAE BRIT REGIS FILIO which I take to read *James III, son of James II, king of Great Britain.* Then below that: KAROLO EDVARDO. That's him all right, Prince Charles Edward Stuart,

The Stuarts' Mausoleum

popularly known as "Bonnie Prince Charlie".

There's a reference to HENRICO also, the younger son, Prince Charlie's brother who became a cardinal, and who, after the death of Charles Edward, styled himself Henry IX. That would have been a hard act to follow and how ironic, if he *had* been king, for a cardinal to follow in name, at least, that arch anti-Catholic and womaniser, Henry VIII!

Well, Henrico may have called himself "king" and so may his father who was never king either, but it doesn't alter the facts. Nevertheless, here it is, written in stone as if it were a fact. One thing is certain, however – Shakespeare was wrong when he made Juliet say: "*What's in a name? That which we call a rose,/By any other name would smell as sweet*". I bet the Old Pretender, James Stuart, thought Iabaco III sounded a whole lot sweeter than either of those other monickers.

"Can you tell us about them?" This is my reward for declaring an interest. Yole wants me to address the group on the Stuarts. Probably she doesn't know much about them and wants to learn so she can pass on the information to her forthcoming customers.

So I tell them about the Old Pretender and the First Jacobite Rebellion in 1714 and the Young Pretender and the Second Jacobite Rebellion in 1745, and the retreat from Derby and how, if Bonnie Prince Charlie's troops had only gone on, if the promised support from France had not failed to materialise – London could well have fallen and we might all be Catholics now. I expand about the retreat and the inconclusive second battle of Falkirk and the butchery of Culloden, the last battle fought on British soil in 1746, and how after that, the wearing of the tartan was forbidden and the playing of the bagpipes also. I pause for breath.

"That was very interesting," Yole jumps in. "Thank you."

I am warming to my task. "Ah, but the story didn't end there. You see –"

Someone is putting a steady pressure on my foot. When I follow the foot up I come to the face of La Belle Dame Sans Merci and it is saying: *Shut up!* I have my mouth open, ready to tell the group all about Charlie's flight to Skye and his escape to France, dressed as a washerwoman, Flora MacDonald and all that, but clearly they are going to have to remain in ignorance as we are already making our way to the exit.

"What's the matter?" I hiss as we bring up the rear.

"Couldn't you see that everyone was bored to tears?"

"Eh? Were they?"

"Course they were! They didn't want a bloody history lesson!"

Ooooh! She swore in a church and in St Peter's as well! She must be really mad at me for embarrassing her again.

48

A Fantasy and an Emergency

in the Piazza

OUT in the piazza, we are reunited with the shorts people. God knows what they did with themselves all this time in the frying-pan heat of this cauldron of a piazza. They do look a bit fed up. Well, nothing new for the Guttings I suppose, but Gordon and partner don't look too happy either. Maybe they've got an attack of the miseries from the Guttings having spent all this time with them in this intense heat, exchanging few words.

In front of us, in the centre of the piazza is an obelisk brought to Rome by Caligula in 36 AD. Nero's Circus used to run through half of the present-day piazza, the basilica and beyond. The obelisk supposedly marked its centre. Interesting to note, unusually, it does not have any hieroglyphics. Maybe Caligula's men nicked it before it was finished or else he told them: *I want one of those pointy Egyptian things, but not with any of those stupid carvings on it or I'll stick it up your toga*, and so they had to sandpaper it down smooth until it

Caligula's Column

was as bald as a pharaoh's pate. You didn't mess with Caligula.

The piazza is Bernini's design and is breathtakingly splendid – a complete contrast to his dire *baldacchino*. In a parallel to *whoever framed* the *awful symmetry* of Blake's *Tyger*, but who was also responsible for designing the humpy-backed and bad-tempered camel, it does make you wonder how the person who designed that monstrosity could be responsible for designing the perfection of this piazza.

The twin arms of the four-columns-deep colonnade sweep round in an encompassing arc which remains open at the side which gives on to the Via della Conziliazone. Bernini had planned to build a triumphal arch there but it was never built, so the arms of the colonnade remain symbolically open as if welcoming the world into the piazza and the protective arms of the Catholic Church. Which proves Bernini was not quite perfect, as we know.

In the piazza, Yole adds, but doesn't say whether by accident or design, there are a couple of slabs, which – if you stand on them – the seemingly impenetrable forest of columns all melt into one single row. Isn't that an incredible thing! Must go and check it out.

Of course, the present-day Via della Conziliazone wasn't anything like what it was in Bernini's day, so perhaps he wasn't so wrong with his triumphal arch idea. This was part of Mussolini's settlement with the Church, the so-called Lateran Treaty of 1929 when the Vatican was accorded independent city status. Mussolini tore down the houses to make way for this broad avenue, infuriating a great number of residents at the same time. Actually, the houses on the street are not perfectly in line, so a row of columns was introduced on either side to convey the impression that the road runs perfectly true and straight. The best view of the piazza and the Via della Conziliazone is from the top of the dome, and I shouldn't think there's a person here who hasn't seen that view on a million postcards and posters.

Over to the left, Yole indicates the papal apartments and says that the second from the end is the Pope's bedroom. There's no chance of us catching a glimpse of him today. The air in Rome is too hot and he's retreated to the mountains, so Yole tells us. If he had known I was coming I am sure he would have stayed. Too bad. I was hoping he would be able to tell me if the itchiness between my shoulder blades is due to budding wings or not. But if they can't be sure yet about John XXIII, I don't suppose I would have got a definitive answer anyway.

Swiss Guard

To our left are a couple of Swiss guards. They were first introduced by Julius II in 1506 to protect the Holy See. You have to be aged between 19 and 30, unmarried and Swiss of course. But you don't appear to be able to see that well to protect the See apparently, as one of them is wearing spectacles. You just don't have to mind making a spectacle of yourself dressed in that yellow, blue and red stripy outfit, designed by Michelangelo on one of his off days.

"Are there any more questions?"

It's time for Yole to go. Her last office for us is to explain how we can go back by tram if we want to avoid the Metro. Don't we just! Only, if we take the tram, we are to watch out for pickpockets. True enough, there isn't room for pickpockets to operate in the Metro, their arms are pinned to their sides.

"Erm... could you tell us, where are the toilets?" says Tom.

I hated that as a teacher. You've just finished explaining something and you ask if there are any questions, hoping that the pupils want elucidation on some arcane point and they say something like, "Do French sheep speak French?" or, possibly even worse, "Do we *have* to know all this?"

They are right behind him, which is why he can't see them of course, but just as soon as Yole goes, that's where I am going. In Iona's bag I have my shorts and I can't wait to get out of these trousers and expose my legs to the fresh air.

I dive into the nearest cubicle. I take off my pouch, colour co-ordinated with my shirt of Lincoln green of course. Naturally, as best dressed tourist of the year, I would ensure that it did. It contains my visa card and, unusually, some euro notes which Iona has allowed me to carry which is only fair really as she is carrying my clothes. I place it on top of the cistern. I wish I had my kilt with me. How comfortable it would be to stride across the piazza and the Via della Conciliazione with the air circulating freely as it would as a true Scotsman.

Suddenly, a thought occurs. What if I had turned up at St Peter's wearing my national dress? Would I have been allowed in? And if not, what fun I would have had at the Race Discriminations Board. Only it's Italy and probably they would never have heard of it. Wait a moment, though – it's not Italy, it's the Vatican. Maybe *they* have heard of it. The scenario intrigues. I imagine presenting myself for inspection in front of the business-suited.

"No!"

"What do you mean, no?"

"No skirts on men allowed."

"This is not a skirt! This is a kilt."

"And *this* is a church. We can still see your knees. Don't care what you call it, it's still a skirt. And you look like a man, sort of."

"You insult my national dress. I am going in!"

"Oh no you don't! Guards!"

I slip out of my reverie and into my swimming trunks. When I get back to the piazza, everyone has gone except for Iona and Bill and Pat, and Tom, Dick and Harriet.

"What took you so long?" says Iona with more than a hint of irritation in her voice. I have apparently been keeping them all waiting. How was I to know? Besides I hadn't taken any time at all – just time enough to change out of my trousers. I hand them over with my panties discreetly rolled up inside them but for some reason she doesn't want to touch them and presents her back so I can stuff them into her rucksack.

As I unzip her bag, suddenly I go ice-cold as if someone had squeezed all the blood out of my heart. I can't say whether it was the act of unzipping the bag or something else that triggered the memory. My pouch! I don't know why I took it off in the first place but I can see it now, lying on top of the cistern. I drop my trousers and bolt down the stairs without explanation and make straight for the cubicle.

Thank you, God! The cubicle is unoccupied and there is my pouch, just as I had left it. I seize it, relieved beyond belief to see that it is not a mirage. If we had had to cancel our visa with the holiday not yet half over and very little cash... The wrath of La Belle Dame Sans Merci doesn't bear thinking about. Imagine us lying round the pool next week in Sorrento, unable to do the exploring we had planned because of my stupidity. It doesn't sound all that bad to me, relaxing in the sun around the pool but it would have been intolerable for Iona who hates the heat and for whom sitting around a swimming pool for longer than an hour drives her to distraction. Life for her would have been unbearable and she would have made it unbearable for me also.

It's with an enormous sense of triumph therefore that I return, waving my pouch in the air like a conquering hero.

"Oh, for goodness sake!" says the trouble and strife in exasperation.

Apparently it had not dawned upon her until now the reason for my precipitant departure. You might have thought she would have been pleased and full of praise for my remembering the loss so quickly and relief at my good luck for finding it still there. But no! Not a single word of appreciation or even admiration at my quick thinking.

Sometimes you just can't win.

49
The Crypt

YOU would never guess it from in the piazza far below, but up here on the roof and on which the saintly figures on the balustrade have rudely turned their backs, it's like a little village. In addition to two mini cupolas which crown the ends of the transepts, there are little buildings like garden gazebos as well as a whole lot of other buildings with terracotta-tiled roofs. There's even a post office. If I had a postcard, I could post it here in the blue post box and it would arrive quicker than if posted in Italy, so they say.

I make for the lift, post haste. My companions will be fed up waiting for me again I imagine. I am right. They are. Time now for the highlight of the afternoon: to go to the opposite extreme, to descend into the bowels of the duomo, to head down to the crypt and visit some dead popes. The ladies, however, are wearied after the rigours of the ascent to the top of the dome and from the crowded descent in the lift and just want to sit and rest their legs. There aren't any seats but they prop their bums as much as they can on some poor blighter's monument. Not the Stuarts'. Bill is off to the loo, so I go to seek out the crypt by myself. The good news is it's free. I would have actually *paid* to have been amidst such illustrious company.

It's wall-to-wall popes. Some hopes amidst all these popes, of finding one that means anything to me. Some of the sarcophagi look very old indeed, but wait a moment, here's one that looks very new. I can scarcely believe my luck is continuing to hold. Normally the gods are agin me. If there's one pope I would have hunted out it would have been this one, and I didn't even have to look for him. IOANNES PAVLVS PP I. Before I came here and learned about popes who were megalomaniacs or patrons of the arts, or both, this is about the only one I'd heard of, apart from and John XXIII (whom I'm going to see in the shortly in the flesh I hope), and Julius II who, apart from his part in giving the world the Sistine Chapel ceiling, was the one who refused to give Henry VIII dispensation to divorce Catherine of Aragon so he could marry Anne Boleyn. The rest altered the history of England.

If my memory serves me well, John Paul was the first to have a double-barrelled name and his pontificacy only lasted a month. Some say he was murdered. And here I am, standing, not at a memorial, but where he actually lies, separated from him by only by a few inches of stone. You can't get much closer to a dead pope than this. I wonder how he is getting on in there. I would love to have a peek but I could never shift that slab even an inch on my own. Have they brought lifting tackle down here to check him out, to see if he's a saintly candidate? Maybe they only had to do it once.

No need to do that amongst those older popes who had kids by the score like Julius II, the so-called "warrior pope", Michelangelo's pain in the neck, not the Sistine Chapel, if not fundamentally elsewhere. Julius had one illegitimate daughter, at least one mistress and allegedly was not averse to a bit of

Tomb of Pope John Paul I (Image Credit: Pixabay)

the other, if you get my drift. Michelangelo began his tomb before his death, as you will undoubtedly remember, dear reader, but was interrupted to paint the ceiling of the Sistine Chapel which took four years, as you know.

Not long after Michelangelo got back to his labour of love, Julius inconsiderately died and if he made it to heaven, I would be very much surprised indeed. In fact Erasmus wrote a very amusing satire on his trying to persuade St Peter to let him through the gates of heaven. When he wouldn't, Julius took the hump and said he would be back with an army to capture it. Well, he would, wouldn't he?

The tomb that Michelangelo and his apprentices made was not completed until more than thirty years after Julius' decease which is why he was not planted where the much-scaled down completed version is in the San Pietro in Vincoli. Instead, what remains of his remains after they were desecrated during the Sack of Rome by disenchanted followers of the Holy Roman Emperor, Charles V, were taken here. It's only fitting after all. He laid the foundation stone.

I'd like to pay my respects to Pius IX, of Immaculate Conception fame, but where is he? As far as I can see, there's neither rhyme nor reason as to the way they have laid them out down here. Perhaps they are organised in order of death but, if so, you would have to know your popes a darn sight better than I do.

There is a main thoroughfare with serried ranks of sarcophagi on either side. It's altogether too easy to visit dead popes down here, like shooting fish in a barrel. What's more, it doesn't mean a thing. Here's Innocent IX for example. Sorry, pope, but I don't know anything about you. My fault I'm sure. It probably means you were a good, average sort of pope or I would probably have stumbled over you on this trip by now.

I zip through the shoals of dead popes down here, my appetite whetted to see a real live dead one. Pat and Iona are still where I left them, Iona fanning herself with her Chinese fan and Pat flapping some sort of pamphlet, probably a lot less effectively. St Peter's greatest fans, I don't think. All this magnificent cathedral to explore and there they are, still sitting on their bahookeys.

Bill is down in the crypt they say, yet I didn't see him. A cryptic puzzle. I remember how he side-stepped me on the Spanish Steps. I'm beginning to think he doesn't want to be left alone with me, regards me as a bit of a dead loss. He would have been behind me and perhaps he was following me, ready to duck down behind a sarcophagus in case I turned round.

"Right, I'm off to find John XXIII. Anyone coming?"

The fans flutter agitatedly as if I'd farted and they were wafting away a foul smell, instead of issuing an innocuous invitation. As if I would do such a thing in such a holy place! All right. I'll go on my own, but go I must.

I head off to the right and it doesn't take me long to find him. After all, he is lit up like a fish in an aquarium. He is in a glass coffin beneath a huge Renaissance painting of wot I know naught. There are candlesticks burning above him and spotlights burning inside the coffin. He looks like a wax-work, like something out of Madame Tussaud's, but if he *were* just an effigy, surely those lamps would have melted him by now, especially that famous nose which comes within a centimetre of the top of the glass coffin. In life, some people love to grab the limelight. Who would have thought that in death, and I'm sure he never asked for it, that he would be so much under the spotlight?

If this is death, it looks all right. Maybe it's worth the ignominy of being gussied up like Santa Claus to have this kind of the biggest sleep of all. He is wearing a red nightcap, trimmed with white fur, a red cape with gold trimmings, a white nightie and red slippers to keep his feet warm, resting upon a plump, red cushion. At the other end, his head rests upon another of the same ilk. All is equal in death: neither brain nor toes have dominion.

Yes, very comfy indeed. Very composed. Precisely. He's doing exactly the right thing. As long as he does not decompose (and there's no sign of that), and it must be as hot as Hades in that confined place under those bright lights which would accelerate the process, my money's on he's going to make it. When you think about it, since he is already in heaven, it's only a small step. The snag is he needs wings to get him there.

373

They have arranged rows upon rows of seats so people can sit and view the corpse in comfort. There are only two others, apart from me. How ironic! You can't get near the *Pietà*, made of marble, yet here lies the real body of a pope, and no-one seems remotely interested, except for an agnostic like me (at best) and a couple of others. How odd life is, or should that be death!

I wonder if, in heaven, good old Pope John minds being made an exhibition of like this. Would he mind, would any-one, if I fished out my camcorder and filmed him? There are no notices to say I shouldn't, yet I am hesitant. It doesn't seem right somehow to film the body of a corpse. Seems like some sort of perversion.

I have a good look around me. The coast seems clear so I take a chance, half-expecting a lightning bolt to strike me down dead from the skies. But nothing happens. No-one in heaven, or here on earth, appears to have noticed. If they do, they don't seem to mind, especially my subject who sleeps on regardless.

He looks a lot more comfortable than I am feeling, that's for sure. I am desperate to get out of my trousers, although there is a lot more to see in this place. We haven't even scratched the surface, never mind the Vatican museums. Hav-ing said that, I am anxious to scratch somewhere else and to tell the truth, it comes as a bit of a relief that when the ladies pronounce themselves too tired to do any more sightseeing, I say nothing at all and, to be perfectly honest, am a tad re-lieved.

We are going out tonight as a group and we need to con-serve our energies, agree to call it a day. No regrets. It's been a pretty successful day. One confirmed saint in an enormous sarcophagus; one saint-in-waiting in the confines of a glass coffin; three Scottish kings-in-waiting who will wait forever; one pope out of hundreds whom I will add to my collection of famous dead people I've met. These meetings tend to be a bit one-sided but I totally understand. I would hate to be woken out of a deep sleep to be interviewed by non-entity like me.

Oh, and there was the Sistine Chapel ceiling. Nearly forgot.

50
Rome with a View

I test the spot on the piazza where the columns are supposed to meld into one and it works! I wish I could do a disappearing act like that! It could be very useful at times of extreme embarrassment. There is another one at the other side, but I can't get on it as there is an American standing on it whilst his Italian friend tells him his life story. Some people just don't know when to stop. I give up waiting.

The plan is to have some lunch and then we will make an ascent of the dome then pay another visit to the basilica. We exit the piazza through the colonnades to the left and make our way down the Via di Porta Angelica and there, on the left, is another of the Swiss guards. This one has the same style of uniform, only his is one shade of blue with a black beret and leggings and white gloves. He seems to be some sort of traffic-calming device, stepping in front of the oncoming traffic to allow that coming from behind to pass. The street is so narrow it will not allow two cars as well as him to be all abreast at the same time. An unconventional but effective way of controlling the traffic. We have sleeping policemen to do that but here they have real, live, Swiss guards. They do things differently in this country, as I said before.

At the Bar Moretto, we split up; Iona and I stay outside, the others in search of air-conditioning on the inside. I don't want anything to eat really; liquid refreshment would do me nicely, but Iona insists I must eat something. She says I need my protein. And me with a hump like a camel, except I carry mine at the front, not the back, being a perverse sort of person. Or should that be beast?

It looks like you can order a slice of pizza, not the entire thing which comes as a relief. We ask the waiter, who looks Jewish and a bit puzzled when I ask if we can just have once slice each. In a very heavy accent he says, yes we can, and do I support Manchester United?

"Not on your life! Me not English. Me Scottish. Me support Aberdeen."

He looks blank.

"Aberdeen. You not heard of? Aberdeen. Football team, same colours Man U."

He shakes his head. "Two pizza. Cheers, mate."

I am surprised and impressed at his use of the idiom. "Where you learn speak like that? *Cheers, mate?*"

"Lots of English visitors. I pick it up. Like to talk English."

"You English very good," I compliment him, although it is not.

"Cheers, mate," and off he goes for my beer, hopefully. I could drink a well dry.

I look up to see La Belle Dame Sans Merci glaring at me balefully.

"What? What have I done now?"

"Why are you speaking to him like that?"

"Like how?" I thought I had been perfectly polite, extra-specially friendly, telling a porky pie saying his English was good, when it was really rather halting.

"Talking to him like he was an idiot and you mentally defective. *Me Scottish, me support Aberdeen*, indeed!"

I am stunned. She is right of course. I was hardly aware of having done it. His English had been so halting, it had seemed right to reduce it to baby language for easier comprehension. I see now how wrong I was and his English would never improve if native speakers insist on sounding like American Indian chiefs, though I should of course say "Native Americans". Never can get anything right.

I am not unduly surprised, when the food comes, to find we have a whole pizza each and they are not that small either. I hate eating a big meal in the middle of the day. It takes me to about this time of the day to shake off the surly ties of sleep and a heavy meal just makes me want to go straight back to bed. But this is my humble piece (several actually) of pizza pie and I do not complain in fully-fledged English about his inability to understand my form of simplified speech. Instead, I just eat it and swallow hard when the bill comes and I discover it's what we spent on the evening meal last night.

I leave the waiter a tip, although I never felt like less like it in my life.

"Cheers, mate!"

I am unhappy also at the prospect of having to wear my trousers again, made worse by the thought of all those stairs in prospect. There is nothing else for it but to go down to the toilets and put them on again. For some reason Iona demands my pouch before I go.

Eventually we find the ticket office by the side of the Sistine Chapel and also discover a lift will transport us part of the way. Tom, Dick and Harriet have gone back to the hotel for a lie down so it is only Bill and Pat, Iona and I, we intrepid upwardly-mobile travellers, who are going on the mission.

We are first in the queue for the lift, but by the time it comes, we have been joined by many more. There is a lift driver and he crams us all in but does not whisk us upward until even more people have been pressed inside. The atmosphere is unbearably hot and humid. For this brief period where our lives cross, I avoid eye contact with my fellow passengers. It's quite intimate enough without gazing into the eyes of the person whose body is pressed against you. I fix my gaze on the panel of buttons at the door. It has "Schindler's" written above it. Ah! Schindler's Lift. That explains it.

We are decanted into a courtyard. Over to our left I can see the backs of the statues which adorn the top of the façade of the basilica, so I know just exactly how high we are and how much higher we have yet to climb, for the dome towers over us to our right. I'd like to go and have a closer look at the statues, but that can wait till later, once I've achieved the summit.

Like the duomo in Florence, we emerge initially inside the dome. Now we are so close, we can indeed see that the "paintings" in the medallions above each of the great plinths are mosaics. Gazing up at our destination, where the light comes bursting through the cupola, the panels spread out like a starburst. Below is Bernini's *baldacchino*. At ground level it looked immense, which at 66 feet high it is, but from here it looks tiny and such a long way down to the top of the cross that draws the four corners of the canopy together.

The four arms of the church spread out from this central point, though because of the wire mesh which prevents would-be suicides or husband-hating wives from casting themselves or their spouses onto the variegated marble floor beneath, it is not possible to lean over, so I can only see two of them. From here it impresses more than from ground level, just how enormous the scale of this building is. But I have to remember I am inside the largest church in the world, ironically, in the smallest country.

From the splendours of the interior, it's but a small step to the exterior or rather the gap between the inner and outer dome, but a giant leap as Neil Armstrong might have said, in terms of architecture. With its glazed gold tiles, it's a bit like entering a public toilet, but without the graffiti which normally adorns such establishments, or which defaced the inner walls of dome of the duomo in Florence.

It's well worth the climb. If only one could escape the birdbrains chattering on their mobile phones, it would be perfect

Rome with a View

for a bird's-eye view of Rome.

I can see the famous view of Bernini's twin colonnades sweeping like a pair of cupped arms with Caligula's obelisk marking the centre of the piazza. Even from this height it still looks enormous and at the far end, like a gaping wound, the Via della Conciliazione leads straight to the Tiber.

It's fun trying to spot other landmarks. The Pantheon, circular and grey, looks like a flying saucer. I can see the Forum and the arch of Septimus Severus. The Wedding Cake rears huge and white over everything, like a great white pimple, easily the most recognisable structure in the landscape, and, you would have to say, looking completely out of place. The Colosseum is much harder to spot, only confirmed by the use of the binoculars, indistinct and grey amidst the tumble of terracotta roofs and much smaller than I expected. There is a surprising amount of greenery all over the city.

And at our feet is more greenery, the elegant and spacious Vatican Gardens, mature trees and manicured lawns and a couple of formal gardens, one shaped into a coat of arms on the lawn in the centre of a huge villa but what it is and whose coat of arms it is, the guidebook does not say. The railway station is to the left, only used for freight nowadays and the papal heliport is at the furthest extremity of the gardens and not visible from here. And there's the courtyard where we had our talk on *The Last Judgement* and the ceiling paintings of the Sistine Chapel, so all those buildings must be the Vatican museums. Blimey! (Because I am remembering where I am.)

I take a last look around. Even if I do come back to Rome, I'll probably never come here again, I reflect, as I make my way down to the courtyard where the lift stops. That's why I make my way over it to have a closer look at the saints stand-

The Vatican Gardens

ing patiently on the roof of the duomo. I can look along the line of them, but I can't get as close as I would like because of the ten-foot high railings, no doubt intended as another suicide deterrent.

Just as well really, as it would have confused the nuns if I had suddenly appeared amongst them with my budding wings.

"Who's that new saint up there?" one nun to the other does say.

"Search me. The one standing next to David Addison, do you mean?"

A bird's eye view of Rome

51

Trams and Tenors

A T the Bar Moretto we stop for the compulsory daily *gelati*, where, to my relief, there is no sign of my former English pupil. We continue down the Via di Porta Angelica until we come to the Piazza del Risorgimento. This is where we are to catch the pickpocket tram back to the hotel.

It's a leafy place and very crowded – good for the thieves and good for us too as it means we probably won't have too long to wait for the tram. According to the timetable there should be one in five minutes.

"Hop across to that corner shop and get me some water," Iona tells me. "This stuff is revolting."

She's right about that. The water, even in its insulated bottle, feels as warm as a baby's bathwater but just "hopping" across the road is not the sort of casual thing you can do in Italy. It's more like risking life and limb.

The stream of traffic seems as if it will never cease. Time is passing as fast as the cars, and the tram may appear at any moment. I don't even know from which direction it will come. Meanwhile here I am still stuck on the pavement. There's only one thing for it – I am going to have to take the plunge and let the drivers steer around me. I take what may be my last look at Iona who is sitting on the kerb in the shade, chatting to Bill and Pat apparently unaware she has just given me the 21st century equivalent of one of the labours of Hercules. The things we do for love. Or fear. I know which this is and what's more, there is much more to my fear "than fear itself" as Franklin Roosevelt put it, adapting an original line from Francis Bacon.

If I could, I would have done it with my eyes shut – obviously not because it's something I am accustomed to, but because I would be spared the sight of the vehicles bearing down on me, not to mention the irate faces of the drivers having to swerve around me without slackening speed. I raise my right hand as if to fend them off, as futile as Canute ordering the waves to retreat but it does serve to hide the face of the *pazzo* who is attempting this death-defying feat.

Phew! Safely across! Since the tram may come at any moment, I do not linger but liberate the first bottle in the chiller cabinet that my hand encounters. I grab my change and flee.

I can see a slight gap in the nearest lane after this black Mercedes but not in the next where a red car is coming up fast on the outside. I step off the pavement once the Mercedes has passed, intending to hop from lane to lane but then an incredible thing happens. The car which had been haring after the Mercedes stops. I am almost paralysed with shock. I risk a quick look at the driver. He doesn't seem in the least put out, and unbelievably the red car has slowed down and stopped too! I feel like Moses must have done when he parted the Red Sea. I make a gesture of thanks to these two untypical motorists and sprit across to the safety of the other side. Wonders will never cease! And there wasn't even one of those black-and-white stripy street decorations in sight!

I needn't have worried I was going to miss the tram though, as there's still no sign of it. I hand Iona the dearly-wrought water.

"It's not *frizzante*," she complains. She clearly has no idea how lucky she is to get me back in one piece. "It'll do though," she adds hurriedly. She must have seen the signs of rebellion clouding my brow but no doubt considering it an overreaction to such a small request.

As usual, she is right. In my haste, I hadn't bothered to look at the bottle I had picked up and I'm damned if I am going to cross that river of death again, however charmed a life I seem to have at the moment. If I'd been a cat I would have used up two of my lives.

And still the tram does not appear. Mussolini may have made the trains run on time, but he seems to have completely forgotten about the trams. Meanwhile, more and more would-be passengers have arrived. When the tram does come, it's going to be a mad scramble for a seat. So what's new? If we don't get on we will be facing a long wait for the next one, which will be just the same anyway. Get on we must.

At last a tram does shamble into view and stops. It must be the oldest, most rickety tram in Italy and must surely have been dragged out of retirement. It has varnished wooden slatted seats and I wouldn't mind betting it was built in the thirties, if not the twenties. It is redolent of the sort of smell that comes from the ingrained dirt of decades. Amazingly, everyone finds a seat. Maybe some passengers decided not to get on, not trusting to a museum piece like this to get them to their destination.

Although it is twenty minutes late, it does not move off and the slats are starting to bite into my bum. I can imagine the excess material of my swimming trunks dripping through them like the ruched curtains in an undertaker's window. We sit and wait. And still we wait. No purple-clad matriarch this time to get this show on the road.

Suddenly there is a mass stampede; everyone seems to be getting out. The doors were never closed and the would-be passengers stream out like lemmings until, in a matter of seconds, we are left alone. We look at each other in speechless bewilderment. What on earth is going on? The world has suddenly gone mad. Has there been some word of a terrorist attack? We decide we'd better follow the exodus too.

As soon as we step out of the tram, it becomes apparent why everyone left. On a parallel track, a brand-new tram has just pulled up. This is more like it! What a complete contrast to its neighbour: much more comfortable seats, which although plastic, are moulded to fit the shape of the posterior. I wonder how many tests, how many moulds they made before they got it right. Not only does it have air-conditioning but a LED display, so you know which stop is coming next. Very useful – if only we knew which one was ours.

Hope it's going where we want. What if it's not? I presumed because the tram was so late, two had arrived together, like buses. But wait a minute! What's happening now? The driver from the old rickety tram is standing in the doorway, haranguing the passengers. He sounds very angry indeed. With one movement, without demur, the passengers get up and rejoin the old tram. One or two others stay put, as do we. What to do? We remain where we are in an agony of indecision. Oh, to be able to understand a little bit of Italian!

At last we glide away from the stop, leaving the old tram still standing. You would have expected it to go first, but not according to the rules of Italian logic of course. Nothing to fear from pickpockets here; we could see them coming a mile off. The big worry is we don't know if we are heading in the right direction or not. Bill and Iona are poring over their maps. We are crossing the Tiber at the moment. That's a good sign. Now we are at an iced-cake sort of building, the Galleria Nazionale d'Arte Moderna on the Viale delle Belle Arti, which is an even better sign as it means we are definitely on the right tram-track.

Bill and Iona reckon the next stop or the one after will be ours. It's nice to relax and put your faith in others, so when

The Galleria Nazionale d'Arte Moderna

Bill says when we arrive at the stop that the next one will do, I slip out of my shoes again to let my feet breathe, only for Bill to change his mind again as soon as I have completed the manoeuvre.

"No, no, this one! This is the one we want!" and up he leaps with us snapping at his heels, me with my feet in my shoes but with not enough time to get my heels into them.

It turns out to be the wrong one after all. But it's a good decision because right next to the stop is a supermarket – the first place I've seen that sells alcohol, and I began my search in Naples nearly a week ago! Apart from the lunchtime beers and the wine at the Villa Borghese in Florence, I've had nothing alcoholic to drink. My poor liver never gets much of a rest at the best of times but on holiday it's expected to work overtime. Looks like this is the end of its holiday at last.

I decide I'd better buy a couple of bottles of gin whilst I can. Gin is the preferred summer drink, especially on the continent. With a week in Sorrento to come, there will be plenty of time for aperitifs. As they klink into my basket, I catch Bill looking at them. He doesn't have time to disguise the shock on his face.

"One for today and one for tomorrow!" I explain. "Hopefully I'll be able to get some more in Sorrento."

He gives a half-hearted laugh but I can tell he doesn't know if I'm joking or not. On balance, I think he thinks I'm probably not.

The walk to the hotel gives us a chance to see Rome off the tourist track. It's a leafy suburb, obviously one of the more select areas. The streets are lined with oleander and the buildings are elegant edifices with stone balconies. Here's one that's different however, wedge-shaped, with wrought-iron balconies boasting luxuriant foliage and windows with green shutters.

The House with the Green Shutters, one of my favourite Scottish novels. That's just about where the similarity begins and ends. And just as well too. It's a pretty grim tale.

I hope it's not an omen.

52
Dining with the Tenors 1

WE are all dressed in our finery as we foregather in the foyer prior to our visit to the restaurant. To-night we are dining with the tenors. Tenors it may be, but it sounds more like "terrors" to me. I ask Angela what we can expect.

"Don't worry," she says, "it's very light stuff."

That doesn't help much. Will it just be some background singing I'll be able to shut out, like musak in a supermarket, or will it be something more obvious? As long as it's tenors and not the female of the species – those ear-splitting sopranos.

We have to catch the bus again – for the first time a rela-tively empty one – and then walk to the restaurant in a street somewhere near the terminus. To be honest, I am not paying a great deal of attention to where we are going, just following our leader. Perhaps those warm gins I had before we came out have blunted my interest. (There was no ice and not enough time for my bottle to cool down after I had removed the min-iatures.) I had made the most of Iona's time in the shower to keep my glass topped up.

We pile downstairs into a basement and it becomes obvious as soon as we arrive that, unlike the meal at the Palazzo Borghese, we are not going to be the only ones. It's rather a large room set with lots of round tables and three for us. Iona and I find ourselves at the same table as Bill and Pat, the young Scottish couple, and the Guttings. Usha, Gordon and partner and the Yorkies are at the table adjacent to us. Behind the Guttings, who are across the table from me, is a small stage with a grand piano on it. It looks like it is going to be live music, just as I suspected.

There are only two bottles of wine on the table. I should have sat at a table with fewer people at it, since, regardless of size, each table has been provided with two bottles, one red and one white. That's not enough to drown a gnat. But maybe it's going to be the same as the Palazzo Borghese and we can get more on demand.

Here come our fellow diners, trooping in. Hundreds of them. The guides, including our Angela, have their own table.

"Welcome to our friends from Japan!" says our host and MC when everyone is seated. (Clap! Clap!) "Welcome to our friends from Israel!" (Clap! Clap!) "Welcome to our friends from England!" (Clap! Clap!)

"And Scotland!" someone shouts out. It sounds a bit like my voice. I hate it when people say "England" when they mean the UK.

"Anyone here from Scotland?" asks the MC.

Cheers and raised hands from our table.

"Welcome to our friends from Scotland!" (Clap! Clap!) "Anyone here from Wales?" Silence. "Anyone here from Ireland?" Silence.

"They haven't got the clap!" This sotto voce, under the influence of the gin, to Iona who returns my witticism with a look that says: *How pathetic! Why don't you just shut up!*

"Now may I present to you the artistes for tonight!"

First to appear is an older man in a white tuxedo with a red rose in his buttonhole, one of those bootlace ties and his grey hair tied back in a ponytail. Second is a younger man in a penguin suit, and to my dismay, a woman in a black evening dress. Her mouth is a gash of red lipstick and she has her raven-black hair scraped back in a bun. Her shoulders and bust are erupting from the top of her dress. Not too much bust, so perhaps her singing will be commensurately restrained. But it's still against the Trades' Description Act to have her in the act, although she is much more comely than the others by a mile. The trouble is she's not just there for the looks – she's going to be opening that mouth of hers.

Having made their appearance, they now bow out to let the waiters perform their duties. After a slight hiatus, Bill starts to pour the wine. My tongue was hanging out but I didn't like to be the first. It looks better for me coming from him. Uh! Uh! Here's mine host coming over. Wonder what he wants?

"Excuse me," he says addressing me. "Sorry for my little mistake just now."

"Erm?"

"Saying you were from England just now."

"Oh, that's all right. A lot of foreigners make that mistake."

"I'm from Lancashire. Been here five years now!"

I am a bit stunned and amazed by this revelation. "I *thought* your English was very good!" That's what I say but I am thinking: *In that case you should have known better, you English ignoramus.*

"Anyway. Is everything all right? Can I get you another bottle of wine?"

What a wise man! What a nice man! Yes, he certainly can. He comes back a moment later, not with one bottle, but one in each hand! What a really, really nice man! I catch Gordon's eye at the next table and tip him a wink, raising my glass in salutation as if to say: *It's easy when you know how.* He looks back: *I wish I had your charisma.*

The first course is some sort of risotto. I notice Guttings hasn't touched his. The waiter wants to know if he can get him something else, but he just shakes his head and the waiter clears away.

Pause for a song. A young man, casually dressed in a black T-shirt and jeans makes his way to the piano. It looks like this is going to be the pattern, a song for every course. We're going to be here all night at this rate. The younger tenor takes to the stage and lets his tonsils warble, followed by the soprano. She may not have the build of the stereotypical soprano, but she can screech with the best, I mean the *worst*, of them. Then the older man joins them and they perform a trio. Bloomin' heck, but these people can project! I expect they are used to being in a theatre, and here, in this room with the low ceiling, it's an assault on the ears. One is powerful but all three at once is deafening and the voice of the soprano soars above them all like the sparrow on the back of the eagle in the fable. It's just as well I keep my glass topped up as there's every chance that at this range, she could splinter it to smithereens.

Some authentic Roman eateries (Image Credit: Pixabay)

The songs don't mean anything to me. They might be Neapolitan or arias from an opera. The Japanese kids at the table to my right are ending themselves. I don't suppose they have ever heard or seen anything like it in their lives. Neither have I really, not so many, not all the way through and certainly not so loud. I don't think it's anything to laugh about but I'm glad they are enjoying themselves. I am getting more fun from watching them helpless with mirth than I am the singing, but then I am a bit of a Philistine. Just ask Iona.

Phew! Relief! They've gone now – for the moment. Now for the main course. It's pork in some sort of sauce. Oops! *The Last Supper* tapestry in the Vatican Museum revisited. I watch with interest to see what will happen when it's served up to our Israeli friends. The meat is smothered in sauce, so it may not be immediately obvious what it is, especially to people who have never had it put on a plate before them before.

Will they gobble it all up, wondering what this delicious new Italian delicacy is?

I needn't have worried. Whatever the Israelis are having, it is not the same as us. Maybe Guttings is Jewish, because he's not eating this either. He picks at some of the potatoes and some of his vegetables, but leaves the rest alone. No wonder you can hardly see him side on. Mrs Guttings explains he's very picky. I feel like asking if I could eat it, to prevent the waste, but it would only have gone to my waist.

One good thing about this entertainment is that although we can't eat, we can drink. In fact, with nothing else to do, even with our extra bottles, we need more wine now the main course has arrived.

"Would you like some more wine?" I ask Bill.

He would. Good. I make my way over to Angela's table.

"Excuse me, er... What's the deal about the wine?"

Angela looks up and fixes me with what can only be described as an astonished stare. She cannot have failed to notice how we had already received two extra bottles. She doesn't know, I hope, that the Guttings are generously donating most of theirs towards the common weald since they are still on their first glass.

"I mean, if we want any more, do we have to pay for it or is it included?" Sensing an atmosphere, I plough on to cover the awkward silence. "I'm just a delegate. Bill was wanting to know," I hasten to add, giving a nod in his direction.

"Just see your waiter," Angela replies in a tone as if I'd asked her how to breathe. What she's actually saying is: *Look, you're not fooling anyone. You've got a boozer's face if ever I saw one and you'll drink as much wine as you can get as long as it's free.*

"Er... right thanks!" I beat a hasty retreat. "Waiter!"

Best not to lose any time. It would be hell to be stranded during the next piece of entertainment without anything to make it more bearable, to dull the senses, to flatten out the soprano's piercing high notes.

53
Dining with the Tenors 2

ALREADY! Here they come again to assault the eardrums. This time it must be a Spanish song because the soprano is striking a flamenco pose and playing air castanets as the younger tenor serenades her. Enough to make her run a mile I would have thought, someone waggling his tonsils at you like that with the power of a ten-force gale. Now the older one is wandering amongst us singing to individual tables, which sends the Japanese kids into further paroxysms of hysterics.

The younger one comes back on the stage. I think there may be something familiar about this song. Well, I recognise one line. Suddenly the older one makes another appearance and has a verbal dual with the younger one. We are caught right in the middle. I can see now how the walls of Jericho fell down. To think that people actually part with good money (and a lot of it too) to listen to this! I would almost pay as much to make them shut up.

At last they stop and everyone claps, including me. The difference is, as far as I can tell, that I am clapping because I am glad they are finished. This part is concluded by the soprano and the older tenor hurling notes at each other. It sounds as if he's made a very improper remark, the way she's screeching notes back at him: *No I will not... not... not – definitely not rip them off, rip them off, rip them off! Screeech!* But it's all right really, they seem to make some sort of compromise because they end up having a little waltz together and above all, praise be, they stop singing. If this is meant to be light stuff, what the heck is the heavy stuff like? My head is throbbing. Thank God for the analgesic properties of wine to make the pain go away.

"Waiter! More wine here!

The artistes are mingling, accompanied by a photographer. I am used to this sort of trick. On our silver anniversary, on the Caribbean cruise, I was even photographed with a pirate with a parrot on his shoulder, very appropriate since it was a form of daylight robbery. I have a secret weapon, however. I am so unphotogenic that even they would not expect me to buy a photo. At least I *hope* I am unphotogenic, that the camera *does* lie and I am not so ugly in real life as I am in photos.

Determined to mark this millstone [[sic]], Iona was reduced to covering my face with foundation makeup before the professional photographers were let loose on me at the captain's reception. As anyone who has ever been on a cruise knows, you are photographed endlessly and each evening our dining companions would seek out my photograph from the hundreds of others for their daily post-prandial entertainment.

Here, when we get the results, true to form, I have not come out well. I have to admit it's better than many photos of me I've seen. At least both eyes are open and I do not look like a drooling idiot, just an idiot. My face looks like a side of raw beef or as if I had been dragged over a glacier, so we have an excellent reason not to purchase a photograph, even although we could have it signed by the ponytailed terror [[sic]] to remind us of how much we have enjoyed his singing and so attractively priced at an eye-watering €20.

The sweet is a gâteau. It's not been the best meal I've ever had in my life or even an Italian one, but we're here not so much for the food but the music – and if music be the food of love, play on! Play on and on and on, because this is our last night in Rome and it has yet to be consummated. How I wish I had earplugs because they are sure to be back for a finale, and I have a feeling I am going to have a headache and the consummation of Rome will just have to wait until we come back to Rome another time.

I donate my sweet to Iona as I am not a sweet person, as you know by now. I'd rather have more wine. This will be my sweet course and hopefully the sweet people will not want any more wine after this, so there should be plenty for *little moi* and perhaps it will induce me to have a more tolerant attitude towards the music even if it can not totally anaesthetise the ears.

Guttings is not a sweet person either. He's eaten practically nothing. At least I've eaten the other courses and am drinking more than my fair share of wine, but he's had practically nothing of either. Perhaps he likes the music, but he doesn't look as if he is. He doesn't look as if he likes anything, ever.

I like this music now. Actually I don't; it's doing my head in, but the entertainment makes a good cover as my partner's rapt, singing along in bits and clearly enjoying herself. And this wine, a bit thin and watery is beginning to seem quite palatable, even if it can hardly crawl out the bottle, being a meagre 11.5%. No more red left. Oh, well, I'll just have to move on to the white then. Hmm! A bit warm and a trifle acidic. But the second glass is better and by the third I scarcely notice these faults at all.

Now the pony-tailed tenor is wandering amongst the audience of diners singing something which I do actually recognise. It's from *The Marriage of Figaro* with lots of la-la-la's and repeated phrases. He has now got a hold of Usha and is leading her reluctantly up to the stage, all the while doing his la-la-la's. Poor Usha looks a bit embarrassed, especially when he points to a place on the stage and seems to be singing to her: *Stand there and don't move!* whilst he goes in search of a second victim. He is back a moment later with Mrs Yorkie whom he places on his left with Usha on his right, all the while blasting them with: *Figaro! Figaro! Figaro!*

Behind his back, Mrs Yorkie is imitating him. As he raises his arm to declaim, she raises both arms, one of which nearly delivers a resounding slap to his chops and at the same time shaking her hips and waggling her bosoms. The tenor pulls her arm down, never missing a beat, but she breaks free singing: *Figaro!* and comes to the front of the stage and waggles her assets in time to his tonsils.

"Figaro!" we sing back, even me.

The tenor continues his aria or whatever it's called, whilst Mrs Yorkie spreads her arms out wide like some member of the chorus in the finale of some popular musi-

"Figaro!"

404

cal. She is completely upstaging him. Poor Usha doesn't know where to look or what to do. She raises an arm in weak imitation of Mrs Yorkie but no doubt she's not had as much wine as she and in any case has a much more retiring personality.

I think it's the funniest thing I have seen in a long time, or perhaps ever, as the tears are rolling down my cheeks. The room is in an uproar. The Japanese kids are in serious danger of splitting their sides or laughing themselves to death. Meanwhile, Guttings watches the whole performance, impassive, unmoved. It really is incredible that he can sit through all this poker-faced. It's a kind of a talent in a way. He should dress up like Tutankhamun and stand on a box in the Piazza Navona. He'd make his fortune.

Mrs Yorkie goes back to her seat amidst rapturous applause. Of all the people in all this room the tenor could have chosen, he picked probably the only person who would have reacted in this way. It is almost too good to be true, as if somehow they had secretly been rehearsing this little act. But of course they hadn't. Had they? I would never have suspected she had such hidden talents. Perhaps she didn't know herself until she found herself on the stage, Italian wine coursing through her arteries and arias blasting through her vocal chords.

They should have stopped there, the tenors, but they have to spoil it all by *deiving* us some more, this time with a tambourine and the soprano trilling above the cacophony as before. At last it is over. Once again rapturous applause breaks out; they take their bows and leave. I applaud also, it would be churlish not to, but not too much – don't want them thinking they have to come back and do an encore. Oh, God, please, God no! But it's all right, they've finished. The waiters materialise again to serve coffee.

I go over to congratulate Mrs Yorkie on her performance and tell her I think it's the funniest thing I've ever seen. They are all looking very mellow at this table, compared to the sober people at the one I have just vacated, so I stay and talk.

It's only fair after Mrs Yorkie has entertained me so royally, that like Soutar Johnnie in *Tam O' Shanter,* I regale her table with my funniest stories whilst they top up my glass.

54

Party Time
and Question Time

I T'S time to go but there's still the best part of a bottle of wine at our table. Pity to waste that. The waiter will probably just pour it down the sink. I'll smuggle it out. Couple of problems though. How to get it past Iona and carry it home on the bus without a cork? It's not so much she'll think it's stealing; it's because she's the self-appointed Drinks Police and my crime is I am too fond of what Keats called the *blushful Hippocrene.*

I let everyone else at the table leave first and hold the bottle down by my side. It's pretty obvious really and, as I pass Gordon's table, he notices my prize. He's chatting to the soprano as if they were long-lost friends. He gives a nod of approval. I remember how he has past history – liberating a bottle from the Palazzo Borghese. There are a couple of unfinished bottles at his table. I bet I'll see them later.

"The trouble is there's no cork," I pause in the passing to let him know. "Hope I don't slop it all over the bus before I get back to the hotel!" I don't mention the other, the bigger, the Iona problem. She's bound to notice as soon as I catch up with her.

It's another of those close Italian evenings. I breathe in the warm, scented air. It is the scent of fear and it's coming from me. I trail behind, walking alone behind the group which has Iona in it. At the bus stop, I engage Tom, Dick and Harriet in conversation. The longer I can put off the appointment with fear the better. In due course along come Gordon, Blondie and the Yorkies. As I predicted, they have purloined their wine bottles, only they have corks in them.

"How did you manage to that?" I ask.

"I asked the soprano," Gordon replies as if it were as simple as producing a rabbit from a hat.

I am suitably astonished. "And she just went and got them for you? What did you say to her?"

"I said: *Excuse me, but didn't I meet you before in New York?*"

"And have you ever been to New York?"

"Never!"

I look at him in admiration, then chuckle at his boldness. I would never have thought of saying something like that. After that it was easy: he charmed her like a bird off a tree and she went to fetch a couple of corks. It's a great thing to have charisma. If I'd tried that she probably would have said: *You're not allowed to take wine off the premises. Besides, by the look of your face, you're taking plenty back inside you.*

In the bus, I stick a finger into the neck of the bottle. No-one else needs to have any if they don't want to. All the more for me. Strangely, the Drinks Police says nothing. Perhaps she doesn't want to create a scene or perhaps Gordon's trophies have put my contribution into perspective. I am feeling a bit more relaxed. It looks as if I may have got off with it after all.

In the lounge of the hotel, we commandeer a couple of flowery Chesterfields and some chairs. We are nine: The Yorkies, Gordon and Blondie, Tom and Harriet (Dick has gone to e-mail his friends), Angela, and Iona and me. We need glasses. Gordon is dispatched to procure them; who else? Presently he comes back armed with an armful. Unfortunately it is also a meeting of the smokers' union: Mrs Yorkie, Angela and Blondie, confirming the statistics that more women than men smoke nowadays.

So we drink and chat, we who have only known each other for less than a week and who know really nothing about each other at all – not even each other's surnames. It's inevitable I suppose, that we should ask each other what we do for a living. Mr Yorkie admits to being an art teacher. Hah! Hah! I knew it! Harriet, I have marked down as a primary-school teacher, a nursery teacher actually.

"I don't work," says Harriet in answer to my question.

"Yes," I pursue, "but what did you do before got married?"

"I was a primary-school teacher."

"Which class?" I can hardly wait for her answer.

"The babies, the new ones."

I can scarcely resist the urge to get up and punch the air. It's impossible, however, to guess what Gordon and Blondie do, nor Mrs Yorkie, and they're not telling. Tom's a doctor. I had him down for that, or a lawyer, or a vet.

I regale the company with my jokes and their laughter is ready chorus. Encouraged, I could go on all night like this, as long as the jokes keep coming. Why don't I tell them the one about when the Pope was caught speeding next?

Rome by night (Image Credit: Pixabay)

And so the evening passes until all the wine is drunk and we are merry. But now Iona is standing over me as if about to make a Drinks Police arrest.

"It's time we were going to bed," she says. "We've got an early start tomorrow."

Eh? We're free tomorrow, free to do our own thing. Why this precipitate rush to bed? I'm just coming alive. Tomorrow, Rome is ours for the taking. We could start the day with a really long lie in; that would be music to my ears. But I know all too well that Iona wants me to leave before we head for the bar and I get settled for the night. Hmm. Maybe she has a point. That might be expensive...

Tom and Harriet decide to call it a night too. As so often happens at parties, it just takes one party pooper to start the ball rolling. That just leaves the hard core, as in Firenze. I could have been a member of that club had things been different. Mrs Yorkie and Blondie have just lit up another cancer stick. I can see this party could go on for some time even without my hilarious jokes to entertain them. Maybe it *is* time to go after all. Who wants to die of secondary smoke inhalation when you can live to die another day of sclerosis of the liver?

* * *

Next morning, as we're having our second cup of coffee as afters, Mrs Yorkie comes over to our table. Not the prima donna of last night but I would say in an incredibly shy way. Looking sheepish even.

"'morning!" Pause. I was wondering..." Another pause then a nervous glance at Iona. I notice it's not me who is being asked. "I was wondering..." she repeats, "...if you wouldn't mind... posting these cards for us?"

At last she has managed to spit it out. But what an odd request! Why can't they do it themselves?

"Certainly," says Iona with alacrity. A moment later, she accepts the bundle of cards Mrs Yorkie must have been concealing behind her back.

"Thanks."

What's going on here? They've still got half-a-day in Rome, like us, not to mention the airport where they could post them. Even the hotel reception would post them – eventually. No wonder she looked nervous. I presume they have stamps on them.

She must feel some sort of explanation is necessary, the unspoken question in my eyes hanging in the air between us like something you could hang your hat on. Iona, on the other hand, doesn't seem to think there is anything even slightly peculiar about the request.

"I don't trust the hotel to do it and we're not going out today (why not – what a waste of time!), and in case there isn't a post box at the airport..." her voice tails off again. So? There is still something not right about this. Aware of the awkwardness in the atmosphere, she plunges on: "Actually, we'd like them posted in Sorrento – if you don't mind."

Ah, hah! This sounds a bit more like it. I don't mind at all, but I do mind not knowing why.

"It's just a joke, really," she says, unconvincingly. "Thanks!" And with that, she turns on her heel and goes back to her table before she can face any questions from the Scottish Inquisition, aka me.

How bizarre! What kind of joke would that be? Maybe when I read the postcards, I'll get a clue. But, up in our room, preparing to go out, Iona will not let me read them.

"They're private!"

"No, they're not! Everyone reads postcards! Especially the posties! And that's what we are."

"You do, maybe."

"Aren't you in the least curious to know why they have to be posted in Sorrento?" I can't believe her lack of curiosity, her total indifference towards this intriguing mystery.

"No!" The tone has a ring of finality about it.

God give me strength! There's no point in arguing. She'll not change her mind. I should have held my *wheesht.* She'll make a point in hiding them now I've expressed an interest. I don't think it's nosiness at all, just natural curiosity. My mother was always irritated by my insatiable thirst for knowledge or as she put it more pithily: *You always want to know the far end of a fart.*

Methinks I will die of curiosity long before secondary smoke inhalation or sclerosis of the liver gets me. It seems a very unsatisfactory thing to die of, though it must be very satisfying indeed to finally have the answer to the most intriguing question of all: Is there life after death?

But imagine if there's not. You would die never knowing and never find out. I really hope sclerosis of the liver gets me first.

The Forum Revisited

55

The Pleasure Palace
and the Palatine

WE are going back to Roman Rome. There are so many other things we *could* do, but we're more interested in archaeology than art, so we've decid-ed to revisit the Forum to try and make more sense of it with the help of our newly-purchased book with the transparent overlays. Such an aid to the imagination! The trouble with the Forum is that it is not frozen in time but with so many ruins spread over so many centuries, the brain tends to melt at trying to imagine how it may have looked at any particular period of time.

We also intend to go to the Palatine where the infant Romulus and Remus were said to have been suckled by a she-wolf in a cave called the Lupercal (after the Latin *lupus* for wolf). The hill was the snobby part of town in the Republi-can period and continued to be so in the early days of the Em-pire when Augustus, Tiberius and Domitian lived there. The ruins of their villas can still be seen.

We buy travel passes at the nearest tobacconist's kiosk. If you have an aversion to smoking (and why should you not?) or never read a newspaper (especially in Italian), nevertheless you should direct your steps to these marvellous institutions which provide an essential service for the independent traveller. If you cross their palms with euros, they will provide you with the means of travel to wherever you want to go. How convenient!

After another gruelling journey by Metro, we arrive at the Colosseum. Facing it is a ruined building on the hill with half-a-dozen or so white columns standing sentinel on either side of it. It turns out to be the apse of an enormous basilica, the Temple of Venus and Rome, another of Hadrian's building projects. This was the largest temple in ancient Rome, actually two temples with their apses back to back. The pillars, so far away from the basilica as to seem part of another

The Temple of Venus and Rome (Image Credit: Pixabay)

construction altogether, are actually all that remain of the 150 which once formed the portico.

The temple facing us is the Temple of Venus Felix (the Bringer of Good Fortune) while that of Roma Aeterna (Eternal Rome), faces the Forum. They were goddesses with a special affinity with Rome. Venus was the mother of Aeneas, the father of Romulus and Remus, whilst Roma was the protectress of the city. Apollodorus of Damascus, the foremost architect of his day, remarked that the seated statues of the goddesses were too big, that if they were to stand up (as if they would!) they would bang their heads on the top of their niches. For this unwise advice, Hadrian had him executed. Which just goes to show you it doesn't pay to criticise the architect, especially if he's also the emperor. If I'd been around, I could have told him that. Never criticise your boss. That's why I have stayed married for so long.

It doesn't look much now, but in the first century it was really something as our book with the transparent overlay shows. And here's the thing. This massive twin edifice stands on just the *vestibule* of Nero's palace, the Domus Aurea, or House of Gold. After the fire of 64 AD which some allege Nero started, he decreed that a stately pleasure-dome should be built.

No expense was spared. The walls were covered in gold leaf and mother of pearl. The bedrooms showered guests with flowers and perfume, but get this – the ceiling of the dining room actually rotated to mirror the movement of the night sky. No mystery about this; just the ingenuity of those who devised it and the pedal power of the slaves who made it work. And in the baths you could have a choice of water – sea or sulphurous. No wonder you needed to be showered with perfume if you've just come from the latter: *You've been bathing in that pongy pool again, Domestus. You're driving me clean round the bend.*

But the lake would have been the best – banquets on barges and brothels on the shore and high-class hookers to boot – none of your common-or-garden prostitutes here, if you please. As things turned out, Nero committed suicide in AD 68 so he didn't have much time to indulge his perversions in the new place. The Colosseum now stands where the lake used to be. Perhaps their ghosts are still here, hovering in the air.

The Colosseum was Vespasian's contribution to the expurgation of the hated Emperor's memory. The Temple of Venus and Rome was Hadrian's. And in its turn, it too became a marble quarry. The popes looted it for their own constructions. How handy to have a marble quarry right on your doorstep! The gilded-bronze roof tiles were used by Honorius I (625-638 AD) for the roof of his basilica to St Peter in the Vatican. In its turn, it was demolished by Julius II (1503-1513) to make way for the present church. And you'll never guess where *he* got his marble from! Forget *caveat emptor. Caveat emperor* more like. Nero, Vespasian, Hadrian: no building was safe. And who's to say what will happen to St Peter's in the centuries to come? If we learn anything from history (and usually we don't), it will not last forever. On the bright side, anything they do to Bernini's *baldacchino* would be an improvement. They could try melting it down for a start.

We circumnavigate the Colosseum, peering in, through barred gates, to see what we can see. It can be seen on postcards anyway, what looks like a pile of bricks mainly. Time is short and we have other priorities, so we decide not to bother going in.

We have come halfway round now – and what's this? They have put a lift in! No kidding; are you looking at this, Vespasian? See what they have done to your monument! It's good to see that the tradition of desecration of ancient monuments is alive and well in the 21st century (though this was probably done in the twentieth), that the ancient customs are still holding good. Is no building sacred or safe! If I were you, St Peter's, I'd be shaking right down to the depths of your foundations (which must be considerable). I foresee a day when

Palatine Hill
(Image Credit: Pixabay)

a nice, speedy, glass elevator will take the disabled (why should they be discriminated against?) or those who can't manage the steps, such as the arthritic and obese, or even the pure-dead lazy, and whisk them up effortlessly to the top of the dome.

Of course there were lifts in antiquity too, and since 2015 a reconstructed one of those that hoisted the wild animals from where they were kept in the basement up to the auditorium, where they were released to fight for their lives or eat Christians for their supper, though actually the current thinking is that was a bit of a myth invented by Christians themselves.

We are heading upwards ourselves, up the hill towards the Palatine. There we can see people wandering around in the cool, green leafy slopes, separated from us by high railings like animals in a zoo.

Eventually we come to a turnstile, but there's a problem. Iona pushes it, yet it won't budge. I find a similar problem, but manage to move it a bit and by sucking in that lump of emergency rations I carry around in front of me, just in case I am ever stranded in a desert without any food or water, I manage to squeeze through. In the Palatine at last!

Bang! Bang! Bang! Bloody hell, what was that? At the same time, Iona is yelling, "David! David! You've to get out!"

I look up to see she is pointing to a man in a green wooden booth a few yards away who has been banging at his little window and gesticulating at me, not so much waving but shouting. I can't hear him but I am supremely glad I don't understand Italian and certainly not expletives. All at once it dawns on me – I have gone in the exit, that's why the turn-stile would not turn. It turns all right when I push it to come out. The man in the booth gives me a contemptuous scowl as we pass by.

Should I explain I hadn't realised that was the exit? No, it's not worth it; I'd prefer to let him think I'm dishonest. Better by far than admitting I'm an idiot.

The real entrance is further along, up a steep flight of stairs where there is a sign which says *Tickets*. We have a choice. We can either go there and visit the ruins of the em-perors aforesaid, not to mention the sprawling ruins of the house of Livia, Augustus' ghastly wife, the hut of Romulus (yes that will be right!) and other such attractions, or we can go down to the Forum. Now I see the extent of the ruins on the Palatine, I realise we don't have time for both.

We opt for the Forum. I want to see if I can make more sense of that jumble of ruins that once was the hub of the Roman Empire.

56

Signs of the Times

FROM the Palatine we make our way down to the Forum, this time to explore it first from the other end, from the arch of Septimius Severus. We saw it before, looking down on it from the Via dei Fori Imperiali but it's only from this close up, standing looking up at it, that you appreciate the true scale of its immensity.

It's looking a bit the worse for wear these days. It was half-buried up until the 18th century but it's had two hundred years of exposure to the Roman atmosphere and pollution since then, and it's as pockmarked as a youth with a severe case of acne.

Wedged between the arch and the end of the Rostra is the stump of a red-brick pillar. On it a marble plaque has been attached inscribed with the words VMBILICVS VRBIS ROMAE – the belly-button of Rome, the centre of the Em-

**Umbilicus
Urbis Romae**

The Forum (Image Credit: Pixabay)

pire, the place from where all roads began or ended. It was probably erected as early as the 2nd century BC but what we are looking at, such as it is, dates from the time of Septimius Severus (193-211 AD) who shunted it along a bit to make room for his arch.

In 20 BC, at the other side of the Rostra, Augustus erected a marble column or a gilded bronze column – the Milarium Aureum, on which were carved, in gold letters or perhaps not (the experts are unsure), the distances to major cities of the Empire. They are not even sure where the column was situated precisely. Almost certainly it was *not* the little stump of decorated column with the little plaque at the bottom telling tourists that that is what it is. Since the Romans did not decorate the bottoms of their columns, it's probably a bit from the top of some column or other that was lying about and someone thought *I know what I could use that for* and plonked it on top of the remains of pedestal that was handily sticking up nearby. That doesn't bother me so much as wondering why the Romans felt the need to have two columns doing precisely the same thing.

It's another thing the Romans gave us, signs like at John o' Groats for example, only not so grand, where it is just a plain white wooden signpost. On it are the distances to such places as Land's End, New York, and Orkney and Shetland. One arm has been left blank onto which movable letters can be inserted so you can have your photograph taken telling you how far you are from home: *Thurso 20 miles.* Strange place to put the sign though – John o' Groats is not the most northerly point on the British mainland, just as Land's End is not the most southerly.

Like John o' Groats (and Land's End especially), I can imagine the Milarium Aureum being something of a tourist trap: *Clever Dick's Instant Portraits* and a whole lot of similar sketchy folk lining up to fleece the hordes of barbarian tourists come to gawk at all the cultured folk in the capital. You can imagine the spiel and the response: "*Only seven sesterces, sir, to prove to the people back home you really have been to the hub of the Empire!*" "*Well, OK, but only six sesterces and are you sure you know exactly how many miles it is to Corinium Dubunnorum? And don't draw the column growing out of my head, Dick.*

What remains of the Rostra that we see today was unfinished at the time of Julius Caesar's assassination and completed and extended by Augustus and dedicated in 42 BC. It gets its name from the tradition of decorating the speakers' platforms with the *rostra* or the "beaks" of enemy warships, actually bronze battering-rams which were fitted to the prows of their ships. Where they are now, no-one knows, but they live on in the name we give to a speaker's podium today.

It was on the rostrum that Caesar built that Antony offered him the crown three times. Caesar turned it down, to the cheers of the crowd. It was actually a test of public opinion and had the response been different, so too would Caesar's have been.

It's also where, in 44 BC, Mark Antony incited the mob against Brutus by delivering his immortal lines during his funeral oration, or at least, the words written for him by Shakespeare. A year later, in the same place, he ordered Cicero's head and right hand (the one that was guilty of writing the *Philippics* against him) to be displayed from the beaks of the Rostra, while for her part, Antony's charming wife, Fulvia, stabbed his tongue with a golden hairpin in revenge for all the vile things he had said about her. She was a scary woman, Fulvia. You might have thought a silver one would have been more appropriate given Cicero's prowess as an orator, but I for one would not have dared point that out to her.

"Where are you going?" Iona wants to know. It's perfectly obvious where I am heading, but she is one step ahead of me even before I take my first up to the little of what's left of the Rostra. Her tone stops me in my tracks. It's unbelievable! How could she tell I was intending to give the *Friends, Romans, Countrymen* speech I was made to learn at school and which I've never had a chance to use since? All that time committing it to memory wasted. I'll probably never get another chance.

To the left of the Rostra is the Temple of Saturn. There had been a temple to the god of Bounty and Wealth (and plenty of other things too) on that site since 497 BC, making it the oldest continuous temple to a deity on the Forum. Appropriately enough, at one time it also served as the Treasury where the Republic's gold and silver was stored. It was rebuilt several times and the present eight incredibly tall columns date from 42 BC. They stand upon a high platform and, taken together, dwarf the people below. The symbolism is obvious: the power and might of the god over puny little man – even if he was the one to build it in honour of the god.

Saturn would undoubtedly have been my favourite deity had I been around in those days. The poor and slaves (which knowing my luck, is probably what I would have been and most likely the latter) were especially fond of him. He was a mythical god-king under whom there were no such things as slavery, private property, war or crime. His reign is still celebrated today, except we call it "Christmas" – they called it "Saturnalia", a week when the feet of the god were released from their woollen bindings and all hell broke loose. The normal social order was reversed, the world was turned upside down, slaves were served by their masters (even if they had to slave over a hot stove first), criminals went unpunished as the courts were closed, as were the schools, and no war could be declared. If only it were so all year round!

In their homes, people would exchange gifts. In accordance with the madness of the season, they were of little value, such as wax dolls. That doesn't sound like such a good idea to me. I wouldn't give my wife a wax doll of me for a lorry load of pins, never mind two. They were often accompanied by a gift-tag on which was written some doggerel, the worse the better. And if that's not the origin of the dire verses on Christmas crackers, then I don't know what is.

Even in those days there were the Scrooge misery-guts (and I have to admit to being one myself). Pliny writes about secreting himself away in a room in his villa whilst the madness went on all around him. He must have been heartily glad when Saturnalia was over and his world returned to sanity. I know I am when Christmas is.

Running at right angles to this, along the Via Sacra, is the Basilica Julia – another of Julius Caesar's building projects, and paid for by more unwilling contributions from the Gallic tribes. Building began in 54 BC and the basilica was dedicated in 46 BC whilst still unfinished. It was completed after the untimely demise of its founder by Augustus, his prodigy, but it burned down shortly thereafter. He ordered its reconstruction, only bigger and better than before. It was damaged by fire again in 283 AD when Diocletian picked up the tab for its reconstruction and once again in 410 AD when Alaric I, king of the Visigoths, sacked Rome.

It used to house the civil law courts, some shops and government offices. There's not much to see now, only the steps and stumps of pillars like ground-down molars, and seems to stretch along the Via Sacra forever. There were 180 magis-

The Via Sacra (Image Credit: Pixabay)

trates, all sitting separately, in four rooms which had remova-
ble partitions. Lawyers would hire spectators to applaud pal-
pable hits at their opponents and boo and hiss at their rivals.
Pliny the Younger tells us they were paid three *denarii* for
their enthusiastic contributions. It was all a bit of a pantomime in fact. Another thing the Romans gave us. Anyway, it
probably was more entertaining than going to the real theatre
and better by far than going to the shows running daily with
gore at the Colosseum.

Having said that, if you were sentenced to death, execution took place in public by barbaric methods such as impale-
ment, and – as everybody knows – by crucifixion. The Romans also had rather a quaint law, namely that it was illegal
to execute a woman who was a virgin, so part of the execu-
tioner's duties was to rape her first.

According to our guidebook, on the steps, we should be
able to see board games scratched onto the surface by bored
punters waiting to be hired by the lawyers. I wonder if this is
one. It's a whole series of shallow holes of regular size and
depth though there doesn't seem to be any recognisable pattern to them as far as I can see. I press my thumb into one and
it takes it quite comfortably. I've no idea how it was played,
but I'm sure it must be a game of some description. Maybe
some sort of solitaire.

Here's something else interesting but I don't think it's a
game. It's a big circle with the letters ORMO at the bottom
and some other letters too faint to make out. My long-
forgotten boyhood Latin is not up to the task of even hazard-
ing a guess at what they may be, far less from being able to
decipher the whole thing. Besides, there's a piece broken off
anyway. My guess is it's a piece of graffiti. That is maybe all it
is, but it's Roman graffiti!

Have pity on the poor Roman vandal. Some poor blighter must have sat here for hours laboriously carving this into the stone. He was probably whiling away the time until he was hired by a lawyer to add his vocal support to his case.

They make it so much easier for vandals nowadays: one quick spray with your can then you can skulk off. They must have been much more tolerant of graffiti artists back then!

A general view of the Forum

57

The Column and the Curia

THERE is a path here, to the right of the Basilica, and on a whim, we decide to take it. It's another one of those serendipitous finds. There are some steps going downwards, some ancient brickwork, a recess in which is set a barred gate and a white marble plaque on which is written CLOACA MAXIMA. I don't know why I remember it, but the Cloaca Maxima is one of the few things I do remember from my days of studying Latin. Now here I am all these years later face to face with it, but to be honest, there's not that much to see from here. There's a whole lot of Italian written on the plaque but I don't need to be able to understand it to know what this is. It's the sort of thing that a guide would never take you to. It's the main sewer of Ancient Rome and goes all the way to the Tiber. I mean what sort of person would get a thrill out of seeing a sewer?

Nearby is a tall, slender, single column. No-one knew what it was until the pedestal was excavated in 1813 and an utterly stomach-churning, sycophantic inscription was revealed. At the risk of reacquainting you with your last meal, I'll only give you a flavour of it: *To the best, most clement and pious ruler...*

The Cloaca Maxima

for the innumerable benefactions of His Piousness... this stat-
ue of His Majesty, blinking from the splendour of gold here
on this tallest column for his eternal glory...

It was erected in AD 608 to commemorate the visit of the
Byzantine Emperor, Phocas, thus making it the youngest column still standing in the Forum. The architect was Viagra.
No, I don't know his name really, but it ought to be. Fourteen
centuries is an impressive amount of time to maintain an erec-
tion, unlike Phocas himself who did not last much longer after
his gilded statue was put on top of the recycled column. Only
two years later, he was deposed and murdered in a most gruesome way.

In the account of his death in his *Chronicles*, John, the
Bishop of Nikiu, lets us see that far from being worshipped, he
was utterly detested. (Those of a sensitive disposition may
wish to skip the rest of this paragraph.) This is what the sena-

tors and army officers did to him. They cut off his private parts, flayed him down to his legs, disembowelled him, beheaded him, burnt his body and scattered his ashes to the four winds. The order of the procedure is important. Is there any other atrocity you can do to what's left of a dead body? I suppose they could have peed on him, but only before the pyre was lit as they wouldn't have wanted to put the flames out.

If it comes down to whether he was more admired or detested then I'm with the bishop. I don't think they cared for him very much.

So what had he done to deserve this dreadful death, humiliation and mutilation? Well, he put his predecessor and his five sons to death, seized their property and assets, and for a bit of light entertainment, raped the wife of a famous nobleman.

"Where are you going now?" Iona says in a suspicious tone.

"Er... erm. Nowhere really."

Bloody hell! She can read me like a book. I thought I might just go and give that long-standing column a stroke for good luck. You never know, some of its power might rub off on me. I missed out on stroking that boar's nose in Florence and now this. Even if it did work, it probably wouldn't have done me much good anyway, I reflect ruefully.

Just beneath the wall of the Rostra, there is a hole in the ground with iron railings fencing it off. What could it possibly be? A flight of steps leads down into the bowels of the Forum and on the wall is a plaque bearing the legend: "NIGER LAPIS" and in smaller letters beneath, "TOMBA DI ROMOLO". Wow! What a find! Can I count this as part of my collection of famous graves I have been to, even if I can't get any closer? Not to mention the slight matter of it being the grave of a mythical figure in the first place.

The *niger lapis,* or black stone, was the capstone of a shrine (before they lifted it off to see what lay beneath). They found an altar and a *stele* (gravestone) with a rather interesting inscription. The oldest known in the Roman world, the letters more akin to Greek than Latin, it is written vertically in what is known as *boustrophedon,* that is to say read from left to right, then right to left, and so on, literally as an ox ploughs a field. The experts were able to make out *rex* for king, and also, significantly, some dire warnings about not desecrating this sacred site.

Ignoring this advice, the brave archaeologists excavated it regardless, and to the best of my knowledge did not die of some mysterious illness as if they had opened a mummy's tomb. They found no evidence of a body. But then they wouldn't, would they? It is supposed to be the grave of Rome's mythical founder, after all.

The extremely modern-looking Curia Julia is nearby, so we wander over to have a peek inside. In a sort of neat symmetry, it began life the same year Julius Caesar died. As with Caesar's other unfinished building projects, Augustus stepped up to the plate and completed it in 29 BC.

As I said earlier, the building we see now dates from 1938, Mussolini having ordered it to commemorate the two-thousandth year of Augustus' birth. It was built to the same specifications as the completely new building that Diocletian ordered after the disastrous fire of 283 AD. That, in its turn, replaced the building that Domitian built after the fire of 90 AD.

Rome was always going on fire. To name but a few, there was the famous one that some say Nero started in 64 AD, followed by another in 69 AD and yet another in 90 AD. Three in a generation, can you credit it! The city of marble that Augustus claimed to have built seems to have been burnt to cinders several times.

We can't go in and look around, but we can see all there is to see as the big bronze doors are wide open. If the Curia looks austere from the outside (which it is), it is no less so inside, apart from the ornate *opus sectile* floor which runs in a strip down the centre. Pardon me if you already know this, but *opus sectile* is a mosaic, usually of a geometric design, which is filled in with various pieces of coloured stone or marble, even glass or seashell or mother of pearl.

As you would expect, it was very much different in Augustus' day. The walls once were decorated with marble and paintings, and the ceiling was gilded. It used to echo to the sound of silver-tongued oratory but now it's a repository for bits and pieces of marble statuary, including two relief panels which once decorated the front of the Rostra. Experts are divided, but most say they depict Trajan destroying records of unpaid taxes and thus freeing the citizens from debt; providing money for the support of poor children; and making money available for mortgages on farms. I bet that made him popular all right, and there was no harm in reminding everybody of the fact each time they come to the Forum to hear someone get something off their chest like they do at Hyde Park Corner today. Another thing we got from the Romans.

At the far end of the hall is a porphyry statue of a headless figure in a toga. It glistens like a wet seal. If you could hold it, it looks as if it would slip through your fingers like a piece of raw liver. Being headless, we don't know who it is, but must have been someone extremely important to have had the honour of being sculpted in this special stone. My guess it was

Trajan, commissioned by a grateful people in gratitude for the tax break. Indeed, where it is situated was the place of honour where the emperor and consuls sat when the senate was in session.

On each side of the highly-coloured strip of *opus sectile*, there are three very wide steps at each side, as shallow as they are wide. It had seating for three hundred senators who took along their own collapsible stools and placed them on these steps. Those not on the front row must have experienced a great deal of difficulty in seeing over the heads of those senators in front. And if you wanted to go to the loo, it would have been just like at the cinema today – everyone would have had to stand up, collapsing their stools to let you past. Maybe it was a tactic they used if they felt the debate was not going their way: *No, by Jupiter, I'm not letting you past,*

Trajan's Panel

Incontinentus. You should have gone before you came. You're always "having to go" when Cicero is speaking...

It comes as a bit of a shock really. These masters of architecture were perfectly capable of building proper tiers of seats with plenty of legroom as they did in the Colosseum, so why didn't they here? Curious. It is certainly wide enough to have done so. And another thing: why does it look nothing like it is depicted in films? Anything I've ever seen of the Senate in films or TV had the seats arranged in a horseshoe shape or semicircle, not in adversarial style, like our House of Commons with the Speaker keeping order at the far end, sometimes with varying degrees of success. Another thing we got from the Romans.

At least I happen to know why the Curia is so incredibly high. It was built to the specifications of the architect, Vitruvius, who wrote all there was to say about architecture in his seminal *De Architectura*. He advised that in order to achieve the best acoustics, the height of the chamber should be half the sum of its width and the length.

I suppose, it being a debating chamber, it might have occurred to Vitruvius to allow a lot of room for the hot air from the speakers to rise.

58

Funeral Pyre and Fire

HAVING seen all there is to see of the Curia, we make our way to the other end of the Forum where, facing the Rostra, is the Temple of the Deified Julius Caesar or the Temple of the Comet Star.

It was unusual in being the only temple dedicated to the cult of a star. Strange but true. But as Hamlet said, "There are more things between heaven and earth than are dreamt of in our philosophy", and if a shooting star is not betwixt heaven and earth then I don't know what is. Shortly after Caesar's death, a comet, what the Romans quaintly called a "long-haired star" appeared in the sky above Rome for seven days. To the superstitious Romans this meant a sign of something significant.

They saw it as the soul of Caesar ascending to heaven to join the gods, and thus the tradition of the emperors that followed him actually being gods-in-waiting, was born. But, you will remember, the recently deceased dictator claimed divine descent through Venus Geneterix – it was only a matter of time before he got his wings and flew to join her in heaven.

Augustus was not slow to seize the initiative and make the most use of this phenomenon. He made a great speech in which he announced that the soul of his adoptive father streaking through the sky was also announcing *his* birth as the new leader of the world.

In an unprecedented honour, the Senate voted to give Caesar a public funeral in the Forum followed by his cremation on the Field of Mars. Accordingly, his body was borne to the Rostra on an ivory couch covered with cloths of gold and purple, the symbols of wealth and power. Mark Antony made his rousing and well-crafted speech heavily laden with irony, at least as written by Shakespeare. By contemporary accounts, the reality was actually rather different, though he did make good use of a visual aid – the blood-stained and dagger-ripped toga Caesar was wearing when he was murdered. When he got to the bit about the will, under which the people were granted Caesar's gardens on the Janiculum Hill (outside the city walls), not to mention 300 sesterces to every male Roman citizen living in the city at the time, that did it for the plebs: they loved Caesar. Death to those who murdered him!

It was no mean sum – the equivalent of four months' pay for a Roman soldier. The people wanted to take him to the Capitol, the spiritual heart of Rome, right there and then but the priests put paid to that, arguing if they did so, it may not just be the pyre that would catch fire but the wooden houses there too. At least that is what they said, and maybe they had a point. It was the practice for cremations to be held outwith the city walls and as you know and the gods know, the city was very prone to fires.

And so it was that the body was taken to the front of the Regia, Caesar's official residence in his office as Pontiff Maximus, the high priest of Rome, a position he had held for near ly twenty years – since 63 BC. Indeed it was in this building his body had lain before the funeral and it was in front of it now that he was cremated on an impromptu pyre built from benches, chairs and tables from the shops, any bits of wood they could find. They must have found plenty, because the pyre is said to have burned all night.

In 42 BC, the triumvirate of Octavian (Augustus), Mark Antony and the lesser-known today, Marcus Lepidus, decreed the building of a temple to the dear-departed god. It was built on the spot where Caesar was cremated. It was dedicated in 29 BC by Augustus after the Battle of Actium, where the navies of the fallen-from-grace Antony, and the femme-fatale Cleopatra, were defeated. The beaks from some of their ships were placed on the high platform on which the temple was built, and this new rostra was used by later emperors to deliver funeral speeches. On one notable occasion there was a spoken duet performed by Tiberius and his son Drusus: the former delivering his speech from the Rostra of Augustus and the latter from Caesar's.

Alas there is very little to see now, the marble having been looted for palaces and churches in mediaeval times, only the remains of a straight wall with a curved one behind it, like the apse of a church. They have an ugly temporary-looking roof over it.

Standing in front of it, a guide is rabbiting on endlessly in Italian to a small group of tourists which includes two kids who, fed up to the back teeth, are tracing patterns in the dust with their feet. I want to squeeze in the space between the straight piece of wall and the apse but I can't because the group is blocking the way.

At last, however, the guide leads them away and I squeeze into the narrow passage. Inside is a stump of a broad pillar

443

and on the top, a bunch of wilted flowers. According to one of our guidebooks, this is where Mark Antony made his funeral oration. You can't trust everything you read in guidebooks; nor can you trust Shakespeare either, as I point out to Iona.

"Surely Mark Antony should have said: *Friends, Romans, Countrymen, lend me your ears. I come to burn Caesar, not to praise him. The evil that men do lives after them –*"

"Shut up!" I have managed to sneak in my speech after all, even although it's in the wrong place.

"Of course, if he *had* said that," I plough on, "the next bit wouldn't make much sense. *The good is oft interrèd with the bones –*"

"I told you not to do that."

Quite right. It must be forty years since I was made to learn it at school so it's not surprising I'm unsure how it continues.

We make our way up the Via Sacra and now we are on the territory we trod earlier in the day. Here is the Temple of Antoninus and Faustina, Picasso's cow still peering forlornly over its pen at me: *Yoohoo! Moo! You back again? Say pal, you can't get me outta here can you? I haven't even room to turn around in this bloody pen!*

Across the way is my favourite building on the site – the Temple of Vesta. I like the curved shape and how the slim pillars seem to soar into the air, especially as we see them from below like this.

What we didn't see earlier however, was the House of the Vestal Virgins which is nearby. All that's left are the ruins of the house around the central courtyard. Known as the *Atrium Vestae*, it once was a two-storey building – "palace", I should more properly say. Apart from tending the sacred fire in the temple that formed part of their duties, their home was not immune to a greater fire than that (like the rest of the Forum), being burnt down in Nero's Great Fire of 64 AD. The ruins we are looking at date from the rebuilding.

The Atrium Vestae

The office of the Vestals had nearly a thousand years of illustrious history, but the beginning of the end came in 382 AD when the emperor Gratian appropriated their income, forbade the leaving of legacies to them and abolished their privileges. When compulsory Christianity was introduced by his successor Theodosius I, the last emperor to rule over both the eastern and western parts of the empire, the sacred fire went out for the last time in 394 AD and officials of the imperial court moved into the Vestals' former home. After that, it was home to the papal court until the 11th century.

Today it is an oasis of green amidst all the burnt grass and broken columns which make the Forum look like a bomb site. There is a central strip of emerald grass, with a couple of fishponds (hence the *atrium*) in the middle, and round the perimeter, marble statues looking coolly white on their pedestals. These are statues of some of the Vestals. Most of them have lost their heads. Maybe that's symbolic of their decision to turn their back on the world of men and adopt this nun-like existence.

One of them, Cornelia Concordia by name, had her name removed from her pedestal after bringing the cult into dispute. No, she did not lose her virginity, but she did something far worse – she became a Christian. It was a sign of the times which were a-changing. It only happened twenty years before the end of the empire.

Well, that brings our visit to an end. Although I have a much clearer idea about individual buildings in the Forum, if you were to give me any date you'd care to choose, I still couldn't picture it as it would have looked like then, which buildings were there and which were not, let alone what they looked like without referring to the transparencies.

Anyway, we had better be heading back. Mustn't be late to catch the bus, whatever we do. Some people have flights to catch.

Last Gasp

59

Music and More Troubles on the Metro

ACK at the Colosseum there is a *gelati* van, unfortunately. €10 for two ice creams! You can buy a whole
businessman's lunch for less than that. As for the ice
cream man, he's definitely in the right business, doing a roaring trade.

We go off to a low wall nearby to sit and eat them. Of
course I sit in the sun whilst Iona chooses a place in the shade.
You would think we weren't speaking to each other, to look
at us. I plonk my posterior on the stone and leap up immediately with an involuntary cry of pain and surprise. The stone
is red hot and I've burnt my bum. I have a good mind to rub
the ice cream on the spot. That seems a more appropriate
place for it. It's the worst ice cream we've had since we came
to Italy (and we've had a few), or is it the price that is leaving
a nasty taste in my mouth?

Over to my left, in a swathe of grass in front of the Colosseum, there is some entertainment to take my mind off the

burning issue. A bride and groom are having their photographs taken. She is in the traditional white dress and he is in a white suit, complete with waistcoat. He must be sweltering under all that. There's a long-haired photographer with cameras strapped across his body like a guerrilla's bandolier, appropriately enough, as he's going to do plenty of shooting by the looks of it. To his left a young man holds a microphone with the wire disappearing into a shoulder bag. To his right, an older man with a ponytail and a power-pack on his back is in charge of a massive camera with a microphone projecting over the lens like the snout of a swordfish. As he hefts the camera onto his shoulder, his knees buckle under the weight. What a way to earn a living! Should have been an ice cream man.

The young couple are posing for a still. He has his hand resting on the pocket of his trousers so that the tail of his jacket is pushed to the side, all the better to show off the cut of his suit. She is snuggling up to him, her voluminous dress totally obscuring his left leg, her bouquet of white lilies held across their waists. He is staring adoringly, not at her, but at the Colosseum whilst she gazes off into the middle distance at something to the right of the camera.

A lot of the time they are apart. At the moment, he is striding up and down like a man with something on his mind, while – for her part – she stands demurely, holding her bouquet. Now she is picking up her skirts allowing a breeze to balloon them out and I get a flash of white shoes and ankles. It's probably pretty sweaty under all that brocade.

Meanwhile, at a hotel somewhere in Rome, the wedding guests are waiting. These two look as if they have got all the time in the world. But the photographer, with euro signs in his eyes suggests: *Why not have one in front of the Temple of*

Marriage in ruins

Vesta to commemorate your last day as a virgin? Heh! Heh! Heh! (Well, pretend then!) These bloody photographers! They are up to all the dodges and rule weddings nowadays.

But a feeling is beginning to dawn on me about this. I don't think it's a real wedding. There seems to be too much equipment and the man with the movie camera seems to be more interested in the Colosseum than the couple. They're not in the shot he's filming just now, for instance. But what is the young man holding the microphone here for? Is he going to be interviewing them for the radio: *Tell, me you happy newly-weds, have you got any special plans for tonight at all?*

And then the penny suddenly drops. No wonder they are apart so much of the time. No wonder they are not gazing fondly into each other's eyes. No wonder the movie man is so interested in the Colosseum. No wonder the microphone man is ready. Voice over: *Tired of him already? Marriage in ruins?*

Don't want to see him? For free advice, call in at our office near the Colosseum. (We'll fleece you later.)

Well, I'm glad I worked that out before we had to go. One mystery is plenty. I've still got the riddle of the Yorkies' post-cards on my mind. The *gelati* are finished and we must get going. We cross the road and burrow down into the Metro.

There is no sign of a train so, faithful to my maxim that in cities, you should grab a seat whenever you can, I sit down to wait.

Gradually, I become aware of the woman to my right. She's a flamboyant character dressed in a yellow-and-red dress. To say it is loud would be an understatement. It is positively screaming at me. Although I judge her to be in her forties, her hair is jet black and tied back in a pony tail and unless I am much mistaken, it's not out of a bottle. She is wearing massive hooped earrings, two on each side and so big I could put my clenched fist through them. The bangles on her swarthy brown arms jangle and set up an accompaniment with the earrings so at each slight movement she's like a human Aeoli-an harp. The line from the nursery rhyme floats into my head: *And she shall have music wherever she goes.*

And indeed, she certainly seems to be listening to music, though there is no sign that she is plugged into a Walkman or CD player, for although she is sitting down, her feet are mov-ing, not just tapping in rhythm to some inaudible and invisible source of music, but moving in some sort of dance rhythm. I don't know much about dancing, but I would say these are dance steps. I wonder if I went up to her and asked: *Are you dancing?* she would say: *No, it's just the way I'm sitting.*

I nudge Iona in the ribs and give her the eyes-right sign.

"I think she has a touch of the gypsy in her, don't you think?" I whisper.

Iona agrees, suitably impressed at her eccentricity. Both of us watch fascinated as the performance continues. Suddenly it stops as Rose Lee stands up and takes up a position on the edge of the platform as if expecting the imminent arrival of a train. And indeed, a few seconds later, I hear or rather sense, the rush of air that always presages the emergence of a train out of the darkness. But she knew about it *before* it happened. Did she have some sort of sixth sense that the train was coming?

We scramble on board. As usual, it is packed, but not so solidly as on that nightmare trip to the Vatican. In fact, there is sufficient room for a quartet of musicians. They are dressed in gold shirts and black trousers with black cummerbunds. The instant we depart, the band strikes up. The sound of the fiddles and Pan-pipes give it an unmistakeable Romanian gypsy-like air. What! Two gypsy events one after the other like this? A co-incidence, or what? Could it possibly be that our gypsy-looking lady on the platform who seemed to anticipate the arrival of the train was actually tuned in to the music of this gypsy band? Surely not, but yet how else do you explain it?

The music is certainly very catchy and I don't mind in the slightest throwing a euro or two into the hat one of them is passing around. Unfortunately, they get off at the next stop – Cavour. We have just one more stop to go.

But there seems to be a problem. The train is not moving. The doors have closed, we are all ready to go, but we're not going anywhere. The doors open again. Some people get off but the majority stay put in the train that looks as if it is going nowhere. Time seems suspended while nothing happens.

Suddenly there is a banging at the window. Someone in uniform is gesturing that we should get off. Get off? But why?

He has already disappeared down the platform, banging on the windows as he proceeds. I wouldn't have been able to ask him anyway, but no one else is getting the chance to either.

The platform is now crowded with people, the train is empty, the guard (as I now perceive him to be) hops on to the last carriage and without further ado, the empty train draws out of the station. What on earth is going on? It just doesn't make sense. But that's Italy for you. Obviously, the train is working perfectly well, at least as far as we can tell. The natives are restless. It's plain to see they are as mystified as us and more than a little peeved into the bargain at the lack of information, not even a tannoy announcement I couldn't understand to tell us the reason for this bizarre behaviour.

After five minutes without another train appearing, Iona is getting worried. What if the next train has been cancelled? What if they have all been cancelled? How are we going to get back to the hotel in time?

Although I don't say anything, I am a tad worried myself. I am worried I am going to have to pay for a taxi. We should be all right for time – we still have half an hour before we are due back at the hotel to catch the bus. Still plenty of time – if a train comes soon and we don't have to wait too long for a bus once we get to the Terminus. Iona hates this sort of situation but I tend to thrive on it. I hate arriving early for anything and having to hang about. I like the excitement of arriving just in time; she loves the quiet life, to leave plenty of time for possible unforeseen events like this. It looks as if it's going to be my sort of day.

Iona looks at her watch agitatedly. "We're never going to make it!"

"Oh yes, we will!" Surely if we are a little late, they will wait for us, for a little bit anyway, but she is clearly getting her knickers in a twist. To be honest, I'm getting quite stressed myself. "If you hadn't insisted on getting those bloody *gelati,*" I just have to add, to let her see it wasn't *my* fault. Just because we're in Italy and they make the best ice cream in the world, there's no need to go bloody mad about them.

But fortunately before it turns into a full-blown spat, like a balm to soothe frayed nerves, the train arrives just at that moment.

60

Life in the Slow Lane

WHILST we have been waiting for the train to arrive, people have been drifting into the station and now there's a whole new train-load to get on to a train which was already a train-load, so once more it's sharpened elbows to the fore as we fight our way on. We *have* to catch this one. We can't afford to wait for another one. I follow close behind Iona. No-one is going to stand in *her* way, my very own WMD – woman of mass destruction – as she cleaves a path through the mass of bodies...

Out of the Metro, and a mad dash to find the stance for the bus to the hotel. We need an 86 or a 92. But where to begin? It seems this is the Terminus for all of Rome. With impeccable logic for once, that's why the Italians call it *Terminus*. There are buses everywhere, but of course there appears to be no logic in the way that they are distributed. We race from stance to stance, from bus to bus, looking for the magic numbers, splitting up in order to optimise the chances of hunting one down, and at last I find the one we want. Now I have to find Iona before the bus goes. Phew! There she is! No mistaking her. She must be the pinkest person in Rome.

Sitting, waiting for the bus to depart, in an agony of impatience, Iona kneads her knapsack. She kneads it even more than I need a beer and I need it a lot, or rather, I need a lot of beer. All this rushing about in the heat has given me the mother of all thirsts which the warm water in the insulated bottle does nothing to assuage, but to tell you the truth, at least half of my mouth's dryness is due to the fear, not that the bus will have gone, but they are waiting for us and cursing us for putting their flight in jeopardy. This holiday began with a missed flight and it might end with missed flights for half the company thanks to me. It's not the disapprobation that worries me, so much; it's the thought of the compensation I might have to pay which terrifies me.

As we draw near the hotel, we are scanning the street for landmarks. We can't afford to over- or under-shoot our stop. The trouble is there are no landmarks that automatically leap out and hit us between the eyes. Is this it? Iona and I look at each other. Yes, we think it is. It seems we have been on the bus for about the right length of time. We press the bell and are decanted, mercifully at the end of the street that we want and hasten our steps towards the hotel which is half-a-mile distant, if not more. My watch says we have ten minutes to the deadline. The way Iona is charging up the street, we are going to make it with five minutes to spare at least. That's what I call good timing. An otherwise dull journey has been turned into an exciting adventure with this race against the clock.

The bus is parked outside the front of the hotel and some of our fellow passengers are already on board, while others are hanging around in groups. But there is something about the way they are standing which tells me they have been waiting for some time – an atmosphere, as they watch our approach, which strikes fear into my heart. What I expected to see was luggage being loaded onto the bus, travellers idly chatting and joking, taking a leisurely departure. But there is no luggage on the forecourt and the luggage compartment gapes ominously open. Angela is looking down the street,

Traffic, Roman-style
(Image Credit: Pixabay)

in the direction from which she would expect us to come. She spots us and looks at her watch. Have we possibly got the time we were to meet wrong? I can believe I would, but not Iona; not both of us.

As we skid to a stop, Iona pants out a breathless apology. "I'm so sorry! Did we get the time wrong?" she asks of Angela. It's too hard to tell as she is so pink already, flushed as she is with the rush and the heat, but she's probably blushing. She blushes when she's innocent, at the mere thought that someone may suspect her of something even so slight as a solecism. In a court of law, the jury would always judge her guilty.

"No, no, it's just I like to get away as promptly as possible. You never know with the traffic. And we've *got* to get to the airport on time," she adds, I think, rather darkly.

I wonder how long they have been waiting as we go to fetch our luggage from the luggage room. If we had been there, would we have gone perhaps half-an-hour ago, even more? Well, that's not our fault if we make the most of our time in Rome; yeah, even unto the last minute.

Everyone is aboard when we return with our luggage and see it safely stowed away by Giancarlo in the bowels of the bus. I am practically hugging myself with the masterly management of my timing. I think I have a bit of a genius for this sort of thing. If we hadn't eaten those *gelati,* if that train hadn't dumped us, we would have arrived far too soon.

We negotiate the suburbs of Rome without any hold-up and in due course hit the A1 or E45 if you prefer, and travel, on course and on time, hopefully, south to Naples, to journey's end and which was also journey's beginning. Perhaps there, the Guttings will be reunited with their luggage.

Something is wrong. We are slowing down. Ahead, traffic is piling up, red brake lights are coming on and further ahead, traffic is at a standstill, stretching as far as the horizon. How wise of Angela to allow time for this eventuality! That's the trouble with Roman roads; efficient but boring. Pity the poor Roman soldiers, marching, marching, marching, wearing all that armour, carrying all that equipment in the fierce sun and not even a slight bend or even a curve in sight to relieve the monotony. Tramp, tramp, tramp in their sockless sandals in a straight line, mile after mile, towards the horizon. How utterly sole-destroying.

Our situation is scarcely much better. We are barely moving, sometimes not moving at all, and whatever is causing the hold up is not even in sight yet. I don't know how far we can see ahead, but it looks like miles. At this rate, we are going to be here for some time evidently. Presumably it is an accident.

But what a rare thing! In all the weeks, in all the hundreds upon hundreds of miles we've travelled in Italy, this is the first accident we've come across. And this despite the aggressive way they drive, like bats out of hell, practically bumper to bumper, lights flashing to say: *Get out of my way!* So unlike our own dear country, where flashing lights mean: *Please go ahead, old chap, after you!* or *Thanks, mate!* depending upon your social status.

I might have known it! Trust an Italian driver to deal with a traffic jam in a typically Italian manner. We are in the slow lane – well, of course, we are all in the slow lane now – but I am on the right side of the bus and on my right is the emergency lane, and on that a car is tooling down it quite the thing. The cheek of it beggars belief. "I hope the cops catch you, you cheeky bastard," I say, but only to myself.

But Nemesis takes a different form. A driver, in front of Smart Alec, seeing this performance in his mirror, straddles both lanes, leaving not enough room for him to get past on either side. As he tries to pass on the right, so the other driver pulls right and as he tries to pass on the left, so does the other. Thus they zigzag their way at a snail's pace down the motorway.

"Ya beauty!" I can't help but cry out, like Tam O'Shanter who couldn't control his enthusiasm for the delectable Cutty Sark and thus revealed his presence to the witches.

Iona and I watch the proceedings with interest over the heads of the Guttings and Giancarlo. Guttings is staring ahead, his face mask-like as usual. What will happen next I wonder. We are moving so slowly there is nothing to prevent Smart Alec from leaping out of his car and in a rage, hauling our hero out of his car and giving him a good doing.

But the gods have a laugh up their sleeve. The cruel injustice of it! A lay-by off the emergency lane appears like a *deus ex machina*. Smart Alec swerves into it, overtakes our hero on the wrong side, nips out of the lay-by again and zooms off down the emergency lane once more. Curses! Well, let's hope the cops catch him. Iona and I look at each other in dismay. The good guys don't always win, not in real life. My guess is the gods will see to it that Smart Alec gets off with it completely.

If Angela is feeling worried about this delay, she's not showing it too much. Once again I reflect on the perils of being a travel rep. She's got to decant all these people at the airport on time and is at the mercy of idiots like us who prevent an early start and unforeseen circumstances like this.

At last the traffic clears. A lorry has shed its load of onions. Onions all over the road. It's going to take forever to pick them up, and there's nothing to indicate what caused it to happen in the first place. Alas, there's no sign of Smart Alec having been detained by the police either. Damn!

At Cassino again, we stop for a toilet break and refreshments. No wonder Angela wasn't looking agitated. If needs be, we could just have missed this out and if anyone was desperate, well that would just have been too bad. There are levels of desperation.

Before too long, we are back on the bus, bowling along the motorway to Naples.

It comes upon us suddenly, Naples airport. It's all bustle as we retrieve our luggage from the hold of the bus, apart from the Guttings of course. Angela has told us that a couple of taxis will whisk us away to Sorrento. Meanwhile, she has gone into the terminal to find out at which desk the homeward-bound people have to check in.

A man in a short-sleeved white shirt appears holding a card with ADDISON written on it. I identify myself.

"Follow me, please," and he seizes Iona's bag and starts marching off.

What! So soon, just like that! We haven't had time to say goodbye to anyone. I seize the handle of my case, wave to my ex-companions. "Goodbye, everyone!" I call. Half of them haven't even noticed, they are still lugging their luggage from where Giancarlo has placed it; some have already gone, presumably looking for a trolley.

"Don't forget the postcards!" shouts Mrs Yorkie.

"Don't worry!" I shout back.

And that's the last I see of my fellow passengers.

Whatever happens in Sorrento, it won't be restful. No sitting by the pool all day soaking up the sun. There's Herculaneum just up the road, and probably Pompeii again, Vesuvius to climb and the Amalfi Coast to explore and that's just for starters.

As I stow my luggage in the mini-bus, I hope I can keep embarrassments to a minimum and avoid disasters completely. Like Queen Victoria, I will try to be good. The trouble is, as Harold Macmillan feared, events have a habit of happening...

About the Author

A native of Banff, Scotland, David M. Addison is a graduate of Aberdeen University. In addition to essays in various publications, he has written eight books, mainly about his travels.

As well as a short spell teaching English as a foreign language in Poland when the Solidarity movement at its height, he spent a year (1978-79) as an exchange teacher in Montana.

He regards his decision to apply for the exchange as one of the best things he ever did, for not only did it give him the chance to travel extensively in the US and Canada but during the course of the year he made a number of enduring friendships. The story of his time in North America is recounted in his *Innocent Abroad* series, also published by Extremis Publishing.

Since taking early retirement (he is not as old as he looks), he has more time but less money to indulge his unquenchable thirst for travel (and his wife would say for Cabernet Sauvignon and malt whisky). He is doing his best to spend the children's inheritance by travelling as far and wide and as often as he can.

Also Available from Extremis Publishing

An Innocent Abroad
The Misadventures of an Exchange Teacher in Montana: Award-Winner's Edition

By David M. Addison

An Award-Winning Book in the 2015 Bookbzz Prize Writer Competition for Biography and Memoir

When, in 1978, taking a bold step into the unknown, the author, accompanied by his wife and young family, swapped his boring existence in Grangemouth in central Scotland for life in Missoula, Montana, in the western United States, he could never have foreseen just how much of a life-changing experience it would turn out to be.

As an exchange teacher, he was prepared for a less formal atmosphere in the classroom, while, for their part, his students had been warned that he would be "Mr Strict". It was not long before this clash of cultures reared its ugly head and the author found life far more "exciting" than he had bargained for. Within a matter of days of taking up his post, he found himself harangued in public by an irate parent, while another reported him to the principal for "corrupting" young minds.

Outwith the classroom, he found daily life just as shocking. Lulled by a common language into a false sense of a "lack of foreignness", he was totally unprepared for the series of culture shocks that awaited him from the moment he stepped into his home for the year – the house from *Psycho*.

There were times when he wished he had stayed at home in his boring but safe existence in Scotland, but mainly this is a heart-warming and humorous tale of how this Innocent abroad, reeling from one surprising event to the next, gradually begins to adapt to his new life. And thanks to a whole array of colourful personalities and kind people (hostile parents not withstanding), he finally comes to realise that this exchange was the best thing he had ever done.

This award-winning book, the opening volume of the *Innocent Abroad* series, charts the first months of the author's adventures and misadventures in a land which he finds surprisingly different.

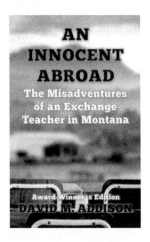

www.extremispublishing.com

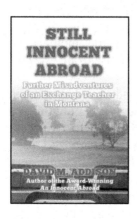

Still Innocent Abroad

Further Misadventures of an Exchange Teacher in Montana

By David M. Addison

In the sequel to his award-winning *An Innocent Abroad*, Scot David M. Addison continues his account of a year spent as an exchange teacher in Missoula, Montana in the western United States.

When he embarked on the exchange, the author vowed he would embrace every experience (within reason) that came his way and mostly they *were* reasonable, though there were some he would not care to repeat.

In the course of this book, he experiences seasonal activities such as Hallowe'en (American style), Kris Kringle and Thanksgiving. He also sits his driving test in his wreck of a wagon which he not-so-fondly dubs "The Big Blue Mean Machine" and whose malfunctions continue to plague him in this book, just as they did in the last.

Nevertheless the author and his young family put their trust in it to take them, in winter, on the 1,200 mile round trip over the snow-clad Rockies to visit relations in Canada – just for a long weekend. Which just goes to show you that although he may have learned some things, this author from a small island is still very much an innocent abroad in this vast and mountainous land to even contemplate embarking on such an expedition – particularly since he set out so ill equipped.

Meanwhile, at school, he is on his best behaviour as he tries not to repeat the shocks and alarms of the first few days when he found himself up to his neck in trouble with parents out to get his guts for garters. The reader will not be disappointed to discover that he still finds some parents and students challenging. At the same time, he is also on his guard for attacks from the "enemy" within – his practical-joker colleagues who are all too keen to exploit his innocence for their own amusement.

The narrative ends with the traumatic events on Christmas Day. It would have been a memorable day whatever happened, but no-one bargained for the Addisons turning their hosts' Christmas Day into one they would not forget in a hurry.

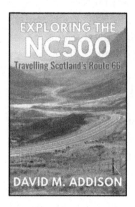

Exploring the NC500

Travelling Scotland's Route 66

By David M. Addison

Travelling anti-clockwise, David M. Addison seeks his kicks on Scotland's equivalent of Route 66. Otherwise known as NC500, the route takes you through five hundred miles of some of Scotland's most spectacular scenery. No wonder it has been voted as one of the world's five most scenic road journeys.

There are many ways of exploring the NC500. You can drive it, cycle it, motorbike it or even walk it, even if you are not one of The Proclaimers! And there are as many activities, places of interest and sights to be seen along the way as there are miles.

This is a personal account of the author's exploration of the NC500 as well as some detours from it, such as to the Black Isle, Strathpeffer and Dingwall. Whatever your reason or reasons for exploring the NC500 may be, you should read this book before you go, or take it with you as a *vade mecum*. It will enhance your appreciation of the NC500 as you learn about the history behind the turbulent past of the many castles; hear folk tales, myths and legends connected with the area; become acquainted with the ancient peoples who once lived in this timeless landscape, and read about the lives of more recent heroes such as the good Hugh Miller who met a tragic end and villains such as the notorious Duke of Sutherland, who died in his bed (and may not be quite as bad as he is painted). There are a good number of other characters too of whom you may have never heard: some colourful, some eccentric, some *very* eccentric.

You may not necessarily wish to follow in the author's footsteps in all that he did, but if you read this book you will certainly see the landscape through more informed eyes as you do whatever you want to do *en route* NC500.

Sit in your car and enjoy the scenery for its own sake (and remember you get a different perspective from a different direction, so you may want to come back and do it again to get an alternative point of view!), or get out and explore it at closer quarters – the choice is yours, but this book will complement your experience, whatever you decide.

For details of new and forthcoming books
from Extremis Publishing,
please visit our official website at:

www.extremispublishing.com

or follow us on social media at:

www.facebook.com/extremispublishing

www.linkedin.com/company/extremis-publishing-ltd-/

Lightning Source UK Ltd.
Milton Keynes UK
UKOW01f2302180917
309440UK00001B/3/P